THE PURGATORY TRAIL

By

Cleo Lorette & Greta Manville

Dear Pauline,
If I played bridge
half as good as you,
I wouldn't be sitting
around writing fiction!!
Hope you enjoy this little
adventure. Greta Manville
Sept. 2006

This book is a work of fiction. Any resemblance to events, persons, names or characters, living or dead, is entirely coincidental, and are products of the authors' imagination.

ISBN: 0-75962-459-3

This book is printed on acid free paper.

1stBooks - rev. 04/26/01

For

Audrey, Cecile, Cherie, Kaï-dee, and Nancy
and of course
Our husbands, Ray and Wally

For their support, suggestions, and endless patience
with our project

Cowboy. Deep in most mature hearts, male and female alike, lies a childhood dream of being a cowboy. Layers of care and responsibility accumulate through the years until the dream lies, dormant and forgotten, in a corner of our hearts. Decades later, let one boot toe of possibility nudge our dusty dream, and it springs full-blown to take control again. More powerful than in childhood, it drives out reason ...

- Audrey Hankins, Cowboy Poet

CHAPTER ONE

A FINE MESS

Lindsey's heart sank. What else could go wrong?

Uncle Simon's death was sad but not unexpected. Then the Taylors, she and Cody, got the rude shock of their lives at the reading of the will.

"Now, Cody's broken his damn leg and gone back to Arizona, leaving me alone here in Colorado to deal with Uncle Simon's 'legacy.'" She found herself muttering out loud half the time with no listeners, and that annoyed her too. Lindsey gunned the motor of the battered green pickup as she drove up the gravel approach to the ranch and skidded to a halt in a shower of dust and pebbles.

She mopped the sweat from her face with a denim sleeve and looked around the empty yard. "Damn." Where was the young cowboy Cody called to meet her there at five o'clock? At ten after, the old "horse kicked my Timex" routine wouldn't work unless he had his arm in a sling.

She opened the pickup door and swung her long legs to the ground. Still wearing the boots and leather chaps needed for riding horseback in deep brush, she'd planned early in the day to ride out to check the cattle. But that was before Cody's accident. Lindsey heaved the door closed with a satisfying slam.

"Is anyone out there?" she called. No pickup around. Perhaps the cowboy was watering his horse behind the barn or out of sight beyond the corral. Surely he would have waited. Only the far-off bawl of a calf broke the quietness.

How she loved this high plains country east of the Rockies and north of the Arkansas River, with its captivating history of pioneers, miners, and adventurers who traveled the old Santa Fe Trail. Surrounded by late summer crops of golden wheat and green milo that studded vast rolling prairies of grassland and desert scrub, Lindsey understood the mingled richness and utility of the land. Now, with fall approaching, much of the alfalfa stubble and grama grass was dry and grazed out in spite of early summer's abundant rainfall.

An eagle wheeling over a distant field caught her attention until she realized that it lacked the power and graceful flight of an eagle. It was only a common hawk in search of prey.

A chain-link fence surrounded Uncle Simon's old one-story frame house, which was sadly past needing paint. The fence, intended in bygone days to keep foraging deer and rabbits away from thriving shrubs and bedding plants, now protected a yard dominated by weeds interspersed with a few late summer sunflowers and occasional lupine. As Lindsey swung open the gate, the metallic "squeee" of its galvanized hinges sounded forlorn. She stepped carefully over the tilted, uneven sidewalk with the blossoms of impertinent yellow dandelions poking between its cracks. If she tripped, she could become the final casualty in the diminished household.

She shivered as the first hint of cool air filtered through the ever-present breeze. She didn't like being alone, but she had work to do. After one last look down the road, she strode through the back door of the ranch house and hung her jacket and range hat on a nail behind the kitchen door.

Lindsey pulled the coffee pot noisily forward on the wood burning cook stove—so typical of Uncle Simon's holdouts against modern appliances. She opened the door to check the coals. Not even a flicker.

She threw a handful of kindling into the stove and lit a sheet of crumpled newspaper under the shavings. Carefully placing several ragged pieces of wood over the tiny flame, she watched to make sure the fire caught. Satisfied, she closed the door, adjusted the damper, and waited for the coffee to reheat.

The barn cat, a huge gray-and-white tabby named Felon, had followed her into the house. Lindsey started to shoo him out, then relented and rewarded the mewing beggar with a saucer of milk. After finishing the last tasty drop, the grateful creature brushed against Lindsey's leg and nuzzled his milk-sopped whiskers against the roughness of her chaps. Lindsey reached absent-mindedly to stroke the coarse fur of his battle-scarred head. Grateful, the cat leaped into her lap.

"Felon," Lindsey said, "you're too big to be a lap cat, and I hate to say it but you're kind of ugly. You're definitely not much for conversation, but at least I'm not talking to myself."

The cat stared vacantly into Lindsey's face, his purr a vibrating engine that dispensed satisfaction as she stroked the shaggy coat. "I guess you appreciated that delicious treat. I wonder why Uncle Simon named you Felon. If I had to guess, I'd say it had something to do with breaking and entering. I hope it wasn't felonious assault on anything other than a rodent."

Felon ran a paw across his whiskers to capture the last drops of milk, then flexed his tufted toes and stretched his thirty-odd pounds across Lindsey's lap.

"You have no idea what a mixed-up summer this has been, cat." Her voice echoed through the sparsely furnished house. "But no one promised it would be easy."

When Uncle Simon became seriously ill, he called asking the Taylors to come up from Arizona to take charge of his affairs. Without hesitation, they put their ranch in the hands of friends and hurried to help Lindsey's uncle. Cody handled the cattle, and she looked after Uncle Simon. He refused to go to a hospital, always so sure that his health would return.

After Uncle Simon died, Lindsey assumed she'd inherited his ranch and livestock, enough to ease the Taylors' everlasting financial worries. Instead, she found she had ten days to get her inheritance, a fine herd of Hereford cattle, off someone else's ranch or forfeit the cattle.

"As if matters weren't bad enough, Felon, Cody broke his leg this morning." She choked on the words, but Lindsey refused to give in to tears. When she thought how, after spending hours at the local hospital, Cody insisted on going home to Arizona to have his long-time family doctor make sure his leg was set right, her aggravation reached a new peak. She'd reluctantly put him on a plane only an hour ago.

"Lord knows, Doctor Evans has set enough of Cody's broken bones, but isn't that just like a cowboy? Breaking his leg now when he's needed the most?" She would never make such a baldly irrational statement to Cody, but it felt good to get it out in the open.

The cat sat up facing her and yawned.

"Phew," Lindsey said, picking him up and dropping him on the floor. "On second thought, mouse-breath, I think you belong outdoors. Back at your post."

She nudged the overweight, reluctant cat out the door and started to pour a mug of hot coffee when she heard the crunch of tires on the gravel drive. Pulling back the yellowed curtain over the kitchen sink, Lindsey watched the pickup's driver get out and head toward the house. She was relieved to see the young man Cody had spoken with last week about moving the herd to auction before the first snowfall.

She took a quick peek in the old mirror beside the door and fluffed the tangled mass of silver-frosted short dark curls with her fingers. Too late to dig out a lipstick. At least, her wind-burned cheeks glowed sufficiently to make her look healthy.

Lindsey opened the door to the startled young man who stood on the porch poised to knock.

"About time," she said, without rancor. "I was beginning to wonder if you were still interested in the job. Come on in."

Tall and rangy, he ducked through the low doorway. Still in his early twenties, his cheerful face with its open, boyish grin showed no sign yet of the weathering cowboys like Cody earned before too many years on the range.

He removed his battered felt hat and offered a handshake. "Afternoon, ma'am. Billy Ray's my name."

Though annoyed by his tardiness, Lindsey liked his firm grip and polite manner. She waved him to a seat at the big oak rectangle that served as a dining table.

"I heated up some coffee. Want a cup?"

"I'd sure appreciate it, ma'am. Sorry I'm late, but I didn't forget." The young man grinned again and carefully placed his dusty hat at his side on the bench. "I got over here quick as I could. My boss sent me over to do a job for old man Potter."

Lindsey nodded and turned to the stove to pour their coffee.

What a good-looking young man he is, she thought. All blue-eyed, wavy blond innocence. Bet he keeps the local gals two steppin', shufflin', and slappin' leather at the Saturday-night cowboy dances. He's a lot like Cody when I met him at a Saturday-night dance twenty-six years ago. Well, Cody won't be dancing or much of anything else for a month or two.

Lindsey placed the young man's coffee mug on the table by the sugar bowl. She returned for the milk and picked up her own mug.

Sitting across from him, she began, "We have some business to discuss. You talked to Cody last week and came to some sort of understanding about driving Uncle Simon's herd to the auction yard and railhead in La Cholla."

"I did."

"Well, there's a hitch or two. The time frame has changed, and my husband broke his leg this morning. He won't be able to help with the drive, so I'll be taking his place."

"I see."

"I need a crew of at least four cowboys. We have to move the cattle off this property and auction them no later than the tenth of September. I've talked to a cattle buyer who has an interested party, but he can only be at the auction on the tenth. As you can see, the timing for moving the cattle is critical. Do you think you can handle it?"

The young man took a leisurely sip of the thick hot coffee and swallowed. His amiable smile faded to a look of unease, and he avoided meeting her eyes. Lindsey could see beyond the young man to the little boy, much like a twelve year old—about to tell a lie.

"Well, ma'am, that's what I come to talk to you about. I thought I had these guys lined up last week, see, but now I don't if we have to move the herd this soon. There's this ropin' goin' on over at Plainview, and the stakes'r pretty high. A good roper can earn more in an afternoon of ropin' than he can drivin' a herd of cattle for five days."

"So, what are you saying?" she asked, running her finger slowly over a chip on the rim of her coffee mug, unwilling to comprehend his meaning.

He hesitated. "It's just that I don't have the crew."

"What about you? Can I count on you? Could we do it with just the two of us?"

"The truth of the matter is, ma'am, I sorta got tied up with the ropin' myself. I've signed up to team tie and for the bulldoggin'."

Lindsey knew ropers. No point in suggesting they forego their damned roping. The event could go on for two days and well into the nights. Nothing short of a major catastrophe came between a roper and a roping. And, it wasn't just the winnings but the sport and the competition that attracted them. A roping could be organized overnight and somehow the word got around.

Lindsey looked down at her hands. She was struck by another possibility. "Is there something more to this? Are you refusing to work for me because ... I'm a woman?"

"No, ma'am!" the young man protested, but his caged look belied his words.

"Can it be that in this new century there are still ranchers and ranch hands who claim working for a woman is bad luck? I suppose you all will use Cody as an example, since it's *my* herd, and look what happened to him."

"No, ma'am!" he repeated, looking as wild-eyed as the cat had when she set him down.

"I only have a few days." Lindsey shrugged and looked away. She felt very, very tired.

"I'm awful sorry, ma'am." The young man picked up his hat and rose to leave.

"By the way, I don't know your last name."

"Worthman, ma'am. Billy Ray Worthman." He fumbled with his hat, as though searching for the proper words to express his regret. "Hope there ain't no hard feelin's, ma'am. If it weren't for the truckers' strike and the local independent truckers takin' off for Denver ..."

"Truckers' strike?" She had counted on trucking the cattle as a last resort. Lindsey tried to conceal her dismay. "Well, trucking's out, anyway. These Herefords are show ready. My husband says they get beat up and scarred when hauled by truck. He said they should be walked slowly, no more than three miles an hour, five or six hours a day. With sixty, seventy miles of rangeland between here and the auction yard, walking them shouldn't be a problem."

"Ordinarily wouldn't be, ma'am." He looked embarrassed.

"Do you have any suggestions? I'm new to this part of the country ..." Lindsey let her words trail off, not wanting him to see how unsure, how totally vulnerable she felt.

"No'm, all the cowpokes I know are goin' to the ropin'."

"Well, thanks for stopping by. I'll just have to think of something else."

She showed him to the door, noting the relief he exhaled as he hastened down the steps.

Lindsey sat down at the table and stared into her empty coffee mug. "I wonder what that 'something else' is going to be?"

CHAPTER TWO

SHARING THE BAD NEWS

The ringing phone startled Lindsey, though she welcomed the outside contact. If the caller wanted to sell an insurance policy or a condo in Sedona at this point, she'd buy it—if she had any money. She knew it couldn't be Cody calling to say he'd reached home safely. His plane could scarcely have landed.

"Hi, it's CC." The girlish voice vibrated with energy, sounding nearby rather than three states away. CC was not young, but her youthful optimism and bawdy tales made her popular with her friends. She had a mercurial side to her nature too, and people who crossed her soon found with what devastating quickness she settled arguments. This talent earned her the nickname "The Terminator."

Lindsey was relieved to hear from her friend. CC's stories always made her laugh, and she could use a good chuckle right now.

"What's up?"

"Precious little since that woman cut off her husband's dicky-doo. Ace refuses to get his out now, saying, 'You can't trust a temperamental woman.' But what I called about—we critiqued your poem, 'After the Harvest,' and I thought you'd like to have our comments before your reading at the cowboy poetry festival."

Lindsey groaned. Until coming to Colorado, she had met regularly in Phoenix with a group of six other women to share their writing experiences and dreams of success. They laughingly called themselves the Future Famous Writers of America, later shortened to "Foofwahs." The women had become close after their literary sessions veered into critiques of their families, friends, and careers. In the spring, Lindsey had finally published a book of poems derived from her ranching years and had been asked to read them at the cowboy poetry festival in Flagstaff next week. Now she wouldn't be in Arizona. One more disappointment.

"Any other time and I'd be eager," Lindsey said, "but right now I'm up to my ears in cowflop."

"Uh-oh." CC's voice became serious.

Lindsey knew she could vent her frustration on CC. She hadn't talked to her all summer, and it felt good to unload on someone who cared.

"When Uncle Simon died, I have to confess, I expected as his only living relative to inherit the ranch and his herd." Her voice broke.

"Easy, girl. What's so bad about that?"

"Uncle Simon's attorney, Sleighton Lerner—" Lindsey interrupted herself to laugh. "His friends call him Sly, but Cody calls him Slow. Lerner chose this most inopportune time to be out of town. Uncle Simon died in the middle of August. Here it is the first of September, and we've only now had the reading of the will. And it was a shocker!"

"How so?"

"Uncle Simon didn't own the ranch. He leased it from a neighbor I'd never met and Uncle Simon had never mentioned, a man named J. Chandler Reed."

"With a pomp-ass name like that, he must be very rich or a plain and simple phony."

"I guess he's rich," Lindsey hesitated. "He looks rich but he doesn't seem like a phony. He has a lot going for him. Good-looking, tall, dresses well, probably in his late forties. He was at the will reading, smiling like an undertaker, sympathetic but confident that he'll get his share in time—and my share too, it seems. He's on close personal terms with Lerner and was pretty much in control of the proceedings."

"Tell me every single detail. I love stories with handsome bad guys in them, as long as my friends don't get short-changed."

Lindsey laughed. "What would I do without you? But remember, you asked for it."

Lindsey settled into a kitchen chair beside the wall phone as she began to describe the events of the morning she and Cody went to Lerner's office for the reading of Uncle Simon's will. Full of hope and dreams for financial solvency, the two were in high spirits.

Lerner's secretary, Elvera Madison, led Lindsey and Cody into the lawyer's office and seated them in front of his desk, which was absolutely bare. Without asking, Elvera brought them each a Styrofoam cup of water from the cooler in the outer office while they waited for the lawyer to appear. Then she placed a solitary file folder on the desk in front of Lerner's empty chair.

"I should have bought you a new ballpoint pen," Cody whispered to Lindsey, nodding toward the file folder.

"What for?"

"To sign all those important papers. The deed and all that stuff."

Lindsey laughed and shushed him with an elbow as Lerner entered the room.

"We'll wait for Reed," Lerner said from the doorway without explaining who Reed was.

Cody frowned and exchanged an uneasy glance with Lindsey but didn't say a word. Making no effort to introduce himself or shake their hands, Lerner sat behind his desk and turned sideways to stare out the window. Apparently lost in thought, the man quietly ran the tip of his letter opener under his fingernails and scraped the gleanings into his wastebasket.

Lindsey looked to see what the lawyer found so engrossing. Nothing outside but a few folks passing by. While continuing to await the mysterious Reed, Lerner progressed to excavating wax from his ears with a large paper clip, all the while never uttering a word. Lindsey stifled a giggle as she puzzled over Lerner's upbringing. She wondered where he might go in his grooming exercise if Reed didn't show up soon.

The minutes passed slowly while the Taylors sat with their eyes politely riveted on their cups of water, their thoughts on the inheritance and visions of burning the mortgage on their Wickenburg ranch.

When Reed finally arrived, without apologies for his delay, Lerner introduced the Taylors to the tall, athletic-looking man whose aura of wealth immediately intimidated them. Seeming unaware of his affect, he shook their hands and offered genuine-sounding condolences over Uncle Simon's death.

Lerner cut him short. "You're late, my friend. Sit down so we can get on with this affair. You can visit later."

Unchastened by Lerner's orders, Reed grinned and settled comfortably into a leather chair at Lerner's side, facing the Taylors.

Lindsey became increasingly alarmed. Something internal warned her that she and Cody were about to be gored, not a new experience for the Taylors. She braced herself.

Lerner read the will granting, as expected, all of Uncle Simon's possessions to Lindsey as his niece and sole surviving relative. What it didn't say was that Uncle Simon also left her his debts.

"As you no doubt know, Simon has been leasing the ranch and the grazing land from Reed here." Lerner smiled at Reed, who nodded in acknowledgment. Lindsey's apprehension mounted.

"No, we didn't know," Cody said. "We thought he owned his ranch."

"According to the terms of the lease agreement between J. Chandler Reed, lessor, and Simon Garland, lessee, the year's substantial grazing fee is due on the tenth of September. If not paid by then, Reed can legally take possession of the cattle. The contract, like many agrarian agreements, was based on paying for the year's pasturage once the cattle sell and the cash is available."

"Your uncle was mighty proud of his herd," Reed jumped in. "Best herd he ever had. I busted my butt to make sure he had the grazing land he needed and at a good price." Reed and Lerner exchanged smug looks.

Here it comes! Lindsey thought.

Without turning to Cody, she could read his mind. How could they come up with thousands of dollars on such short notice? Their own ranch was heavily mortgaged, their Visa and MasterCard maxed out. Raising a large amount of cash was simply out of the question unless the local bankers cooperated.

Cody spoke up. "With the cattle free and clear, surely the local bank will lend us that much money, using the cattle as collateral."

Another exchange of looks between the two men on the other side of the desk disturbed Lindsey. She began to feel everything was out of control.

Lerner replied, "With the estate in probate and you being from out of state, it's not likely you'll get much help from our bank here, but of course you can try."

The implication was clear. Lerner had already spoken to the local banker.

"What about you, Mr. Reed?" Cody asked. "Can you hold off a while until we have time to raise the cash?"

Reed looked pained. "Money is extremely tight right now, Cody, my friend. I'm sure you understand that with a large ranch like mine, my funds are tied up. I have no choice but to insist on payment no later than the tenth to meet obligations I've made, anticipating that money coming in. I'm sorry, but the answer is no."

"I see." Stunned, Cody struggled to look confident. "Don't worry, Mr. Reed, you'll have the money by the due date."

Lindsey grasped her husband's arm. Dear, sincere Cody. He doesn't have the remotest idea how he can find that kind of money, but if it's humanly possible he'll do it.

Reed waved away their concerns with a jovial air. "I'm not the least bit worried." His white teeth flashed in a broad smile that accentuated his deep tan.

Lindsey suspected Reed already knew through Lerner's investigation that the Taylor's financial condition was precarious. "I'm kind of surprised Uncle Simon didn't have more money in the bank," she said, timidly, not wanting to sound greedy. "He certainly didn't live a lavish lifestyle or gamble. If he was making so much profit from his cattle, he must have put something away."

Reed looked sympathetic. "I can understand your thinking, my dear, but there weren't many good years for poor old Simon, not like this one. Any money he had no doubt went for medical bills."

Offering his hand to Cody, Reed clapped him on the back. Tipping his white Stetson, he bowed slightly in Lindsey's direction. "Goodbye, beautiful lady." He took her hand, and for an instant their eyes met. Lindsey felt oddly uncomfortable, as though she and this attractive stranger shared some kind of delicious secret. Her face felt hot. She hoped Cody was too involved getting away from Lerner to overhear Reed's compliment.

* * *

"Then," Lindsey continued to CC, "once we got back to the ranch, WHAMMO! This morning, Cody gets thrown by Ringo, his favorite horse. The one he's been riding all summer. There's nothing more useless than a cowboy with a broken leg."

"Well ..."

"Now we—not *we* anymore—*I* have to get the cattle to the auction barn nearly seventy miles from here by the tenth of September. Nine days to get my act together. I convinced Cody I could do it, now all I've got to do is convince myself."

"Lindsey, if there's anything we can do to help, you know you can call on any one or all of us. You're in a shitpot of a predicament. Maybe among us we could loan you the money."

"No ..." Lindsey paused to consider the offer. "But thank you. Cody wouldn't hear of it. He'd never borrow from friends or relatives."

CHAPTER THREE

HELP WANTED

Bone weary, Lindsey was almost too tired to eat the leftover stew she reheated for dinner. With Cody's emergency, she'd skipped lunch but wasn't hungry even now. Close to dozing over her plate, she came to with a start at the sound of sudden loud hammering. Someone at the front door. Who could it be? On a ranch, no one uses the front door.

She jumped up and headed to the living room. She hadn't heard a car drive up or the squeal of the gate hinges. For a brief moment, she considered dashing into the office to get Uncle Simon's pistol from the desk but thought better of it. She knew it wasn't loaded and didn't know where to look for the ammunition.

Her heart pounding, Lindsey was sure whoever was at the door could hear it. She cautiously lifted the edge of the door curtain to find J. Chandler Reed on the porch, hat in hand, a broad smile on his face. That same annoying smirk he'd had in the lawyer's office.

"Evening, ma'am," he called.

Lindsey opened the door a crack.

"I hope I haven't frightened you, Lindsey."

He used her first name as though he'd known her all her life.

"I'm afraid you did." Lindsey reluctantly returned his smile, though hers felt weak and quivery. She kept the door partially closed. I don't know this man from Adam's off ox, she thought. He could be a serial killer for all I know.

"I heard about your husband's accident. I just came to tell you how sorry I am and to see if there's anything I can do to help."

Lindsey was at a loss to respond to the man's apparent sincerity. Recovering her manners, she smiled and thanked her visitor.

"I'm afraid there's nothing ..."

"I'm aware you're alone and commend your caution, but I'd hoped we'd be friends. Your Uncle Simon and I got along famously. I'd like to think you and I will continue our good neighbor policy."

Hmmm, Lindsey's mind raced. This man claims to have been a good friend, but in the time since Uncle Simon fell sick he never once came to pay his respects. Other neighbors did, but not this handsome devil. How does he know Cody broke his leg? Or that I'm alone?

She hesitated a moment longer, then decided to relax. "I guess standing here like an idiot, holding the door half closed, looks pretty unfriendly. Please come in. I didn't mean to be rude."

When Reed stepped into the room, his large frame made the living room seem cramped.

"Can I get you something to drink, a beer or a cup of coffee?"

The man waved his hand, declining her offer. With regal bearing and a light, panther-like walk, he crossed the room, and with the ease of long familiarity settled into the one comfortable lounge chair.

Lindsey leaned against the wall, arms folded across her chest. She tried not to notice his tanned good looks. He appeared much younger than a man pushing fifty, his close-trimmed sandy hair revealing little gray. He wore obviously expensive clothing, a pearl-gray western suit, shiny gray reptile cowboy boots, and a white Stetson that he tossed casually on the sofa. As she closed the door, Lindsey glanced at the long, low, white Cadillac convertible parked in the ranch driveway.

"Mr. Reed ..."

"My friends call me Chan. My lady friends, anyway, and I'd like you to call me that. Mr. Reed's my old man's name." He laughed at his timeworn joke.

"Oh, of course ... Chan. I don't mean to sound unneighborly, but I've been here all summer taking care of

Uncle Simon and I understand you live nearby and I haven't seen you in all that time and Uncle Simon never mentioned he was leasing from you and I think you can appreciate our surprise when we learned of the lease." She paused for a breath, a little embarrassed by running on so foolishly.

"Simon was real sick, sicker than he told folks around here, so it's no surprise he wanted to concentrate on getting well. I hear your husband is a competent cattleman, and I'm sure Simon knew his stock was in good hands. You said you have a ranch in Arizona?"

"That's right." Lindsey didn't want to talk about their ranch near Wickenburg. Compared to his holdings, their ranch was small potatoes. "Uncle Simon never gave up. He was confident he'd beat the cancer if anyone could. He kept hearing about people whose strong faith licked it, and he was sure it was a case of mind over matter."

"I'd have been over to see Simon sooner, but I've been in Europe all summer, then I stopped by Tulsa on business. I was devastated when I heard Simon had died and I missed his funeral."

"Oh," Lindsey said. The silence between them held for a long moment. "Cody told me you made him an offer on the cattle," she ventured at last.

"I know you've been through a lot of grief, Lindsey, and have a lot on your mind. I'm not here to push you into any decisions, with your husband away, but, yes, I did make him an offer. He said he'd let me know, but the next thing I heard he'd broken his leg and returned to Arizona. I realize you're a woman and perhaps not as experienced—"

"Mr. Reed, I think you should know that my husband and I have been cattle growers for twenty-five years, and ours has never been a limited partnership. We've been a team. My husband has the utmost confidence in my ability to look after whatever business needs to be handled. He left the decision up to me. I understand you offered us less than half of what we could expect to get at auction."

Lindsey went to the desk in the small office adjoining the living room and opened the center drawer. She was glad she had her temper under control, or she might just look around for the ammo and use Uncle Simon's pistol on this self-serving sonofabitch. Instead, she returned with the scratch pad Cody had been doing his figuring on the evening before. She checked his numbers before continuing.

"By our calculations, for four hundred and sixty head in all, including calves, we should get twice what you offered at today's market. Now that we've seen a copy of the lease, we figure we owe you a approximately one tenth of that amount." She wondered again what Uncle Simon had done with the proceeds from previous years. Maybe this man had been cheating Uncle Simon all along.

"If you had the herd at the sale barn right now, Lindsey, you might be close to being right. But you're a long way from getting that beef where it's got to go."

"Not so far—"

"You know, I meant no disrespect, but the cattle business is a man's world, and I'd hate to see you getting messed up where you don't belong. A woman simply cannot move that large a herd of cattle. You know you're not going to get anyone to help you, what with the truckers' strike and all."

"I think you'd best let me decide what I can handle ... *Chan*," she said. Lindsey squared her chin. He's going to find out what women can do.

Reed stood up and faced her. "Dear lady, I don't want to be hard-nosed about this, but I'm afraid I'm going to have to demand you stick to the original terms of the lease." Reed leveled a chilly gray gaze on her upturned face. His look and words, though steely, were suddenly softened by a kindly smile full of patience, sympathy ... condescension, as she saw it.

"We intend to fulfill Uncle Simon's contract to the letter." She was tired but painfully aware of the need for her mind to function clearly right now.

"Then I guess that's it," Reed said. "I was merely curious if you'd made up your mind to take me up on my offer, generous, I think, under the circumstances."

"I've not made a final decision. I have some comparing to do, arrangements to make. Cody's broken leg has handicapped us, I'll admit, but rest assured I'll notify you that we'll either accept your offer by the tenth or will have the lease money in your hands and the cattle off the property by that date."

Lindsey paused, remembering something Cody had told her. "By the way, if we do decide to take you up on your offer, what guarantee do we have that *you're* in a position to pay us such a large amount? I'm afraid we would have to insist on cash or a cashier's check."

"Whew," he whistled. "You are one good businesswoman, Lindsey, but you do me an injustice." He placed his hand on her shoulder, again unnerving her with his show of familiarity. Looking deep into her eyes, he said, "I'll forgive you, because you don't know my reputation. I'm recognized throughout the state, the *west*, as a responsible businessman, a man whose word is his bond. I pay my bills."

He released her shoulder with a little reassuring squeeze, and Lindsey relaxed. His manly, take-charge attitude, his firm touch made her waver, but she caught herself and knew without a doubt she could hang tough in the face of this all-too-charming rascal.

"You haven't answered my question," Lindsey said, her tone chilly, controlled.

"Ma'am, I don't like to discuss my private business with just anyone, but my banker will back my draft for the purchase of the cattle."

Lindsey knew better. After they'd left the lawyer's office yesterday, Cody began making phone calls about this man who had suddenly become so important in their lives. Cody had even been on the phone this morning before his accident, discovering from more than one source that Reed's lavish lifestyle and poor management had led him into financial hot water. He was three years behind in lien payments, and the bank was threatening to foreclose the ranch.

"And what guarantee do I have that the bank will honor *your* draft? I'm afraid I must demand a letter of credit from your bank verifying that they will honor your draft." Lindsey smiled inwardly as a wave of anger flushed to the roots of the man's sandy hair.

"Great balls of *fire*, woman!" Reed turned away, then regaining his equanimity grabbed his white hat from the sofa and bowed in mock humility. "I can see that I've stumbled into a hornet's nest. I should hire you for my business manager. Dear lady, I'm afraid we don't really understand each other yet. I've come here as your friend and neighbor, in good faith and decency, to see what I can do to help, and you start spitting nails. I guess I'm pushing you too hard."

He paused, shaping the brim of his Stetson in his strong, brown hands. He seemed to be considering something. "You've been under a lot of stress lately, and you probably need some room. I sincerely apologize for my bad manners. Tell you what. Tomorrow night, why don't you and I drive into town for dinner at the country club?" Again, that look, like they had a secret, just the two of them.

Lindsey was speechless for a moment. She'd expected him to become angry, and she didn't care. The man was too smooth. Now, instead of being angry, he was apologizing and inviting her to dinner. Caught off-balance for a few moments, she was tempted to say yes. Then she remembered the rapidly shrinking timeframe. The cattle had to be gathered into the corrals, and she had barely enough time to make arrangements to move them elsewhere if that was to be her decision.

"I appreciate the invitation, but I'm afraid it's out of the question," she said, her voice softening.

"You're too pretty a woman to stay cooped up here playing nursemaid to a bunch of smelly cattle," Reed pressed.

"I've a job to do, Mr. Reed ... Chan. But thanks, anyway. If you'll excuse me, it's been a long day."

"As you wish, pretty lady," Reed said, and tipped his hat.

Lindsey walked out on the porch and watched him drive away. This big man is none too pleased at things not going his way, she thought. I suppose he's used to smiling at women and having them jump to accept his dinner invitations. Thank God for the information Cody gleaned about Chan's weak finances—and his extravagance. A person can't be too careful, and, besides, I don't accept dinner dates with strangers—or near strangers. I'm a happily married woman.

Inside the house, Lindsey closed the door and leaned against it, smiling. At first, she tried to deny that she was pleased he found her attractive. But she couldn't miss the look in his eye. For the first time in a long while, she felt heady, no longer tired. He's a charmer all right and great looking. Dinner at the country club would have been fun.

She hurried into the kitchen and began furiously washing the few dirty dishes. Before she finished, she stole a look in the mirror by the door.

I don't look so bad for a woman my age.

* * *

The next morning, Lindsey awoke early, planning to drive into Plainview. She had to get a permit from the cattle inspector to move the herd, and she hoped he might be able to suggest where she could find a crew.

Lindsey had tossed and turned half the night, searching for a solution to her dilemma before she finally fell into exhausted sleep. She'd managed to come up with only one alternate plan—Plan B—to be used only if all else failed. One that could be aborted at the last minute if Plan A worked out after all.

Once in town, Lindsey found that the cattle inspector was out on a call, but the teen-age girl at the desk said he'd be at the ranch in the morning to inspect the cattle. Lindsey asked a few more questions, quickly discovering that the girl knew little, if anything, about driving cattle or hiring a crew. She did suggest checking the Plainview newspaper.

Lindsey stopped by the newspaper office. There were no "Jobs Wanted" ads by cowhands but plenty offering work. The next issue would be too late to advertise for a crew.

The editor was friendly but shook his head when asked about hiring cowhands. "Most of the young people move off to Denver or someplace where there are city jobs. Not much to do here since the awning factory relocated to Mexico."

Lindsey thanked him and moved on. Time was running out. If she were to put Plan B into action, she had to make that phone call to CC before noon today. It seemed clear Plan A would not be feasible.

She needed time to think and something to eat. She knew Evelyn's Cafe down the street to be a hangout for the town idlers and retirees who spent their days swapping lies and playing checkers. She could ask around at Evelyn's.

The cafe was deserted except for two old men occupying a booth along the wall. The tall, rawboned woman behind the counter eyed her briefly, then went about her business filling salt shakers. Lindsey approached the men and laid out her problem.

"Sorry, young lady," the first man said. "Can't help you. I used to ride but I got a bum back an' it'd kill me now to get on a horse."

"I ain't got no good opinion of horses in the first place," the other man volunteered. "And I ain't crazy enough to trust myself to the whim of any stupid animal."

"Well, thanks for listening." Lindsey told them she was Simon Garland's niece and gave them her phone number in case they should run into someone looking for work.

Sliding onto a swivel stool at the counter, she ordered coffee and the number two special, scrambled eggs and bacon. She'd skipped breakfast and was getting a headache.

"How about you, Evelyn?" Lindsey said to the woman behind the counter. Evelyn had been close enough to overhear her conversation with the old men. Maybe she knew someone.

"Huh. Cowhands are a scarce commodity these days. The young folks are only interested in running around on motorcycles and driving hot rods. Now, there's a thought. If you could herd cattle with motorcycles you'd get all the help you could use."

Lindsey laughed. She liked Evelyn's easy manner. To make conversation more than anything else, she asked, "Have you ever taken part in a cattle drive?"

Evelyn grinned, her uneven teeth giving her heart-shaped face a homely, old-fashioned look. "I used to round up cattle on my folks' ranch when I was a kid, but that was a long time ago." A wistful expression played over her face as she rubbed out a spot on the counter with her dishcloth. "Sorry, I'd sure like to help you out, but I gotta look after my business here."

"Thanks, anyway." Lindsey paid for her breakfast, then used the public phone to call CC. She left a message and drank more coffee and reread the want ads while she waited for CC to call back. CC called after twenty minutes and Lindsey easily convinced her that Plan B could work. But then, CC always loved new and outrageous ideas.

She called Cody to explain her plan. He sounded skeptical and worried but had no alternative to offer. "Sorry, honey, but I'm full of painkillers, and my judgment isn't what it ought to be."

"Cody, I may be making the biggest mistake of my life, but I see no options. CC said she was pretty sure she could get at least five of the Foofwahs here in a couple of days. She wasn't sure about Angie. She may be on her way to San Antonio by now."

Cody groaned. "I've seen the Foofwahs, honey. They may be a fine bunch of writers, but that's a far cry from being *riders*. They're all overweight ..."

"Not *all*," Lindsey objected.

"Mostly all, and they're not kids, either. I doubt they'd know which end of a cow to feed. You're going to be driving four hundred and sixty cattle nearly seventy miles, Lindsey. Have you really thought this idea through?"

"I know what you're saying, but I think it would work if you'd get Jake Wiggins to help us out. Between Jake and me, we could almost do it by ourselves. We need the others to keep an eye out for strays."

"I don't like it, Lindsey, but what can I say? I'll call Jake. You make sure you get permission from all the property owners along the route to move the cattle over their land. Ask the owners to provide you with extra hay for the cattle and send the bill here. Grass this late in the year won't be enough, and you don't want the cattle losing weight on the trail."

"Yes." Lindsey made notes of things to do. "And have Jake bring some extra horses."

"Right. Four should do it."

"Cody, what if we were to sell off enough cattle to pay Mr. Reed, then take the others to Arizona to build up our herd of breeding stock? Or find some land to keep them on here? These are fine breeding stock and would give us a fresh start."

"No, Lindsey. Sell them all. It would be smarter to use your inheritance to buy more land here. Land gives you collateral to buy cattle. Besides, commercial cattle do better here. A breeding herd wouldn't survive on the desert."

Lindsey sighed. It was worth a try. As much as she loved this Colorado country, she knew Cody would never leave Arizona.

CHAPTER FOUR

GOOD FRIENDS

The Foofwahs little dreamed of undertaking a real-life western adventure beyond their most capricious imaginings. But bonded by their dogged pursuit of the literary arts and their Musketeerian motto, "Trouble for one means trouble for all," the women from the beginning of their friendship vowed to help a sister in distress.

The women first met in Chloë's creative writing class three years earlier and continued meeting after the semester's end to spark their writing efforts and to critique each other's work. Eventually, social events supplanted the harshness of critiques, and husbands were invited to their parties and picnics. The Foofwahs made no pretense that fun was anything other than their topmost goal and that extended to their writing.

Lindsey's call came when five of the seven Foofwahs were attending the First Annual Writers of the Purple Sage Conference in the central Arizona resort town of Bradford. Founded in the early 1900s by a descendent of the Mayflower Bradfords, the town, with few exceptions, was noted for its puritanical leanings.

The Foofwahs arrived late at the Bradford Inn the night before the conference was to begin. They'd decided to wait for Chloë whose evening class met from six o'clock until nine, so they could drive the hundred or so miles together rather than take two cars. Penny was younger than the others, and the only one of the five willing to drive the curving mountain road at night.

They were devastated to find their reservations for lodging had not been held past six o'clock.

"You mean registering for the conference wasn't sufficient to guarantee our rooms?" Chloë felt her equable manner slipping. Normally, somewhat timid, she preferred to avoid conflict at any cost, but she couldn't conceal her astonishment at the hotel's lack of consideration. "We're not in New York City, you know. Wouldn't you think someone would have had the sense to realize that five conference registrants in *three separate rooms* would be committed enough to show up later if not sooner?"

She turned to CC. "I don't want to appear rude, but I hope he got the message that someone made a dumb mistake."

"It was probably him, the little twerp."

"Sorry, ma'am," the clerk said addressing Chloë, his manner restrained and haughty. "Our rules are standard in the industry."

"Industry, schmindustry." CC, The Terminator, stepped forward. "Find us a room or we'll report you to the FCC, the ICC, the IHC, and the grand jury. You screwed up, buddy."

Uncertain what the woman was talking about, the clerk agreed to call the few other hotels in Bradford. He desperately wanted to get rid of the old bags before his boss heard the ruckus and reprimanded him for not checking the conference list prior to forfeiting their rooms. The writers' conference promised to be a good piece of business for years to come if all went well. The staff had been drilled on this at daily briefings over the past several weeks.

The problem the clerk faced was that a popular arts and crafts festival had begun over the past weekend for a ten-day run, to end after Labor Day. The town was loaded with tourists hoping to find treasures among the products of the many Arizona artisans and retirees with hobby skills who were busily turning out charming and unusual commodities. Early in the day, people had begun arriving at the hotel without reservations and were quick to slip him a few extra dollars for a room. The clerk couldn't bring himself to turn away this kind of money, but he also needed continuing employment. He told himself he was doing the hotel a favor because the conference rates were half the normal room charge, something management should have thought of when they booked a large event to coincide with the festival. He was sure a fair number wouldn't show up anyway, nor would they have the decency to cancel.

"I'm sorry, ladies." The clerk turned from the phone to face Chloë while avoiding CC's piercing brown eyes. He glanced at the other three women sprawled wearily in lounge chairs, waiting for the confusion to be resolved.

Returning his gaze to Chloë's frantic expression, her wide green eyes pinched in a troubled frown and a tendril of carefully coifed auburn hair straggling onto her forehead, the clerk felt a moment's compassion for the women. "There's one more place, though I hesitate ..." He paused and looked at CC, then turned back to the phone and placed another call.

After a couple of minutes negotiating, the clerk returned, relieved to have a solution. He handed them a slip of paper with an address. "Here's where to find the Eagle's Nest. It's out just beyond the edge of town. They have a room that will be ready in an hour."

"A room? One room for five of us?" CC shrieked. "What's wrong with you? Can't you see we're not kids, and we're not into sleeping on the floor?"

"Yes, ma'am. But that's all I could find. Believe me, it's the last room in Bradford, and it's got two double beds."

"That'll take care of four of us. What about the fifth?" Chloë asked, her gentle voice cracking with strain as though she knew she'd be the odd man out, sleeping on what?

"I'm sure they can work something out, ma'am. Probably bring in a rollaway."

Chloë groaned. "Those things are for kids or at best small adults."

The clerk could see his boss standing in the office, ready to come out and check the night receipts. He had to get rid of these people. "You'll probably want to hurry. They wouldn't promise to hold the room."

"I guess we don't have any choice," Chloë said. Tall and regal, her whole body sagged as she slumped in a lounge chair beside Gina.

"Apparently not," CC said. She returned to the desk. "Are you sure you aren't saving a few rooms for last-minute VIP arrivals?"

"Definitely not," the clerk replied.

CC's anger succumbed to reality. "It's eleven-thirty now, and we can't afford to lose that room too. Tell him we're on our way," she ordered. She started to join the others, then turned and approached the man. A picture of maternal sweetness, she offered him a benediction. "May the ravens of hell peck out your brain, one bite at a time, asshole."

* * *

At the Eagle's Nest, the women rapidly discovered that the motel's name should have been "Lover's Roost."

"Twenty-four fifty per hour," the elderly, rheumy-eyed clerk stated with authority. "Or forty-nine fifty per day plus ten dollars extra per person."

"Highway robbery!" Gina exclaimed. The businesswoman of the group, Gina had retired early from a career as a marketing executive for a fast-track conglomerate.

"Listen, lady, you want it or not? I won't have no trouble renting it out."

"We'll take it, we'll take it," Gina relented. Her face felt stony. She wasn't used to defeat in business dealings, and it annoyed her to be forced to accept short shrift first at the hotel and now at this fleabag motel.

In the past, she had managed corporate and customer relations with great poise and knew well the techniques for getting her way. The problem here, though, she told herself, was that she was trying to argue with someone with space for rent between his ears. "Just give us our keys."

"Now hold on, sister," the old man said. "It ain't going to be ready for another hour. It's paid up till one A.M., so you're just going to have to wait. If you want it, that is."

"What kind of a place is this?" Penny called from the doorway where she'd been standing as though braced for a quick getaway. Her taffy-colored ponytail whirled back and forth as she looked from one to another for an answer. Her china-blue eyes widened to form perfect circles. "You rent your rooms for an hour at a time?" Those eyes, usually so merry and now so tired, glared in disapproval, as her small, plump body swelled in repugnance.

"You want it or not?" The old man looked annoyed. "Look lady. I ain't askin' you what five women are planning to use it for. Ain't my business."

The women gasped at the implications of his remark.

Gina was the first to recover. She placed her hand over CC's mouth before her friend could proclaim another benediction. "I *said*, we'll take it."

"Count me out. I'll sleep in the car," Penny said, retreating to the outdoors, each step registering disgust. "What if any of my friends or members of our church saw me coming out of a place like this? They'd never understand. Worse, I'd never have an opportunity to explain. People catch diseases in rat holes like this!"

Kai-ling, the fifth member of the group, stepped forward. Born in Mainland China and reared in Taiwan, Kai-ling had survived deprivation far worse than this. She was a tall, well-proportioned woman with a commanding, intelligent bearing.

"Thank you. We will sit here until the room is ready, but, please, may we have another chair?"

Responding to the kindlier, polite tone, the old man hobbled around from behind the desk, dragging a straight-backed kitchen chair.

"You want some coffee?" he asked. "It ain't too old."

"No, thank you," they murmured in numb unison, eyes at half-mast.

Gina picked up a dog-eared tabloid from a side table and flipped through the pages, pausing at the most lurid captions. "I *never* read this kind of thing ... *What*? A two-headed baby was born pregnant with Siamese twins!" Her lips tight with disapproval, she cast the magazine aside and dropped her head to her chest.

The women sat or slouched in varying states of discomfort on the hard, threadbare, tweed couch and plastic arm chairs, all upholstered in mismatched shades of brown. Kai-ling leaned forward on her kitchen chair, staring at the shoelaces of her Nikes.

Finally, from the rear of the parking lot a car was revved its engine. Lights flashed across the smeared, dusty windows of the motel office as the car bumped over the uneven asphalt before turning off into the night.

"Here's your key," the old man said.

Gina grabbed the key from the old man. "Thank you. Just tell us the room number. It's not on the key."

"It don't need a number. Works on all the doors."

"*What*?" Gina was beyond exasperation.

"Number 33, straight across the parking lot. You might want to wait till my wife changes the sheets and towels. I'll go wake her up." The old man paused in the doorway to his living quarters as though expecting an interruption.

"No, no." Gina's inner alarm sounded at the thought of yet another delay. She was tired enough to die, and it was already one-fifteen. "Just give us the linens. We'll take care of things."

They grabbed their duffel bags from the car, careful not to waken Penny, who was curled up in the back seat, her small, round body neatly tucked into an S-curve to accommodate the limited space.

Gina unlocked the door of the motel room. "Oh, jeez." She choked on the thick, stale cigarette smoke hanging in the air.

"How can we spend the night in this stinking, rumpled room?" CC asked.

"Would you rather sleep on the courthouse lawn?" Gina groaned. In her years of business travel, she'd stayed at upscale hotels, never exposed to sleaze like this. She fervently hoped the writers' conference was worth the indignities she and her friends were suffering.

Chloë's expression brightened. "The park doesn't seem a bad alternative."

"Come on, get real," Gina said. "The wet grass and hard park benches in the cool night air would cause worse grief than we already have."

With a choral sigh of surrender, the others agreed.

"We aren't old, but we're not exactly young either," Chloë conceded.

Gina's strong sense of order resurrected itself, and she got down to business. Without another word, she cautiously picked up an overflowing wastebasket, careful to protect her recently manicured nails. She carried the basket to the rear of the parking lot, making sure her beige linen pantsuit didn't brush against the filthy dumpster.

She felt cross when she returned to the room. Then, laughing at the irony of the situation, she pushed a blonde bang away from her eyes, placed her hands on her hips, and rendered a first-rate imitation of Bette Davis's immortal line, "What a *dump*!"

It broke the tension, and everyone laughed. Chloë and CC set about changing one bed, while Kai-ling pulled the sheets off the other. With the door and window open and the bathroom fan blowing to circulate fresh air, the room was habitable by two o'clock.

CC gingerly slipped into her nightclothes while standing in the bathtub complaining, "I'm afraid to open my suitcase anywhere that doesn't have a clear view of the invading cockroach battalion."

No sightings were declared by the time she finished changing, but CC insisted, "That can of pesticide wouldn't be under the bathroom sink if war hadn't been declared. Trust me." The effervescence that usually fueled her pixie demeanor had receded into a mild froth, and she flopped onto one of the beds, sighed, and fell hard asleep.

Gina lay down beside Kai-ling. She rolled onto her side to face a wall papered with yellow cabbage roses. Thinking of CC's assertions about bugs, she inspected the pattern carefully and found nothing alive. "Wouldn't Angie have loved this?"

"You think so?" Kai-ling asked.

"Not the room, the bizarre experience."

Angie, the seventh Foofwah, had regaled them with tales from her years on the road as a teller of fortunes. With flowing red hair and mysterious, cat-like dark eyes, she dressed in gypsy costumes replete with bangles and beads while she read palms, tarot cards, and crystal balls at carnivals and fairs from coast to coast, border to border. She loved the challenge of plumbing people's psyches, and while that type of life was tough, it bought her freedom. With a sense of humor that recognized the ridiculous in any situation, Angie could indeed have spun a riotous story for the Foofwah chronicles from the evening's events. But she was in Phoenix preparing for the coming season before heading off to Texas and the winter circuit.

Emerging from the bathroom, Chloë said, "We're out of tissue and soap. I'll go to the office and get some."

She stepped outside, but quickly returned. "The 'No Vacancy' sign's blinking, and the office is dark," she reported. "Never mind. I think I have some in my cosmetics bag."

The women muttered thanks, and protest ceased until the alarm screamed at six a.m.

* * *

After a continental breakfast and the first two hour-long sessions of the conference, the women met in the hospitality area for a coffee break.

"What's next?" Gina asked. In spite of the stress from the previous night's misadventure, she felt it was important to look polished and poised in the event she met someone important who took an interest in her writing. She'd dressed in a peach leisure suit, a shade called "Desert Sunrise" by its Italian designer. The collar and pockets were trimmed with hand-embroidered horses and flowers.

"'Too Much Sex?'" Chloë responded. Her eyes, still tired from lack of sleep, had lost their emerald luster and flattened out to an impassive gray-green, like stagnant pools of alkali.

"Poor Chloë," Gina said. "Why on earth would you be thinking of sex at a time like this?"

Chloë snapped, "That's the name of the next session."

"Oh," Gina said, sorry she'd misjudged her friend.

"Yeah, that's choice," CC said. Her high spirits had returned. "Bet we could add a thing or two ourselves. Did you see the T-shirts they're selling with the names of the seminars? Think I'll pick up one of those 'sex' ones and surprise Ace." She hurried toward the vendor tables with the others close behind.

CC loved T-shirts with significant slogans. She sorted through them as though she were picking humorous birthday cards, laughing out loud when one tickled her fancy. Besides "Too Much Sex?" for her husband Ace, she chose a sentimental one for Penny, "Friendships are Forever." Another she couldn't decide whether to keep or give away proclaimed:

> The only way to get rid of a temptation is to yield to it.
>
> \- Oscar Wilde

She tried to get Gina to take it, but Gina said, "I don't wear those things."

"Never mind," CC said. "I'll find a use for it. It's too good to pass up."

Chloë selected one she knew her husband Ray would appreciate:

Chloë
Swamp Lady
I want to be where you are.

After the women made their purchases, CC stopped to scan the bulletin board perched on an easel near the registration desk. She picked up a note asking her to call Lindsey in Colorado, then rejoined her group.

"With Lindsey's problems," CC said, "this may not be good news. She called fifteen minutes ago."

During the drive to Bradford the night before, CC had told the others about Lindsey's woes.

"Maybe Lindsey's decided to join us," Gina offered, more concerned about juggling an array of notebooks, bags, and writing utensils without breaking a nail than worried about the reason for the call.

"Hmmm, not likely," CC said. "Why don't you go on in and find us seats. I'll give her a call."

* * *

CC hung up after reassuring Lindsey she and the other Foofwahs would enthusiastically come to her rescue. Then she placed a call to Angie. When she returned to the lecture room, "Too Much Sex?" was in progress, and the Foofwahs were following the lecture with rapt attention. She slipped into the place saved for her near the door.

"Human nature being what it is, we are interested in sex because it is a mystery." The white-haired lecturer leaned his spare frame casually against the lectern and expanded on his topic. "Sex ranks near the top of our list of motivations, both for our lives and the lives of our characters. We have become so blasé, so inured to emotion, it takes a powerful stimulus to arouse passion in readers today. It's doubtful that most of you will put enough sex in your novels."

"Or our lives," CC added in a stage whisper. Heads turned, and the Foofwahs frowned in her direction.

"Shhh," Penny whispered.

CC scribbled a note and passed it around:

MUST SEE YOU ALL OUTSIDE. NOW!!

Gina let an impatient look escape but quickly retracted it when CC mouthed, "It's important."

The women filed silently out of the lecture room. The speaker paused, looking puzzled as though wondering which of his remarks had offended so many of them, then he shrugged and continued.

CC hurriedly explained Lindsey's call for help. "She just needs us to help her look after a few things for three or four days. It shouldn't be too bad."

"Wouldn't it be dangerous?" Gina asked.

"I don't know. Can you ride a horse?"

Gina hesitated. "Sort of."

"Can the rest of you?" CC looked around. Everyone nodded yes.

"It would be like a grand cookout!" Penny offered. "Without the kids along. What a hoot!"

Kai-ling agreed. "It would be fun."

"I'm not sure," Chloë said, but after a pause, relented. "Okay, I'm game."

Without further hesitation, the Foofwahs headed for their car, united in their determination to help a dear friend. Their luggage was already loaded; they had expected to find better accommodations or to leave the conference at the end of the day anyway. Now, they could be back home in Phoenix in two hours, repack for the trip to Colorado, and explain, cajole, or browbeat their husbands, whatever it took, to be at the Taylor's ranch in Wickenburg by evening. Cody would have horses and advice and someone named Jake waiting.

CHAPTER FIVE

THE GYPSY SPIRIT

Before telling the other Foofwahs about Lindsey's call that motivated them to leave the conference, CC had phoned Angie, fearing she might already be on the road to Texas. She knew Angie's derring-do, flexibility, and enthusiasm would be critical to their task. And just as important, Angie's mobile home, the "Gypsy Spirit," could serve as their chuck wagon.

Through a lifetime guided by misadventure, Angie had somehow managed to keep her own gypsy-like spirit intact. She had severed her ties with her family when she ran away from home to marry Buddy Jessup, the high school football hero. Her family called him "heathen trash," and her father tried to have Buddy arrested for statutory rape. She'd never returned home.

In time, Angie's marriage proved a disaster, but with no marketable skills and two children, divorce was unthinkable. She eventually divorced Buddy anyway after their sixteen-year-old son was killed in a car crash for which Buddy blamed her. She had given the boy permission to use her car that night against Buddy's orders.

After a year of therapy and black depression, she took her share of the divorce settlement and made a down payment on a fortune-telling concession owned by a woman she met in group therapy. The woman convinced her that with a birth number of seven, she surely had extra-sensory perception. Angie puzzled over this, thinking in that case she might have predicted her son's death, but the woman persisted.

"You are wise beyond your years. And you are very caring. I will teach you all you need to know."

Angie had no regrets. She loved traveling and meeting people, and, best of all, the independence. Some of her predictions came so close to reality that in time she began to believe that she did indeed possess some degree of ESP.

When CC phoned, the mobile home park manager summoned Angie to accept the call in the office. It was unusually warm even for Phoenix on this September morning, an indication that the temperature would reach the low hundreds by afternoon. Already uncomfortable as she jogged over to the manager's office, Angie thought perhaps she should avoid the call. Not many people had her phone number. The prophet in her sensed that this was bad news.

With her wide dark eyes, gamin nose, and friendly smile, Angie was known throughout the carnival circuit as the flame-haired gypsy with a story for every occasion, the fortuneteller who delighted children, the energetic vagabond. Now, after she hung up, she was more distressed than happy.

For the past week, she'd been in Phoenix, her home base, working on her schedule for the coming season of carnivals and fairs while laying in supplies. Besides a good store of food, she needed candles, incense, and a new crystal ball. She had planned to take off for San Antonio at the beginning of next week. The hot weather made her lethargic and subject to emotional swings that were totally alien to her. She hated this side of herself. For the first time, she was not looking forward to a new year of being on the road.

"Dammit, it's all the fault of that stupid creative writing class!" Her only audience was the slow-witted fifteen-year-old Tom, employed to do maintenance work around the trailer park. Today, she'd hired him to help her reload the Gypsy Spirit.

"If it hadn't been for that weak moment, my life would be so much simpler. Here I am committed to changing my whole schedule before I even begin, and this afternoon I'll set off on some stupid wild goose—or wild cow—chase. Dammit, dammit, dammit!"

She kicked the case of canned goods she'd tried to lift but dropped. Tom grinned sympathetically, lifted the carton, and stacked it with the other food supplies.

"I spent all last week buying this stuff for the trip and now I'll have to spend most of the day unloading and storing it," Angie called to him.

Maybe it's not me and not the hot weather, she told herself as she and Tom removed the supplies and costumes she'd so carefully packed. Maybe it's the big four-oh birthday party the Foofwahs gave me last week. I'm definitely getting too old for birthday parties and for this rugged life. I've got to find another way to make a living. Traveling from state to state hitting the carnivals isn't as much fun as it used to be.

She and Tom worked silently for a while, shifting the load to an air-conditioned rental storage unit.

Before they finished, Angie inspected the Gypsy Spirit critically. It had entered this world as a GMC two-and-a-half ton, flatbed truck. Someone with more imagination than expertise had converted it into a recreational vehicle by building a room on the flat bed. The roof was peaked and covered with shake shingles. Apparently, the builder had shingles left over and decided to cover the sides with shingles as well. Had the little house been sitting in someone's back yard instead of on the back of a truck, it might easily have been mistaken for a dwarf's cottage stolen from the woods. Resembling a miniature Swiss chalet with a little blue door and small windows outlined with blue against white-painted shingles, the house sported a wooden plaque over the door bearing the inscription "Fortunes."

The Gypsy Spirit served Angie as both home and livelihood. When open for spiritual readings, the studio couch was piled high with pillows and covered with a dark red, Hindustani spread. Cluttered shelves were concealed by red velvet drapes. A tiny, draped table in the middle of her "psychic room" held a crystal ball to complete the illusion of mystery.

Angie viewed the smooth dual rear tires of her truck and shook her head. "The engine needs work, too," she sighed. She had hoped the tires would last until she reached San Antonio where she could make enough money to purchase tires—two anyway.

"Now all this has changed because Lindsey needs help, and I've promised I'll take off for Colorado to help with a *cattle drive,* for God's sake! Will these tires get us there and back?" Tom was still nearby but Angie didn't care if she had a listener. She was used to talking to herself. "Of all the absurd things! What do I know about driving cattle? What do they need me for? I've jockeyed this old truck thousands of miles, but I've never been on a horse." While she talked, she and Tom worked methodically, carrying cartons of supplies into the storage unit.

"How'd you get involved in a cattle drive?" Tom asked, more for conversation than any genuine interest.

"It all started three years ago."

Angie had been told many times that she should write about her adventures, that they'd make a wonderfully funny book with her insight into other peoples' motivations and her own special brand of humor. The last time she'd heard it, she'd made a silent pledge to learn how to write her book. Fate stepped in when, back home in Phoenix, the local paper carried an announcement of a creative writing class to start the following week. Reacting with her usual impetuosity, Angie called the instructor, Chloë, and before she put the phone down she'd enrolled in the class. She could attend in the mornings and wait tables in the afternoons and evenings. Maybe even tell a fortune or two.

Angie was excited about the class but apprehensive because it had been over twenty years since she'd been in school as a student. She felt like an intruder when she entered the classroom the first time, but after looking around she was encouraged by the friendly smiles of the other women, who seemed to be even older than she. Lindsey Taylor, with a warm smile, beckoned Angie to a seat beside her, and they became instant friends, a relationship Angie cherished.

No men, she thought, a little disappointed. But just as well—no distractions.

When the class began, she sat in the front row, with tears in her eyes, thinking this was something she'd wanted to do all her life, then the next moment wondering what in the devil was she doing in a classroom when she should be planning next season's itinerary.

"Now I'm hung to meet the Foofwahs in Wickenburg and be prepared to haul five of them to Colorado for this blasted cattle drive." She sighed. "But Lindsey needs me."

"What are Foofwahs?" Tom asked.

"You wouldn't want to know," she replied, giving him a friendly cuff on the shoulder.

"Kind of sounds like a name for airheads," Tom said, continuing with his work.

Angie put down the carton she was carrying and studied him for a moment, wondering if he might be brighter than she thought. Then, with a look of annoyance at herself and a flash of loyalty to her friends, she responded, "They most certainly are *not* airheads! They're my *best friends*!"

CHAPTER SIX

DECISIONS, DECISIONS

Lindsey fretted over her decision, in spite of the enthusiastic response from the Foofwahs. By early afternoon, she decided it might be prudent to put aside her qualms about accepting Chan's dinner invitation. Just possibly, he was sincere when he said he wanted to help, and he, of all people, could be the source she needed for cowboys to get her cattle to auction. It wouldn't be too late to call off the Foofwahs. Tonight they'd be in Wickenburg where Cody would provide horses and advice, and she could easily stop them. It would be worth a try. For the first time all day, she felt hopeful.

"Let's see if the man really meant it when he offered to take me to dinner." She found his listing in the directory and quickly punched in the numbers.

"Lindsey! What can I do for you?" Chan's voice was full of smiles. His heartiness calmed her, though she still had a few reservations about her own boldness in making this call.

"I thought if you haven't already made other plans, I'd like to take you up on your offer for dinner this evening."

"My dear, I'd cancel dinner with the governor in favor of taking out such a pretty lady. What time should I pick you up?"

Lindsey swallowed hard. This seemed mighty like a date rather than a business engagement. "Six o'clock?"

"Perfect. Wear something upscale casual."

"I have a dress. It's not fancy. My best clothes are back home."

"A dress will be just right. I'll see you at six, and we'll have dinner at the country club."

After she hung up, Lindsey trembled like a teenager making her first date. She told herself she was being ridiculous.

It's been a long time since I've been to dinner with a man other than Cody. It wouldn't be so bad if this one weren't so good-looking. And that look of his, boring inside me, like he knows my deepest secrets. What have I done?

Nonsense, her conscience spoke up. *Have faith in your ability to stay on the straight and narrow. You are merely trying to find help to move your cattle. Chan seems sincere, even though helping you wouldn't be to his advantage. Just go, check him out, and quit all this fussing!*

I should call Cody to tell him.

Fool! Idiot! Do you want poor, injured Cody to lie there in Arizona worrying about you? You're a big girl. Act like one, and you won't get in trouble.

* * *

Over-estimating the time she needed to bathe and dress, anxious to look just right, Lindsey found herself ready and waiting an hour ahead of Chan's arrival. It gave her more time to fret.

This *is* like a first date!

Quit thinking "date" stupid! Her conscience was still on the job. *It's business. Business.*

Lindsey wore the only dress she'd brought from home, a navy blue sheath with a v-neck. When she looked in the mirror, she thought her sun-burnished face was perhaps too red. He might not see it as the glow of good health so much as the face of a ranch woman who's been outdoors too long. Too bad she didn't have any powder to tone it down. She needed accessories to make the plain dress more interesting, but the only jewelry she had was her gold wristwatch and her wedding band. She wished she'd remembered her small, gold loop earrings, but she hadn't thought to pack for dressing up. She had only this one basic, go-anywhere sheath she'd purchased for Uncle Simon's funeral.

It's too plain, she thought.

Cut it out! It's just right, the reflection in the mirror chided.

Her navy heels seemed too tight after wearing boots and sneakers all summer, but they'd have to do. Most of all, she hated to wear pantyhose. Boot socks were more her style.

When Chan arrived, he was dressed in shades of light gray with his western-style shirt open at the collar. An exquisitely cut lightweight jacket emphasized his broad shoulders and slim hips. The grays complemented eyes that twinkled with invitation, making Lindsey think maybe it wasn't too late to back out.

Cody, trust me.

Before she could say anything, Chan whisked her away to the country club in his customized white Cadillac convertible. With the top down, Lindsey relished the feel of the wind in her hair in spite of the slight coolness of the evening air.

Chan pointed out historical landmarks she'd seen many times, and told her local tales passed down by the old settlers.

"Cody and I seldom went out except to shop for necessities. A couple of times we went to movies." She felt easier with him now. "I've read up on the history of the pioneer days along the Santa Fe Trail, but I hadn't heard the local legends."

"Reading the history is good, but it fails to bring true perspective to the hardships of folks who developed this vast land of precious cattle and rich crops."

Lindsey scrutinized the countryside as they passed dense rows of cottonwoods outlining the many streams and creeks feeding the mighty Arkansas flowing to the southeast. This was the beginning of the route along which the cattle would need to be moved. Far off, the long low purple Rockies stretched across the west. They looked to her like a crouching pride of patient lions, and she began to create a poem in her head.

"You're very quiet," Chan said.

Lindsey confided her thoughts about the poem and told him of her modest success writing cowboy poetry.

"Have you been published?"

"A small book of poems. My favorite, 'Your Place or Mine?' was published recently in *The Old Settler's Review*."

The title of the poem picked up Chan's interest. "I'd like to hear it, if you can remember how it goes."

"Oh, I can remember." Lindsey was pleased with his interest. She recited all eight verses of a poignant tale about a tenant rancher who falls in love with the absentee owner's land.

When she finished, Chan whistled appreciatively. "Pretty impressive, lady. I don't think I've known any poets before. I will say, though, I thought the subject referred to something, uhmmm, more romantic." He covered her hand with his and gave it a masterful squeeze.

Lindsey pulled her hand away and straightened up in the seat. She rode silently until they reached the country club, pondering how friendly she should let the man be before telling him to back off. She liked the firmness, the reassurance of his touch. She convinced herself he intended nothing special. She was just being a prude.

Inside the club, Chan seemed to enjoy showing off his importance by leading her to "his" table, permanently reserved beside the window overlooking the eighteenth green.

Over martinis, Chan told her the background of some of the more prominent diners around them. One was a judge, another a banker. Lindsey recognized the banker as the man who had turned down the loan application she and Cody made earlier in the week. She attempted to smile at him, but the man apparently didn't see her.

Sly Lerner entered by himself and, other than a cordial nod, ignored them. He was soon joined by the plain-faced stick of a woman Lindsey recognized as his secretary.

"Sly's wife died last year, so Elvera fills in socially," Chan explained. "And no, I don't think there's anything going on between them," he intercepted the question in Lindsey's eyes. "But then, who knows?" he grinned wickedly. "Old Elvera may have hidden talents."

Lindsey focused on her shrimp cocktail. Lerner never failed to come up with surprises.

At dinner, Chan dazzled her with his knowledge of fine wines and described how the various sauces for the entrees on the menu were concocted.

By dessert, Lindsey felt it was time to bring up business matters. She looked across the candle-lit table into his smoky gray eyes and hesitated. The cocktails and wine had made her light-headed. Now, the after-dinner Tuaca made her queasy. She wasn't used to fancy drinks but didn't want to appear unsophisticated in Chan's eyes. She had a sudden desire for fresh air.

Better get on with business, her conscience nudged.

Without further prodding, Lindsey plunged into the subject. "Chan, I've found it impossible to round up anyone locally to move the cattle."

"I'm sorry to hear that, but I'm not surprised." He reached across the table for her hand. She felt a small quiver run through her body. His hands were brown and smooth, not rough and raw like Cody's. She pulled her hand gently away. "Do you know anyone I might hire?"

"I'd like to help you, pretty lady, but that's one area beyond my power. Between the roping contest and the truckers' strike, to say nothing of the perpetual shortage of manpower in this town, you're up shit's ... excuse me, up the proverbial creek without a paddle. I'd help you myself, but one more person just won't cut it."

"What do you suggest then?" she asked.

"What can you do? I think you're probably stuck with having to sell your cattle to me. Don't think I feel good about it, but as a businessman, I have obligations to fulfill. The best I could do would be to offer you ten thousand more, but that's my top dollar."

Well, Cody, she thought, I hope you realize this dinner was worth ten thousand dollars. Overcome with dismay, she began to feel downright nauseous, certain it was from the failed negotiations, not the alcohol.

"I can't accept that, Chan, I'd be selling us out too cheap. I just can't do it."

"It's your call, my dear. Another thing. Do you have any idea of the permits you'll need to move the cattle over public and private property?"

"Cody gave me instructions."

"But did he tell you whom to contact?"

"Well, no ..."

He began to count on his fingers the names of ranchers and bureaus that would need to be approached.

He thinks he'll discourage me with this information, she thought. He's almost right, but not quite.

Lindsey excused herself and went to the powder room. Before returning to the table, she dug into her purse for a note pad and pencil and quickly jotted down the names Chan had given her while she could still remember them. He'd think she hadn't paid attention if she had to ask him to repeat what he'd told her.

"Do you think we can leave?" she asked when she returned. "You've been very kind, bringing me here for a lovely dinner, but it's getting late."

"Whatever you say, though it's only nine, and we haven't even tried out the dance floor."

Lindsey had noticed the orchestra start up during dinner. She and Cody hadn't attempted ballroom dancing for so many years, she'd hoped Chan wouldn't bring it up. The thought now of spinning around on the dance floor made her head swim.

"Thank you, but I'm pretty much out of practice."

Chan nodded and guided her through the maze of tables by placing his hand firmly in the small of her back. Was it her imagination or did she feel the pressure was slightly more than necessary? It made her whole body tingle.

While Chan went for the car, she shivered in the cool evening. It had been warm enough when he picked her up, so she didn't bring a wrap. The truth was that the only wrap she had was her old denim jacket, and it wasn't fit to be seen. She'd try not to let on that she was cold and hope Chan wouldn't see her goose flesh.

When he drove up in the Cadillac with the top down, she stepped quickly into the car so he wouldn't feel obliged to assist her, though she could see his intentions were to come to her side and hold the door. She smiled weakly at such old-fashioned chivalry. No man had held a car door for her in a long time, and it had a nice feeling.

"You're cold," Chan said, noticing how she clutched her bare arms to keep from shivering. "I can put the top up."

"No, I'm fine." She might be cold, but she needed the fresh air to clear her head.

"Here, take my coat." He placed it gently over her shoulders, and as he leaned close she could smell the musky scent of his cologne. Her head took another whirl, and for an anguished moment she thought she'd be sick. Whether from the drinks or from the intimacy, she wasn't sure. What would it be like to be held and kissed by this man? No! Get rid of such thoughts! She couldn't afford to lose control of her emotions.

Chan turned on the radio to a country music station and sang with a rich, true baritone while he drove her to the ranch, making conversation unnecessary. At one point, he suggested stopping at his place for a nightcap. She politely but firmly declined.

At her door, Chan said, "You're sure you won't change your mind about selling the cattle? I'm just trying to help, you know." He took her hand in his and pressed it to his lips.

"I know." This time, the little thrill that trembled through her body became an engulfing wave. She steadied herself. "But I have help on the way. I guess I didn't tell you. It would have been simpler to find help here, but we'll be okay."

Chan's look of astonishment made her feel it had been worthwhile to save her trump card for last. He had been nice to her this evening, too nice really, but after all, it seemed pretty obvious he was trying to use her for his own gain.

"Would you like to tell me more?" Chan asked, recovering his composure.

"No, Chan, not tonight, but thanks for the lovely evening. It was special."

* * *

As she fell asleep, Lindsey's thoughts revisited the evening's events alternating with despair over her lack of money. Hovering over it all was Chan, sexy and so vigorously male. Such thoughts made her feel guilty but at the same time deliciously excited.

The kaleidoscope of her mind shifted, and she saw herself in her first year of marriage to Cody, nineteen and shy. Cody told her she was beautiful with her long, curly dark hair and hazel eyes. And he was inordinately pleased with her firm, young body. Lindsey was happy. Cody loved her and promised her a good life. She hadn't minded that Cody couldn't afford a diamond engagement ring. The gleaming gold band was enough.

Lindsey cherished the solitude and closeness to the land she found as a rancher's wife. It fulfilled a need in her poet's nature.

On their first morning riding horseback, Cody handed her a pair of rusty spurs with tattered leather straps. "One day, I'm going to buy you the prettiest pair of silver spurs you ever saw, set with garnets—or maybe even rubies," he had promised.

But fortune has a way of eluding some, she found, even those who work hard and are scrupulously honest. Over the years, there was little enough money for necessities. Lindsey worked alongside her husband until the baby came—and died three weeks later. They tried to have more, but the babies were always stillborn. She busied herself by keeping a close interest in the business side of their lives, helping Cody whenever she could, but money was always scarce, especially whenever Cody had to hire a hand to take her place.

Cody was never long on words and after their first year, his compliments were rare, but she always knew he loved and appreciated her. He never again mentioned silver spurs, and she would have been the first to question such a luxury. On the rare occasions when she remembered his unfulfilled promise, she consoled herself with "Cody tries so hard. No point making him feel bad about a promise he can't keep."

As she slipped into a dream-state, the scene shifted again. She and an attractive stranger—it was Chan!—were riding along a wide, wooded path. Chan rode a beautiful white gelding. She was mounted on a multi-colored appaloosa mare. Before them, a sun-dappled green glade beckoned, and they entered the cool retreat. Chan stopped his horse and dismounted. He came to her side and lifted her from her saddle.

"Beautiful lady," he murmured, gently lowering her to the ground. He pulled her close, his hot, hungry lips eagerly seeking hers, while she stood on tiptoe, anticipating his passionate kiss. She placed one arm around his neck and the other pulled his hips tightly against her own. She breathed in his musky, horsy smell and felt his feverish firm lips crushing hers ...

CHAPTER SEVEN

CHAN

J. Chandler Reed, "Chan" to his friends, received at birth a bountiful portion of God's gifts when it came to masculine beauty and a likable personality. He used people, but they lined up for the opportunity. Men envied his looks but still vied to share his company at the Jaycee, Rotary, and cattle growers meetings in Plainview, where Chan served on the school board. Some wisecracked that as long as they knew where Chan was their wives and daughters were safe. Women cast flirtatious glances whenever he entered a room, hoping to be the polar star to whom he'd gravitate. He was charming and fun, with the ghost of a twinkle in smoky gray eyes that penetrated deep as if to say, "I'll not tell our secret."

He had in fact shared secrets with too many of the women, but the only one of his three marriages to come from the local community had been to his first wife, Caroline. Caroline Milledge had inherited her father's vast ranch near Plainview and his stocks, bonds, and financial interests worth forty million dollars. Caroline's first husband was a young man from a neighboring ranch named Chet Tyler, who had pleased her father. He was even more delighted when Caroline and Chet produced two children on whom he lavished generous trust funds.

When the children were still small, Chet died after a car crash while on a hunting trip. Caroline's father succumbed the following year. Distraught but spirited, she enrolled in agricultural extension classes, determined to learn how to intelligently run the ranch herself. She fared well through diligence and a mentality geared toward profit, and she managed to not only keep the ranch running but to increase its profitability.

On a trip to her alma mater, the university in Boulder, for a seminar about new techniques for artificially inseminating cattle, Caroline stayed over to attend a football homecoming game. The quarterback-hero of the day was young Chandler Reed. Chan's prowess on the field thrilled the fans and gave rise to conversation among the younger alumnae meeting for cocktail parties afterward that his prowess off the field was legendary as well. Chan hopped from party to party after the game, welcomed warmly for sharing his many talents.

It wasn't long before Chan met Caroline. She felt that something special clicked between them, unaware that something special clicked between Chan and every woman he met. Caroline thought Chan was sent by God for her alone, the answer to a sad young widow's prayers. She was lost forever in the depth of his warm gray eyes, eyes that were only for her until after their wedding eight months later. Caroline was thirty-four and Chan only twenty-one, just graduated from college, but age was no barrier to their lovemaking.

Chan had grown up in a neighboring town and knew of the Milledge fortune. He'd never met Caroline but had read of the tragic accident that killed her husband five years earlier. He was in high school at the time, and the misfortune meant little to him in spite of endless conjecture by his family and their friends about what Caroline would do with the ranch and all that money.

Meeting Caroline changed Chan's life. She was slim, beautiful, and rich—everything a man could desire. He had planned to become a partner in his father's insurance agency, a career he had no particular feeling for, though his outgoing personality and football stardom would have made him an asset to the firm. Chan preferred the idea of professional football, but an injury in the last game of his senior year kept him on crutches for three months. Combined with meeting Caroline who proposed almost immediately after their first date, he decided that given a choice a life of pain was not for him.

Chan became a gentleman rancher with a doting wife and two ready-made children who despised him, impervious to his good looks and charm. He wasn't their real father and could never take his place. To make matters worse, they were sick of the endless gossip they overheard about their mother and her infant stud. To keep peace in the household, Caroline sent the children to boarding schools and thus avoided dividing her attention among husband and children.

She gave Chan entire responsibility for running the ranch, though she wisely kept an eye on the finances. Chan liked to spend money and suffered no complaints from Caroline about buying his first white Cadillac convertible, expensive imported horses, and fabulous clothing. They traveled to Europe twice a year for winter sports and summer relaxation, enveloped in each other's lust. Chan steadfastly attended to his husbandly duties, keeping Caroline unsuspicious of his indiscretions.

When Caroline died suddenly of heart failure fifteen years after their marriage, Chan was desolate. Not only did he lose his wife, he lost most of her money, which the will divided between the two children. By the terms of a pre-nuptial agreement, she left Chan the ranch, Tres Alamos, worth a considerable fortune itself, and a small trust fund that fell far short of Chan's spending habits. The soaring inflation rate made operating the ranch a nightmare of red ink. The children took their money and planned feverishly to sue for Tres Alamos as well, until the family attorney, Sleighton Lerner, convinced them they had no chance of winning. Sly, though a few years older than Chan, had belonged to the same frat house at the university. The two felt a kinship for one another that centered more on interest in Caroline's money than on brotherly ties. They met frequently concerning business matters and played poker together every Saturday night.

Chan's second wife, Mattie, didn't last long. Chan met her when he was in Las Vegas at a cattle growers' convention. After dropping fifty thousand dollars in a poker game, money he couldn't afford to lose, Chan went on a drinking binge that lasted three days. Awaking to find himself married to a dancer from the Strip, he packed Mattie off to her family in Florida and called

Sly to start confidential annulment proceedings. The experience was costly but not as expensive as becoming the butt of the town's jokes. Chan had long taken a serious role in the community and expected the community to view him as a prominent contributor through deeds if not cash. How would it look if he brought home a bimbo as the mistress of his prestigious estate? Besides, she brought no dowry to the marriage, only phenomenal boobs and a good pair of legs.

The third marriage, when he wed Yvonne, was undertaken with propriety and a good deal of discreet background checking. Chan had remained in a state of ostensible celibacy for ten years after Caroline's death. He had the local matrons' sympathy and casseroles and any other favors they offered, but the men in the community breathed a sigh of relief when Chan announced his engagement to the Tulsa socialite, Yvonne Messerschmidt.

Yvonne stood to inherit a good-sized fortune from her uncle, who owned several large oil refineries. The uncle had raised the orphaned daughter of his only brother and doted on the red-haired, high-spirited young beauty.

The only flaw in Chan's plan was that the uncle refused to die in spite of numerous surgeries, radiation, and chemotherapy, while Yvonne outspent anything Chan could have imagined in his worst fantasies. She renovated the elegant Victorian mansion on his ranch and bought sumptuous new furnishings that were either ultra-fashionable or semi-priceless antiques. Trips to the Denver and Tulsa department stores yielded elaborate new outfits for exotic vacations on South Seas cruises, African safaris, even bear hunting in northern Canada.

Yvonne loved entertaining almost as much as spending. She had a glass-enclosed swimming pool built when the patio was retiled and expanded. The pool and patio added dimension to their parties, both in style and size.

Pressed into leasing or mortgaging more and more acreage, Chan suggested that she might look to her uncle for some of the money she was spending. Yvonne was livid.

"This is your house I'm improving, Chan. And the property value alone has quadrupled from the changes I've made. Look to your banker, if you need money, or ask that reptile Lerner what you're doing wrong. Perhaps you should hire a manager."

Now Chan was furious. He had managed well under Caroline's tutelage and had kept his head above water until he married Yvonne.

"I hadn't reckoned on marrying a spendthrift, sweetheart, and one without money of her own, as it turns out. When can we reasonably expect the old bastard to die?"

White with indignation, Yvonne poured herself a glass of sherry. "If you ever speak of my uncle that way again, I will personally kill you!" Her eyes glared darkly with controlled rage as she nonchalantly set her glass on the marble coffee table before the fireplace. Her body seethed with hostility as she threw herself into a deep lounge chair and noisily ransacked the latest issue of *The New Yorker*.

Angry and frustrated, realizing he'd overplayed his hand, Chan slammed brazenly out of the house and raced his Cadillac down the long driveway. He consoled himself with one of his lady friends in La Cholla, sixty miles away. When he returned the next morning, Yvonne was gone.

What Chan didn't know was that for several years Yvonne had been bored with his endless talk of cattle and horses. She was sick of his poker games and loud-mouthed friends. On their fabulous vacations, she'd eyed the athletic young studs nearer her age and interests ... and wondered. Chan was sensational in bed, but ... She was afraid to play around for fear Chan would discover it and throw her out. As he so aptly stated, she had no real money of her own—yet. But on her last trip to Tulsa, matters changed. Her uncle, who disliked Chan from the outset, recognized her discontent and leaped at the opportunity to suggest that he would provide well for her if she ever had enough sense to lose the cowboy.

For three days, Chan thought Yvonne had merely left in a snit or taken off on another buying trip. On the fourth day, he was served with divorce papers.

CHAPTER EIGHT

GETTING IT TOGETHER

Back in Phoenix, the Foofwahs threw themselves into furious activity, amazing themselves in view of the previous late night's stress. Fatigue disappeared like smoke, however, in the excitement created by responding to Lindsey's call for help.

Gina pulled her minivan into CC's driveway promptly at five o'clock.

"Lord, have mercy," Gina gasped, her eyes round with disbelief at the pile of supplies CC had garnered in the short time since they'd arrived home. "Where will we put all this?" She joined CC at the rear of the minivan.

"You have plenty of room," CC assured her, humming to herself as she began loading what looked to Gina like a ton and a half of food, clothing, and bedding into the minivan. "You'll see."

"This is just a week's trip, not disaster relief for a small nation," Gina complained.

CC's trip to the discount club had netted sleeping bags, canteens, Levi's and flannel shirts, straw hats, sunglasses, tanning lotion, and ugly big gloves Gina vowed she wouldn't wear. Gargantuan amounts of bottled water were stacked in the driveway alongside cases of pork and beans in gallon cans and lesser amcunts of Spam, powdered eggs and milk, Tang, Bisquick, syrup, and, finally, marshmallows for the campfire. There was even a portable potty. CC insisted on bringing her dainty ceramic plates with little basket holders and her stainless steel flatware rather than paper and plastic. "It's just nicer than eating off soggy paper plates," she explained, "and it's better environmentally."

"Where will the girls sit?" Gina grumbled. She handed a case of Spam to CC, trusting CC's logistical ability to find the space.

"It's only forty miles to the Taylor's ranch." CC adjusted several duffel bags loaded over the top of the canned goods. "They can squeeze in between this stuff—or sit on each other's laps."

"Then I'm glad I'm driving." Gina slid into the driver's seat and revved up the engine to encourage CC to get in the car. "Forty miles crammed together with all this *stuff*? Have you heard of spontaneous combustion?"

"There. That's it." CC dusted off her hands in satisfaction and slammed the rear door. "Let's get the others. What great fun!"

At Gina's insistence, they stopped at a U-Haul outlet to rent a small trailer. The women arrived at Chloë's house thirty minutes later to pick up Chloë, Penny, and Kai-ling. Angie, driving the Gypsy Spirit would meet them at the Taylor's ranch in Wickenburg.

"Oh my God! More *stuff*! They've brought enough luggage to fill a baggage car!" Gina exclaimed while she made several attempts to back the U-Haul into the driveway without knocking over the stack of luggage and boxes. She hated pulling a trailer. It was difficult and tacky. On the fourth try, she gave up and pulled across the driveway.

"We can tie boxes on top, if we have to," CC said, assessing the suitcases, cosmetic bags, duffels, and boxes of books.

"Why books?" Gina asked.

"We'll have time to read in the evenings." At Gina's glare, CC offered, "Everyone has a right to travel in the style that best suits her."

"Have you ever tried to read by a campfire?" Gina asked.

Kai-ling and Chloë emerged from the house, filled with the excitement of the journey and proud of being called on to help their friend.

"Where's Penny?" Gina growled. Her brow furrowed at the thought of another delay.

"She called," Chloë said. "She'll be here any minute. Penny said she had to pick up some extra strings for her guitar."

Moments later, Penny's car careened around the corner and screeched to a stop behind Gina's rig spanning the driveway.

"Sorry I'm late, guys. Did I miss anything?" Penny asked. "What's with the U-Haul?" Penny had taught high school girls' athletics for a few years, and excitement heightened her team spirit.

"We had too much *stuff* to get it all in the car." Gina said with growing impatience.

"I thought we were taking horses," Penny said, looking puzzled. "I've never heard of taking a U-Haul on a cattle drive."

"This will be no ordinary cattle drive, my friend," Gina laughed, determined to reassert her good nature. Impatience would only make this a tedious endeavor. She might as well accustom herself to living at least temporarily with other people's disorganization.

"Who knows?" Kai-ling offered. "This trip could become historical as 'The Foofwah Trail.' Think of it! Two hundred years from now, anthropologists will find shards of our ceramic plates and stainless teaspoons strewn along the way, marking our struggles."

"Not my ceramic plates, they won't," CC objected. "They may not be porcelain, but they're good pottery, and I intend to bring every one of them home."

"It will more likely be called 'The Purgatory Trail,'" Chloë sighed. "We may think we've gone to hell and back by the time we get through this venture."

The women laughed amiably and began cramming luggage and boxes into the U-Haul, then tied large pieces to the minivan's roof rack. The backrest of the rear bench had been flattened to accommodate longer and wider objects. In the middle row, Penny sat between CC and Kai-ling, cradling her guitar in her arms and protecting her rhythm and percussion instruments with her legs. When Penny traveled, she always carried extra music makers for others to play in the event of an impromptu hoedown. CC and Kai-ling carried in their laps whatever wouldn't fit elsewhere.

Singing "Vive le Compagnie," the happy group headed for Wickenburg to begin what they considered the greatest adventure of their lives.

* * *

Once on the highway, the women compared notes on the degree of difficulty or guile it took to convince their husbands the trip was necessary and not at all dangerous.

"It was easy for me," Chloë said. "Ray's out of town, so I just left a note. He may die laughing at the idea of me getting on a horse willingly. But I thought he'd be pleased for me to be around the animals again after all the years he wasted trying to convince me to share his love of horses. Ray's idea of heaven still is to saddle up and ride in the Squaw Peak Mountains where he rides once or twice a week with friends. But not with me! Every time he's coaxed me onto a horse, I've barely escaped being killed. The horse knows who's in control, and it's never me."

"At least you gave it a try," Penny sympathized.

"Did I ever tell you about the time Ray boarded his horse, Don Lee, at the Wigwam Resort's stables while we went on vacation?"

She had, but they urged her to tell the story again.

"On our return, Ray stopped to pick up the horse, and like a darn fool I let him talk me into riding Don Lee home, about five miles. What was even stupider, I let him put spurs on me. Ray really wanted to ride the horse himself. I'm sure he sincerely believed he was being generous letting me ride Don Lee home.

"Well, you can picture dumb me thinking I could handle that animal. Every time I bounced into the air, I got spanked by the damned saddle. And every time I bounced, I unintentionally spurred Don Lee. To say the horse was high-spirited would be an understatement. He took off like a demented fiend, tearing through an eighty-acre prairie dog village. I knew one step into a prairie dog hole would be the end for both of us. I could see my battered and broken body tossed into a cactus patch.

"I knew I had to get those spurs off even though I was going fast forward at something like sixty miles an hour, not counting all the up-and-down motion.

"Ray drove the car home along the roads while the horse and I dashed 'as the crow flies,' but we arrived in a dead heat. That incident fueled one of the biggest arguments we've ever had. I accused him of trying to murder me and swore I'd be damned if I'd ever get on a horse again. Until now, I've stuck to my pledge."

"You may have some trouble sticking to your pledge on this cattle drive," Gina warned.

"We'll see." Chloë smiled secretly.

* * *

"I left a note, too," Kai-ling said. "But I'm not sure Hanchen will be very happy with it."

Her husband, Hanchen, didn't quite trust the Foofwahs. He liked them when they had get-togethers and included the husbands, but he made it clear he believed writers of fiction wasted their time as an excuse to avoid working at productive jobs.

Nevertheless, Kai-ling could not find it in herself to refuse to help Lindsey when she needed it. She had planned to use the quarter break from graduate studies in English to clean out closets and to wallpaper a bathroom. Her life as a wife, mother, and mid-life student was a series of tight schedules, hellish at times, but she found satisfaction in successfully juggling all three. Now, this trip spurred her intellectual curiosity. She would travel through a part of America she'd never seen. Kai-ling loved travel and research. Perhaps she could write a book for publication in China about life as a Chinese-American cowgirl. She had a small pang of conscience about lying that she knew how to ride a horse. Really, how difficult could it be? She didn't want to be left out of this worthy quest.

Kai-ling carefully packed her clothing and tied up several cartons filled with oatmeal, fruit, and health food she knew the Foofwahs would overlook in their urgent departure. She then put a chicken casserole in the oven for Hanchen and Wendy and left a note:

> Hanchen, trust me. This is something I have to do. I have arranged for Wendy's care. I will call soon to explain.

* * *

Like Kai-ling, CC was always eager to take on a new adventure, and her enthusiasm bubbled infectiously.

"Ace was wonderful," she said. "He offered to come along." At first, CC seriously considered his suggestion. Ace's ability to know how absolutely everything worked, including people, could be a real help. But it wasn't likely any of the other husbands would be able or even want to go. Besides, Lindsey had said a cowboy friend of theirs named Jake would be joining them. Jake should be able to keep them out of trouble.

Ace had looked a trifle disappointed when she declined his offer but relieved at the same time. He was in the process of remodeling the laundry room and welcomed a little time without interruption. MIT-educated, Ace had been an engineering consultant before retirement. Now, as a home engineer with a perfectionist's attention to form and detail, he found his vast areas of expertise useful for turning their abode into a designer's showcase. Halfway out the door on his daily run to the hardware store, Ace had been surprised when CC arrived home so unexpectedly. Now, he had fleeting fears that the Foofwahs might be taking on something too big for them, but his confidence in CC's good sense, her capability and resourcefulness kept him from expressing his doubts.

"Do you know what the dear man did?" CC paused dramatically. "He gave me his most prized possession, his cell phone, in case we run into trouble."

* * *

"Poor Joe is still up in Pine Ridge, working on our house," Penny said. "He's on a week's vacation, and I was going to join him when the conference was over."

Penny and her husband had spent every weekend and vacation for the past three years constructing a dream home and took justifiable pride in their ability to do the heavy, difficult work themselves. Penny's right-brain creativity didn't interfere with her left-brain manual dexterity. She had been Joe's partner from the onset of the project, and she felt somewhat guilty about running off now to help Lindsey. At the same time, she welcomed a vacation away from lumber and nails—and her natural wanderlust had long been buried under childrearing and house-building. This was the opportunity of a lifetime to travel along the Santa Fe Trail in the footsteps and wagon tracks of the pioneers. She wouldn't miss it for the world.

"Joe was disappointed, but he understood."

* * *

"Well, Ted wasn't so nice," Gina said.

When she raced in the door, Ted was in the kitchen heating a bag of popcorn in the microwave. Gina breathlessly explained the need to help Lindsey move a herd of cattle, certain that Ted would be annoyed by the idea of her taking off on such an uncertain, possibly dangerous, adventure. She was surprised that he laughed. A lecture she expected, but laugh?

"What's so funny?" Gina asked suspiciously. Ted couldn't answer. He was out of control, laughing.

"Well, I'm glad you're having so much fun over this. If you think I can't ride a horse, I'll have you know I took riding lessons when I was young. I can handle a horse."

Ted managed to restrain himself long enough to wipe his eyes and said, "The only riding you've ever done was at a dude ranch. You've never had to ride a horse for five or six hours at a stretch."

"No ..." Gina said, beginning to sense that she was being led into a trap.

"Have you ever slept outside in a bedroll, with the coyotes howling nearby and nothing overhead except the stars? With snakes and bugs on the ground?"

"Yes, when I was a Girl Scout ... but there weren't any coyotes ... or snakes."

"Face it, Gina. You're not the outdoor type. Your idea of roughing it is to stay in a motel where you have to walk across the parking lot for ice. Or where they don't put a piece of chocolate on your pillow at night."

Gina thought of the privations at the ratty old hotel in Bradford the night before and knew he was right. "But ..."

"I really think you should graciously bow out of this one, Gina. I don't think your body has the tolerance for it at your age. You've never been particularly athletic. You've only been on a horse a few times, and then you thought you'd die after two hours in the saddle."

Now her back was up. All Ted had to do was bring up her age or express a doubt about her ability to do *anything*, and she'd prove she could do it if it killed her.

"Well, it can't be that difficult. Ted, I really want to do this. And I can't go back on a pledge to help another Foofwah. Do you think you could do without me for a week or so?" Down deep, she prayed he would go along with the idea. In retirement, she missed the frequent opportunities for travel she'd loved when she worked, and the constant bridge parties and luncheons were wearing thin. Ted hated travel other than short getaways, and, while she would never admit it, she was desperate for something new to stimulate her stalled desire to write a bestseller.

"Ted, this is important to me."

Good-natured, generous and loving Ted had never denied Gina any wish she truly desired. He caved. "You must have enough sense to know what you're getting into. Go ahead. You've earned a little fun, though I doubt you'll find it fun. I'll wager it's the hardest work you'll ever do in your lifetime."

Ted started toward his den with a bowl of popcorn. "They'll be home before dark," he chuckled to himself, thinking he was out of Gina's hearing.

* * *

Furious at Ted's attitude, Gina was unaware that her erratic driving had caused a nervous hush to fall over the group. She laid on the horn, forcing an old couple poking along in the car ahead to pull over to the shoulder while she passed.

"Whoa! What's that in the road ahead?" Gina cried, standing on the brakes and causing the heavily laden minivan and U-Haul to veer to the left, barely missing an oncoming semi. The object of their attention jumped around in the road, waving violently at passing motorists.

Chloë squinted, straining forward against the windshield to try to see better. "It's a short little man with a lot of whiskers, jumping around behind a pickup truck. He's moving in so many directions at once, he looks like a jackrabbit caught in an electric fan. We'd better stop."

Gina pulled up behind the pickup. The weight of the overladen minivan and trailer reduced the vehicle's braking power, and for an instant it seemed the car would pin the frantic signaler to his bumper.

Eyes bulging from the near certainty of immediate death, the diminutive, dust-covered old man, who looked about seventy going on a hundred, squeezed out from between the two vehicles and spat tobacco juice on the ground. Some of it lodged in his stringy, grizzled whiskers, and he passed the arm of his faded blue shirt across his chin to tidy himself.

Gina rolled down her window. The women looked almost as bug-eyed as this dead-ringer for Yosemite Sam.

"Ho, ladies," he said, shifting the wad of chewing tobacco to his cheek so he could talk without gargling. "Mind if I hitch a ride into town? My truck's broke down." His eyes wandered across the women stuffed among their luggage and supplies.

"I'm sorry," Gina replied. "We really don't have room. You can see for yourself."

"I ain't very big. I could just squeeze in," he wheedled, shrinking himself together to appear even smaller. "I'll die if I don't get outa this god-danged heat purty soon." He fanned himself with his dusty cowboy hat and mopped the perspiration running into his squinty eyes with a wadded end of dirty blue bandanna.

"I don't..." Gina began.

"We can squeeze together a little more," CC interrupted. "We can't leave this man to die out here. It's a hundred and ten in the shade."

"Okay, but I don't know how," Gina relented.

"Where're you ladies going?" the man asked.

"We're headed to Cody Taylor's ranch just outside Wickenburg," Chloë said.

"Well, now, ain't that funny. That's where I'm headed too," he drawled, clawing at his whiskers as if trying to reach something deep down and alive. "My friend Cody asked me to come up from Tucson and pull a horse trailer to Colorado."

"What a coincidence," CC exclaimed exultantly. "That's where we're going!"

"Well, now, tell you what," the man said. "To make more room, whyn't I jes' take these big boxes outa the back and put 'em in my truck, then when Cody sends someone to git my truck, they can bring the boxes with 'em."

"Hmmm," Gina said. "I can see you're a born problem-solver."

After he made the switch and stowed Penny's musical instruments safely in back, the man climbed in and snuggled up close to CC. In the rear view mirror, Gina could see her duck as the brim of the man's hat banged against her head. CC's nose began twitching uncontrollably, and a look of panic spread across her face as she unleashed a violent sneeze.

"Excuse, me sir," CC said politely. "Could you lean over to the right a little? Your whiskers are tickling my nose."

"No problem, lady," he said, pressing against the car door. "My name's Jake."

"That's what we figured," Chloë said over her shoulder from the front seat. "We're the group of writers Lindsey asked to help move her uncle's cattle to auction. When we meet to critique the stories we write, we call ourselves 'Foofwahs' for the fun of it. I know it sounds kind of silly."

A rainbow of expressions passed over Jake's face, as he put two and two together. "Well, I'll be dogged ..." He scratched the back of his neck.

As they resumed the trip along the highway, the foulness of unwashed clothing and body odor overlaid with stale tobacco suffused the crowded interior of the minivan. First one window and then another crept silently open to wash hot air through the reeking fumes and sweep them—along with the cooler air—out the windows. Giving up resistance to the gale-force wind, a package of paper napkins in the rear broke open and soon little white paper birds were flying around inside the vehicle and out the open windows.

"See, that's why I like real plates," CC reminded the women. "Paper's always flying around."

Reluctant to close the windows, the women ignored CC and the effect the escaping paper had on the environment.

Jake alone seemed relaxed and comfortable. The rancid little passenger folded his arms and leaned contentedly back in the seat. "Yessir, I been a cowboy all my life. Punched cows in Montana when I was fifteen, then I signed on to herd and stayed for ten years."

He let out a loud belch that sent reminders of earlier meals, noxious, gastro-intestinal waves, searching for open windows, but not until they lingered, almost lovingly, over their nearest victims.

Without noticing the muffled, choking sounds around him, Jake continued with his life's story. "Never went to school after that. Never married. Don't s'pose no woman'd have me," he smiled modestly as if he didn't believe what he said. "Weren't no jobs, and, besides, I liked livin' outa doors. Fer a time I was camp cook fer the resta the hands and got purty good at cookin' beans and biscuits over a campfire or from the back of a chuck wagon. We usta have steaks like you ain't never seen. And that was back in the days when ever'body was poor, and we was the poorest."

* * *

What Jake didn't tell them was that he was the oldest of five children. His mother died when he was eleven. His father had disappeared two years earlier. Jake had heard a rumor his pop had run away with an eighteen-year-old neighbor girl. He never found out for sure what really happened, because his new parents and neighbors always stopped talking when he came into the room. He knew only that his mother had died of a broken heart as much as from the "consumption" that made her cough so hard she spit up blood.

When his mother died, different neighbors took in him and his two brothers and two sisters. Jake knew the farmers were not just being kind. They were looking for free labor. Jake was the first to be picked for he was a good farm hand, having worked side-by-side with his pop since he was a toddler. Jake missed his brothers and sisters but was never allowed to visit any of them. He had come to hate his pop, sure his mother would have lived if his father had only stayed and looked after the farm and his family. Jake made a vow the night his mother died to kill his pop if he ever caught up with him. Fortunately, he never learned what happened to his father so his pledge was never put to the test.

Jake's growing up years had been unhappy ones. The neighbor who finally took him permanently was "Ol' Man Skimpson." Everyone called him that because of his miserliness, although his real name was Simpson. Ol' Man Skimpson was a hard taskmaster, and for four years Jake worked alongside the men, keeping up with them. The one time he disobeyed, he slipped away on a Sunday afternoon to see his baby sister who was living with a family several miles away. He'd asked permission to go, but it was denied. Jake sneaked out when the Skimpsons were taking their Sunday afternoon naps. When he returned, Skimpson almost took a layer of hide off him with a leather belt. Jake never tried it again. He just swore to himself he'd run away at the first opportunity.

When he was fifteen, he escaped from Ol' Man Skimpson and headed west. Jake hated farming. He wanted to be a cowboy. He was hired by a rancher in Montana, and cowpunching became his trade.

* * *

If there was one thing Jake was sure of now, it was his knowledge of the ranching business. His idea of woman's place was learned early. At every ranch where he worked, the boss's wife stayed in the kitchen and left the real ranch work up to the men. Occasionally, they'd drive a pickup to bring in the strays that were too young to walk, but, other than that, they left ranching to men. They didn't organize themselves into clubs and write books and drive cattle. If they had to do something outside the home, they attended sewing bees and made quilts. Something useful. He'd get these old girls shaped up once he was running the show. For now, let them have their fun.

The five women sighed with enormous relief when Gina drew up to the gates of the Taylor's ranch. They reached

Lindsey's place alive but drained of energy after the perils of the trip to Wickenburg.

"Now the fun begins," CC chirped.

Jake smiled to himself. "Ain't that the truth?"

CHAPTER NINE

SURMOUNTING THE OBSTACLES

The Taylor's ranch house was built on a hill overlooking the town of Wickenburg and the purple peaks of the Vulture Mountains beyond. The rock-covered ground visible for miles around was dotted with greasewood and mesquite bushes, powdery from the desert dust. Tall saguaros stood sentinel, some with arms akimbo like traffic officers, others like protective mothers clutching their children to their breasts. The house was low and rambling, built of adobe to protect the dwellers from the intense Arizona heat.

Cody, with a cast on his leg and leaning on crutches, met the minivan with its jumbled load of people and provisions at the gate. He greeted them with forced heartiness, "Been expecting you folks for a couple of hours."

Cody found he had been right to come home. His broken leg had been set badly, and Doctor Evans had to break the bone and reset it. He was supposed to stay off it for a few days. Now, Cody found it doubly stressful to have to rely on women to handle a job he should be doing. Moving a large herd of cattle across Colorado was no job for women, but Lindsey was stranded up there, so far from home, and desperate. All he could hope was that these women would give her moral support, and not get in the way too much. He'd met them a few times, and by no stretch of imagination could he picture them as wranglers. But he knew with Jake's help, Lindsey was competent to handle the job. And Jake was ornery and mean enough to keep the women in line. Foul enough too that there wouldn't be any hanky-panky.

"Lord help us all," Cody said, eyes raised to heaven, as the overloaded minivan began to disgorge.

"Ho, Jake! What're *you* doin' in with these gals?" Cody asked, surprised to see his old friend disentangle himself from among the women.

"These ladies was kind enough to give me a ride when my truck broke down," Jake said, sounding genuinely grateful and oblivious to their sidelong expressions of disgust. He belched as he straightened up and shook Cody's hand.

"These are the lady writers I told you about," Cody said.

"Hmmm," Jake said, reaching deep into his grizzled beard. "I thought you said *riders*!"

Cody laughed. "Sorry, Jake. I didn't mean to confuse you."

Jake turned to Chloë. "And what's that other thing you call yerselves? Fooferahs?"

"Foofwahs!" Chloë said. "It's short for Future Famous Writers of America." She looked into Jake's stony eyes. "It's meant to be a joke."

Cody's qualms about the ability of Lindsey's friends to handle this important venture were not eased by seeing them again. His trust in Jake and Lindsey's faith in the inventiveness of her literary friends were slim guarantee that Lindsey would have all the help she needed. Right now, he felt a little like vomiting.

Chloë said quietly to Gina, "Cody's one of those men who looks like a cowboy no matter how you dress him up. Kind of like Clint Eastwood. Trim his hair, put him in a suit and tie, hand him a briefcase, and he'd still look like a cowboy."

Gina nodded.

Cody was tall and lean and his face a leathery brown from the wind and weather. When he took off his Stetson to wipe away the sweat, he exposed a forehead in pale contrast to the rest of his face. They knew him to be a taciturn man, one who spoke only when it became absolutely necessary, though on occasion, loosened up by a couple of beers, Cody's conversation became spiced with cowboy humor and jargon. Today, his speech was restrained and careful.

The women eyed him with awe. Cody was a real-life cowboy. Jake didn't count.

A column of dust a mile down the road signaled the advance of Angie and the Gypsy Spirit. Everyone stopped talking and watched the vehicle's lumbering progress.

"Jesus H. Christ. What is *that*?" Jake said, mopping his forehead and the back of his neck.

As the vehicle drew through the gate, the women circled around shouting and waving to their friend. Cody stifled a stricken look, and Jake spit a wad.

Gina noticed the disrespect and thought to enlighten the men. "The singular charm of this dwarf's cottage has attracted seekers of fortunes to Angie's concession at fairs all over the country."

After introductions, Angie passed by Jake without a blink or a twitch and began to direct the reloading of the supplies and luggage into, onto, and underneath the Gypsy Spirit.

Chloë pulled out a wide, flat box marked, "Fireworks." "What should we do with this? It's after the fourth of July and fireworks are illegal in this state. Can we leave it here?"

Angie had forgotten about her stash, picked up the last time she drove through New Mexico. "Leave it alone," she said. "They're legal in some states, and once in a while I need something at a fair to attract attention."

Chloë looked skeptical but slid it back under the platform of the Gypsy Spirit.

Jake handed the larger cartons to Gina and Penny, who stowed them inside the cottage. The other women looked over the contraption to see where everyone would fit. They rejected Jake's offer for two of them to ride in his pickup. Penny and Chloë would start the trip riding up front with Angie, then switch off with Kai-ling, CC, and Gina, who would drive the second shift.

CC kicked the front tires with a mighty 'thunk.' "The tires seem to be in good shape. Ace told me never to kick tires, but I feel better knowing they're not soft."

"Where's the toilet?" asked Penny.

"Oh ... ah ..." Angie hemmed, we'll have to rely on roadside rest stops—or bushes for emergencies.

"That's okay," CC volunteered. "I brought a portable potty. Remember?"

"You think of everything, CC." Penny looked relieved, then frowned. "But where is it?"

Jake heard the question. "I left it with those cases of canned goods I shifted to my truck. Cody sent one of his neighbors after it while you were dinking around with the witch's hut over there."

As if on cue, Cody's neighbor, Delbert Hanson, drove his truck through the front gate towing Jake's pickup, which had turned a lumpy reddish brown color similar to wet desert soil.

"What in tarnation happened to my truck?" Jake yowled, running over to inspect the scabrous vehicle.

"Looks like the beans musta blew up from the heat," Delbert replied. "There was beans everywhere. I scraped out the backa the truck bed and dumped ever'thing else. It was a real mess."

"For chrissake, how many cans of beans did you wimmen have?" Jake asked.

CC became defensive. "Beans are important providers of nourishment. High in protein. You could live on beans if you had to."

"How many?" Jake repeated.

"Ten gallons."

Jake looked thunderstruck. "You damn wimmen blew up my truck! Don't you know it's probably a hundred and forty degrees in the sun?" He turned away in disgust and walked toward his bean-plastered truck, a handsome shade of terra cotta.

"It'll be all right," Delbert reassured him. "The truck's okay under the hood. Of course, you shudda had the windows rolled up."

"So much for the beans ... and the portable potty," CC said. The women mumbled their shared dejection at the loss of the toilet.

"Yeah," Jake said. "You wimmen'll get a lesson in the glamour of outdoor livin'." He walked around the pickup. "The best laid plans of mice and wimmen. Goddamit!"

Cody intervened. "Looks like he's getting his sense of humor back. But what did you need all the beans for? You'll only be on the road a couple of days and on the trail maybe four."

"Well ... you know," CC said with uncharacteristic shyness. "People tend to get bound up when they don't eat right and beans help to keep you regular."

The men guffawed and made remarks the women chose to ignore.

"We'll get by, CC," Kai-ling cheered her friend. "We have lots of fruit and cereal."

"But the potty," Chloë said, looking dismayed. "Surely it could have been washed off. We can't just squat in the *bushes*."

"Maybe not, ma'am," Delbert said. "But it was so messed up I just give it the pitch. I couldn't hardly tell what it was."

With grim expressions and tight lips, the women inspected the cramped quarters afforded by Angie's rig. A few polite grumbles echoed a broadening theme, "Do we know what we're doing?"

Gina offered, "I think we're going to wish we hadn't gotten into this."

One rallying cry held them together: "Lindsey really needs us!"

When Cody could no longer stand to watch the women's awkward loading of supplies, he suggested to Angie that he take over directing to give her a break.

"Thanks," she said. "I need a cold drink."

"Help yourself to a beer in the fridge ..." he said. She disappeared into the house before he finished the sentence.

Delbert and Jake helped by carrying cartons, but Jake's bossiness soon got on the women's nerves, and they openly defied his commands.

Noticing the lack of warmth between his friend and the women, Cody reinforced Jake's orders, telling himself he'd have to talk to Jake about being a little more subtle.

Exhausted by the heavy work in the warm September evening and from a surfeit of exciting new challenges, the Foofwahs readily endorsed an offer from Cody for beer all around, all but Penny who had diet root beer.

At eight o'clock, Delbert's wife Mary Lou, who volunteered to cook up a barbecue, flopped thick, tender T-bones on the large outdoor grill. The last glow of sunset fell from the sky as Mary Lou brought out a large kettle of pinto beans that had been simmering all day, heaps of corn on the cob, and piles of garlic bread. Cheers of admiration for the cook sounded from the men and women alike.

"We don't have to cook dinner ourselves!" CC called out. Hooray!"

The women joined in with a rousing toast, beer cans hoisted high.

"I wonder what our husbands are having for dinner tonight," Penny asked.

"Who cares?" Chloë responded. "We're on a first-rate adventure. And I'm starved!"

"Mmmm," Kai-ling added. "I love the aroma of mesquite-grilled steaks. It has been a long time since lunch."

Laughing like schoolgirls, the Foofwahs allowed that they might even learn to tolerate Jake.

Jake, overhearing the remark as he returned from the kitchen where his offer of help had been politely refused, gave them a snaggle-toothed grin. "Back at you," he said, making a gun of his fist. "You ladies better eat hearty." He nailed a fly to the ground with a spew of tobacco. The fly lay in the pool of brown juice, fluttered weakly, then gave up the struggle. "Food won't be like this when we git on the trail."

"No," CC said darkly. "Especially without beans."

After dinner, Jake rendered a loud belch and politely excused himself from the table to start repairing his truck with Cody's tools and Delbert's help.

"I have maps for you girls," Cody said, and the Foofwahs settled around him at the dinner table cleared of dishes. Cody spread out the maps of Arizona, New Mexico, and Colorado to plot the route for the next day's trip. He pointed out the locations for where to water and rest the horses, where to stay for the night, and where to look for emergency help.

Weary from an excess of excitement, hard work, beer, and food, the women could scarcely concentrate. Cody looked at their tired faces and cut his instructions short. "That's enough for tonight," he said.

The women looked grateful, but headed to the kitchen to help Mary Lou finish cleaning up the kitchen and setting it in order for the next morning.

Finally free to unroll their sleeping bags, the Foofwahs started to bed down when Gina asked Angie to give her a tarot reading. Angie was astonished. Gina had always made a to-do about not believing in such things.

"Just in case ..." Gina said.

Angie spread out her cards and spent a long time pondering their meaning. She seemed reluctant to speak.

"What?" Gina asked suspiciously.

"I see disillusionment, disorder, and confusion."

Gina shivered. "What happened to 'You will meet a tall, dark stranger'?" Disillusionment didn't surprise her, but she didn't know if she could deal with disorder and confusion. "Maybe we put that all behind us today," she conceded.

"What about your own fortune, Angie?" Chloë asked.

"Well ... I don't usually read my own," she hesitated, looking around at the expectant faces. "Okay."

She dealt out the rows of cards once more and again studied their meaning at length. "I don't think this is a good idea," she said quietly.

"Tell us, tell us," the Foofwahs chanted.

"I see a new beginning, that could be okay. But I see a radical change from old associations and environments, obstacles, betrayal by a friend."

The women looked uneasily at one another. Gina said, "There's really nothing to this tarot business. I knew it."

Angie gathered up the cards. "Let's go to bed."

* * *

After their evening of liquid spirits and high-spirited anticipation, the heavier imbibers among the women awoke grudgingly the next morning. Nevertheless, they responded to duty and gathered to meet Jake in the corral at five o'clock for final instructions. Cody had made it clear that Jake would be his stand-in, and Jake's orders would be law.

Breakfast wouldn't be ready for an hour. Mary Lou had offered to return to make sure they got a good send-off. Jake brought out a pot of strong cowboy coffee, and the women helped themselves to mugs of the steaming black brew. In the cool morning air, the hot coffee tasted good and re-energized the flagging enthusiasm of Lindsey's champions. Cody struggled out long enough to greet his guests but soon hobbled back inside to take the pressure off his swollen leg.

Once they were fully awake and looked around, the Foofwahs discovered that each was dressed identically in their new outfits. CC had purchased by volume rather than discrimination and the only difference was in length and width. Each had the same shade of blue-gray prewashed Levi's, red-checkered shirt, red-patterned neckerchief, black straw cowgirl hat trimmed with the matching fabric of the neckerchief, and black leather boots with identical white stars on the front. Appalled at their loss of identity, and regardless of team spirit, each woman set about individualizing her outfit.

Angie removed the hat trim and the neckerchief.

Chloë ransacked her duffel and added red bows to her hat, then changed into her own red boots and blue plaid shirt that could be more comfortably buttoned across her ample chest.

"Damn these skinny foreign cuts you buy in the discount places," she muttered as she removed the shirt CC had provided. The tight Levi's had to go too, and she substituted a new pair of navy stretch pants to go with the blue plaid shirt.

Kai ling cut off her Levi's above the knees because the trousers were too snug to fit inside her boots that were already pinching.

Penny tied her shirt into a bare-midriff style, causing Jake to shake his head in wonder at the sight of her plump little tummy roll.

Gina insisted on wearing her own felt Stetson, "Revenuer" model, which she'd protected with mothballs in its original box for many years.

CC refused to change a thing. "Really!" she said disgustedly and walked off toward the barn.

"Each one 'a you wimmen is gonna get a chance to meet yer horse before we load 'em up," Jake said gruffly. "Cody said you oughta be matched up to a horse you kin handle."

Assuming the women knew how to ride, Jake led them to a corral full of raunchy-looking horses that milled about restlessly, nipping at each other's rumps.

"Cody was in too much pain to think about culling out the orneriest horses," Jake muttered, assuming Lindsey's friends were competent horsewomen or they wouldn't be here. "Pick your mount," he called out.

The women eyed the dusty range horses, then glanced woefully at one another. The horses looked huge and mean. Some of the women prayed silently and others began to sweat profusely despite the early morning coolness. Noticing their reluctance, Jake and Delbert—who had arrived with Mary Lou saying he wouldn't miss this event for anything he owned—started selecting likely matches among the horses and tying them to the hitching rail. Delbert claimed he wasn't too familiar with

Cody's horses, and Jake had been off in Tucson for several years, so neither knew the temperaments of the individual animals.

Now began the reality of the situation for the women. "Nothing insurmountable for Foofwahs," they laughed with bravado, while privately agreeing that the next few minutes could be embarrassing.

No one was surprised when mounting proved a difficulty. Jake and Delbert, after saddling several likely looking horses, tried to help by offering a "leg up," but the women's mature figures and the tight new Levi's offered resistance not easily overcome. Neither would stretch in the right directions.

Gina's horse was coal black with one opaque blind eye, a twenty-three-year-old former draft horse named Matilda. Gina had asked for an especially gentle mount, but she thought the selection was questionable and possibly insulting.

"We working girls have to stick together," Gina said, giving her horse a timid pat on the mane and hoping desperately to befriend the beast. "Frankly, though, I wonder if you shouldn't be the one retired rather than I," she whispered in Matilda's ear.

Gina was more than a little afraid of horses in spite of what she'd told Ted, but nothing could have convinced her to reveal her terror at this point.

Jake detected her fear, but for Cody's sake smothered his desire to say something to unnerve the woman completely. He felt like throwing in the towel on the whole danged mess. Cody should have told him these women were greenhorns.

"I don't know," Gina said, with rare indecision. "Maybe I should try a ... smaller horse."

Jake gritted his teeth. "Cody said this'n is as gentle-natured and well-mannered as you can git." But stupid, he thought. Serves the dumb old girl right if she gets a dimwitted plow horse. Some of the women seemed okay, but a couple, like this one, acted a little too bossy.

"I'd like it better if she had two eyes," Gina said.

"Nuthin' to worry about, ma'am," Jake said. "Horses has great pee-riferal vision and only needs one eye."

"Yeah, if it's in the middle!" Gina laughed.

Gina got her left boot in the stirrup, but as she tried to claw her way up onto the back of Matilda, her weight dragged the saddle toward the horse's belly. Gina shrieked as Matilda reared, her one eye rolling wildly, not unlike Gina's two eyes. Gina wrested her foot free of the stirrup while Jake grabbed the reins and soothed the horse. Delbert cinched the loosened saddle.

Shaken by the experience, Gina sat on a stump while she pondered whether there might be a sure way, other than death, to get out of the adventure.

"Ya shudda stood on that stump to mount," Jake yelled, and under his breath concluded, "ya danged nitwit."

Chloë was having her own troubles. With her first effort to get her boot into the stirrup, her new stretch pants popped a seam, and she rushed indoors for a quick change. When she returned, Chloë searched for a horse that looked more docile than the rest and finally chose a muckeldy-dun gelding.

Delbert checked the list Cody had given him and said, "That must be the one called 'Mouse,' probably for his coloring."

Chloë wasn't sure whether she picked Mouse because he was the best looking or because all the other horses were nipping and kicking him, and she felt sorry for him.

Kai-ling's horse was a roan-colored mare whose name was "Romancer."

"Why would anyone give you such an unlikely name?" she asked. "You must be a sweetheart."

Kai-ling and Romancer seemed to have a special rapport from the start. Chloë noticed and commented, "You're such a polite person, always reluctant to offend anyone, even a horse, and I think she appreciates it."

Kai-ling finally got the hang of mounting the mare by putting her left foot in Delbert's strong, cupped hands and then swinging her right leg over the saddle. She was pleased at achieving a satisfactory measure of cooperation from the horse by simply patting the animal on the neck and imploring her, "Please, Romancer, dear. Walk forward, okay?"

Penny took so long to pick out her mount that there were few choices left. She finally selected one called "Old Bushmills." Out of her hearing, Delbert told Jake Old Bushmills had been named after the favorite whisky of his former owner and earned the name from his unsteady gait when he moved at anything slower than a lope. Penny, a teetotaler and unfamiliar with liquor brands, told Kai-ling she thought the horse must have been named for a New England mill pond. "It sounds so familiar. Maybe I saw it in *National Geographic*.

"Looks like a fine working horse to me," Jake lied, thinking to speed things up.

As Penny settled into the saddle, her short legs groping for the stirrups, OB stood on his hind feet, front hooves pawing the air, then took off around the barn at a gallop. "Hi, ho, Silver," Penny yelled gamely as her straw hat sailed off in their wake and her ponytail flip-flopped.

"My God," Jake yelled, pulling Kai-ling off her horse and jumping in the saddle to follow and retrieve Penny, who could still be seen and heard a quarter of a mile distant.

Before long, they returned with Jake leading a now docile Old Bushmills and a flushed and nervously smiling Penny, who had managed to stay in the saddle.

"So much for experience," Penny laughed, reminding the others that she was the only one of the women who actually knew how to handle a horse with any degree of competency.

CC, vowing to mount her horse without making a spectacle of herself, coaxed it alongside the rail and with a determined nimbleness scrambled up from a footstool to quietly and successfully clamber aboard—but from the wrong side, contrary to her husband Ace's instructions beforehand to always remember to mount from the port side.

"Don't do that when you're on the trail," Jake warned her. "The horse won't know what you're doing and is apt to buck. You might get kilt."

Chloë, after three failed efforts, looked around and said, "You know, I don't think there's any way I can get on this monster short of a block and tackle." She was sharing Gina's thoughts about how to graciously retreat from what was becoming a ridiculous and very possibly dangerous situation.

"I've got it," Delbert said. Hurrying into the barn, he emerged with a stepladder.

With the aid of the stepladder, Gina was finally able to board her horse with some remnant of dignity. She stepped over Matilda's back and slid into the saddle.

Everyone was on a horse except Chloë. She turned from Mouse and strode away from the corral, muttering under her breath, "You're not getting *me* on any damned horse!" She plunked herself down in a lawn chair to watch the unfolding of a ridiculous drama that she knew could only end in disaster.

"We must take this stepladder with us," Kai-ling said with practical foresight. She could imagine the difficulties they would have down the road.

"Naw," Delbert said. "You'll git the hang of it fast enough. It's always hardest the first time or two."

CC, astride her horse, felt proud that she alone mounted unaided and undisgraced, other than the small matter of being rebuked for mounting from the wrong side. Her gelding was named Trickster, which she felt was a misnomer she quickly corrected by renaming the plump, docile palomino "Butterball." She clicked her tongue and pulled up on the reins. Before she knew what had happened, the former Trickster bent his knees to the ground and rolled over on his side to play dead.

"Eeiiyh," CC screamed, with her left leg pinned beneath the horse's flank. Jake gave a sharp whistle and the horse rose as quickly as it had lain down, leaving CC lying on the ground clutching her knee and her straw hat.

"Are you okay?" Jake asked the horse, stroking its nose and annoyed at the possible injury to the animal.

"I think so," CC said, "thanks." Though genuinely frightened, she didn't want to appear scared.

"Is your knee okay?" Delbert asked, embarrassed by Jake's lack of concern for the woman's welfare.

"Sure," she said uncertainly. "I'll rub it a minute to get the cramp out."

"Git some liniment for her," Jake said, in a belated offer of help. "In fact, git a whole vat of liniment. From what I seen here this morning, there's going to be some sore backsides on this trip."

"I apologize, ma'am," Delbert said. "I guess this is the one that used to be a circus horse, so you have to be careful how you treat him."

"He'll have to be careful how he treats me, or he'll be dog meat at the first crossroads," CC said, looking annoyed. "Butterball ... Trickster, my foot! This horse is 'Shitears' for the rest of the trip!"

Declining to select a more tractable horse, CC preferred the challenge of bringing the handsome rogue into line. She insisted such a smart beast would soon get the picture about who was boss.

"Maybe it wouldn't be so bad to have a horse roll on you," Chloë said. "It's one sure way to get out of this ..."

"Forget it," Gina interrupted. "I've already thought that one through. The risk's too great. And I hate pain."

Angie was relieved that she'd have the Gypsy Spirit to drive and could dispense with having to ride a horse. Her one performance on a horse was when she was six years old, and even then she was humiliated by her inability to stay in the saddle. She'd long ago written horses out of her life as an unnecessary evil.

As a last resort, Chloë volunteered to serve as camp cook, saying she would ride with Angie. She felt comfortable that her contribution would be keeping the others well fed and healthy with her gourmet flair.

Angie looked aghast. "But we need *riders*, so that means I'd have to ride a horse, while you drive the Gypsy Spirit. You couldn't do that!"

"Sure, I could," Chloë said, hanging on dearly to the life-saving rope this switch would provide. She'd driven cars all her life. A truck couldn't be that difficult.

Seeing the panic in her friend's eyes and thinking of the differences in their age, Angie conceded with what she hoped was fairness and good grace. "All right. I'll do it."

"Now, we only got room in the horse trailer for four horses," Jake instructed, "so you ladies decide which ones to take. Lindsey's got a couple or three up north, so we kin git by with jist takin' four."

The women conferred briefly and decided to leave Matilda behind. They thought it seemed too likely that the elderly, half-blind horse might die on the trail.

Gina would ride Chloë's Mouse, since the camp cook wouldn't need a horse. Romancer, Old Bushmills, and Shitears were the others approved to accompany the Foofwahs on their journey. Angie would wait to see what Lindsey had to offer, as none of the other horses here looked appealing.

After breakfast, Jake and Delbert loaded the horses into Jake's trailer. The women had repacked most of their luggage at Cody's suggestion the night before, leaving Gina's minivan and the U-Haul behind stuffed with excess gear, books, and clothing. Cody had patiently explained that the ladies might have to miss church services once they were on the road, and it was highly unlikely there would be any other opportunities for dressing up. Jake guffawed in a knowing and particularly offensive way, affirming the Foofwahs' intent to shed the filthy little varmint once he'd performed the service of delivering the horses to Lindsey.

"C'mon," Jake yelled from the window of his truck, ready to roll. "You ladies iz in for the time 'a yer lives!"

Angie climbed behind the wheel of the Gypsy Spirit and leaned on the horn to blast a rendition of "How Dry I Am." With Jake following, towing the horse trailer with his hosed-down, bean-mottled pickup, Angie gunned the motor and roared down the road away from Wickenburg. The little caravan headed for Flagstaff and what in bygone days was famous Route 66, now Interstate 40. If all went well, they could be in Albuquerque before dark.

CHAPTER TEN

DOWN THE ROAD

The morning air was clear and comfortable at eighty degrees. A couple of fluffy white clouds, far apart, wandered slowly in the deep blue of the desert sky, a favorable omen for fair weather and good times ahead, Angie told them.

The motley band of Lindsey's rescuers started their caravan to Colorado with Jake leading the way. He said he knew the route and acted insulted when offered a map. Albuquerque was four hundred and fifty miles, and it would be a long day, especially with the bumpety jolting of the Gypsy Spirit whose shocks hadn't been discernible for several years.

Record-setting rainfall during a long Arizona monsoon had colored the desert with verdancy unusual for September. Soon the saguaros and green-limbed palo verdes began to thin out and dark green piñon-junipers appeared on the tops of hills and in slopes of grass. Myriad small sunflowers lined the highway and carpeted the slopes of the foothills with their yellow glow.

Penny and Chloë, riding up front with Angie, thumbed through a handbook on Arizona wildflowers and attempted to identify the many varieties of sunflowers they saw.

"Do you think we can really get along without Jake once we reach Colorado?" Penny asked, reopening the group topic from the night before.

"I think we have to," Chloë shuddered. "He's just too filthy and objectionable for any of us to want to 'camp out' with him. The whole outdoors isn't wide enough to get rid of his smell. Can you imagine four or five days of him giving orders, eating with us—the man has absolutely no manners—even *sleeping* with us?"

"Aaargh!" they agreed.

As the truck chugged along I-17 climbing toward Flagstaff, the white clouds gradually increased and thunderheads began to appear in the northeast. Some clouds looked like puffy, white flowers, others like flat linen sheets with tattered edges. They seemed oddly stationary, casting soft, protective shadows to shield the shrubs and grasses from the baking sun. The high plateaus of the Mogollon Rim country stretched to the east as the caravan crawled along the highway.

In the Gypsy Spirit's little house, wedged between bedrolls, luggage, and cartons of food, the other three Foofwahs listened to the chimney vent and metal window frames clank and rattle as the truck rolled along the highway. The rhythmic cacophony, combined with the warmth of the snug quarters, lulled the women into such a state of torpor that they lacked enough energy to entertain murderous thoughts of Jake.

Shortly after ten o'clock, Angie followed Jake into Flagstaff, past the tall ponderosa pines standing honor guard. At nearly seven thousand feet, the air was cooler than in the desert valleys. The women emerged gratefully from the truck cab and the mystical cottage for a mid-morning snack at "Huldah's Home Cookin'."

"This trip is awfully slow," Penny said, as they settled around a long, rectangular table.

"You ladies ain't probably use ta travelin' in trucks and pullin' horse trailers," Jake said. "We ain't travelin' no seventy-five an' eighty miles an hour like ever'one else out there. Fifty miles an hour is tops for us."

"How long before we reach Albuquerque?" CC asked.

"About another five, six hours oughta do it," Jake said, "Dependin' on how many stops you wimmen gotta take. It's all freeway, but that don't make no difference. We can't go no faster, but at least we won't have cars and campers honkin' and passin' us like we did outa Wickenburg. The horses hate that."

"Bet they do. So do I," Gina said, grimacing behind her coffee mug. "Tell you what, Jake. I'll be driving the next leg. We can't get lost on I-40, so why don't we just go on ahead, and we'll meet you at Albuquerque. Okay, Angie?"

Angie considered the pros and cons, then shrugged.

"I don't like it," Jake protested, pulling crumbs of hamburger bun from his whiskers before licking his fingers. "What if one of us runs into trouble. You're more likely to than me, you know." Talking all the while he chewed the hamburger, he swished it down with a big gulp of coke.

The women thought about it for a minute. Unanimously, they agreed to risk trouble unprotected rather than remain squeezed into their cramped space any longer than necessary. By afternoon it would be warm even at the high altitude, and air conditioning was not one of Angie's luxuries. Jake could worry about Jake.

* * *

Not far out of Flagstaff, thunderheads gave way to smoky-looking grayish-white clouds covering the sky. Mist soon began to hit the windshield.

"Where are the windshield wipers?" Gina cried in desperation, wishing Angie were up front, but she was now lodged in back with Chloë and Penny. "No windshield wipers! They don't work!" Frantically toggling the wiper switch without result, Gina pulled onto the shoulder and stopped. "Damn lucky there's even a place to pull off."

As they sat immobile and frustrated, Angie hurried around the passenger side with a handful of newspapers. CC rolled down her window and said, "We don't have any windshield wipers."

"I forgot to tell you," Angie apologized. "The motor went out a couple of months ago. Replacing it was so expensive, I just pull over and wait out rainstorms. Sometimes it helps to rub down the windshield with newspapers. The ink leaves the glass with a film that will sheet water so you can see."

As Gina stepped from the driver's side, Jake and the horses swooshed dangerously close past them, sending a shower of water to immerse her, the truck, and most of the newspapers.

"Hell's bells," Gina shouted. "To be humiliated by that old goat. He didn't have to swerve so close and spray us, the old tomcat!"

Hail began to fall, and Angie ran around to the safety of the Gypsy Spirit's cottage, while Gina scrambled back into the truck cab. The hail lasted only a short time but sounded like tap-dancing pebbles on the roof, accompanied by the susurrant music of the summer shower.

When the rain stopped and the sky cleared, dramatic cloud formations excited the beauty-loving romantics.

"Great God in heaven, look at that sky," CC exclaimed.

Behind them, a dark purple shade of rain, like a theater curtain with a fringe of white at the bottom, covered the western sky and obscured the San Francisco peaks. Overhead, a thin veil of clear china blue spread to where a large white cloud edged in pink and gold spun an enormous, brilliant rainbow across the eastern sky.

"Oh, I know we're doing the right thing," CC said, barely able to contain her renewed enthusiasm. "It's a sign that everything will be okay! Just like Noah."

"Right," Gina said. "And Jake's probably squatting on the pot of gold right now."

Gina pressed the accelerator to the floorboard, but could only get up to sixty miles an hour. After a while, they spotted Jake's truck.

Kai-ling shouted, "Look, isn't that Jake ahead?"

"It sure is!" CC agreed. "Let's pass him!"

Gina gunned the motor, and they slowly came abreast of the trailer with the horses.

"Let's give him the old cowboy yell!" CC said, rolling down her window and letting out a whoop. "Yahoo!"

"Whoopee," Kai-ling yelled.

In the back, the others caught on and squeezed their heads out the windows to wave their hats and scream, "Wahoo!"

Gina hit the air horn to blast out "How Dry I Am."

Penny stuck two fingers between her teeth and let out a piercing whistle.

Jake stuck his head and arm out his window and waved his hat, frantically trying to get their attention.

"Stop that confounded noise!" he yelled.

The racket startled the horses so that they began to rear and stomp, causing the trailer to weave and hop dangerously along the highway. Jake struggled desperately with the wheel of the pickup, trying to keep the trailer upright while he looked for a safe place to pull off and stop.

The yelling stopped as suddenly as it had started. The women watched in horror while the pickup and trailer swerved and bucked along the highway.

"Oh my God!" Gina cried. "They'll turn over."

The women's hearts beat wildly as they realized what a catastrophe an overturned trailer with four horses would cause on a busy interstate highway. Someone would surely be killed. Plus, there was increasing danger of Angie's truck becoming involved unless Jake could get the trailer safely off the highway.

Gina floored the truck, hoping to get around and out of the way to give Jake more room to maneuver the pickup and trailer. They could see Jake wrestling with the wheel in a frantic effort to keep the pickup on the road and the trailer from overturning.

Finally, Jake regained control, eased over to the side of the road, and stopped. As he did so, the right rear tire of the horse trailer blew. Gina pulled off the highway ahead of him and onto the wide shoulder.

Jake hopped from the pickup, furious at the women's antics.

"You bunch of god-danged idiots, you fluffheads or whatever the hell you call yerselves! D'ya want to get us all killed? Don't ya know better than to spook a bunch of horses? And now I've got a flat tire. Shee-it!"

He continued yelling at them as he ran to the side of the trailer and mounted a fender above the forward tires. The horses were still rousting about, trying to get out of the trailer. "Here, boy. Easy, easy, girl. Mouse, it's okay, guy. Everything's all right now. Easy, boy. Good boy, Trickster." Very slowly, the horses settled down but were still jittery.

The women, in the meantime, had spilled out of the Gypsy Spirit and were uneasily watching the scene, the full import of the near-accident sinking in. They had done a stupid thing. The kind of stupid thing men expected them to do. No one spoke or looked at each other. All eyes were on Jake.

"There's nuthin' for it but to take these poor animals out of the trailer while I change the tire. If we're real lucky, none of *them* will get kilt." It took about fifteen minutes before the horses were calm enough to be backed out of the trailer. Through some act of divine providence, the roadside was flat and wide enough from the highway to the fence for the horses to have ample space safely away from the traffic.

Jake took the first horse out and tied him to the side of the trailer. "Goddammit!" he yelled. "Give me a hand. You caused this mess. Come over here and help me."

Penny was the first to grasp what he needed. She ran ahead and took the rope of the next horse backing from the trailer and began to walk him around. Gina and Kai-ling were close behind her, each taking the lead rope and walking a horse away from the busy, noisy highway. Every time an eighteen-wheeler passed, the sound frightened the women as much as it did the horses. Jake quietly gave orders to the women while he mingled with the animals, patting the horses on their rumps and rubbing them on their manes, talking soothingly as he moved among them. In time, the horses quieted.

They spent almost an hour stopped beside the highway. The women could see they hadn't earned any brownie points with Jake, whose obvious hatred of them unleashed itself in restrained mumblings under his breath that were easily construed as individual personal threats.

Once Jake changed the tire, he hunkered down on his heels, spit into the dirt and reached into his pouch for another wad of chewing tobacco. He didn't look at the women, and no one dared speak.

"These poor animals gotta have water," he mumbled, when he finally stood up. "Git 'em back into the trailer, and I'll drive 'em on to a place near Winslow where I know we kin git a drink, uh, water. Foller me."

He began loading the horses back into the trailer with help from the women. Jake didn't complain but occasionally looked disgusted, particularly when Kai-ling suggested, "Perhaps we should sweep out the bottom of the trailer first. It is knee-deep in horse manure."

"It's a good thing the highway patrol didn't show up," Jake said. "They'd throw the lot of us in jail for public endangerment."

Not sure what he wanted them to do, the women hesitated to question him, so they crawled back into the Gypsy Spirit. Angie took over the driving and followed Jake obediently onto the highway. Near Winslow, Jake pulled into a rest stop and talked to someone on the phone for several minutes. He then waved for the women to follow and took the next exit, heading off into open country. They proceeded nearly five miles before Jake turned into the yard of a ranch house and drove around to the back.

A man came out of a shanty-like building and talked to Jake. He gestured toward the open corral, and Jake motioned somewhat impolitely for the women to get out.

"Make yerselves useful. Unload them damn horses into that corral," Jake ordered, pointing toward an empty corral surrounded by ancient sycamores. Having the man as an audience, Jake took advantage of the opportunity to display his authority over the thoroughly cowed women, reasonably sure they wouldn't attempt to sass him.

"Who does he think he is, giving us orders like we were the hired hands?" CC demanded.

Nevertheless, she and Kai-ling led the way to the back of the trailer and attempted to unlatch the doors. But the exertion of their combined strength failed to budge the latch. Gina and Penny added their muscle to heave against the bar, and the door finally sprang open. Gina reached through the barred windows along the side to untie the horses, and Penny backed them out, one by one. Kai-ling was waiting to grab a lead and walked the horse around for a minute or two before taking it into the corral. They continued until all four were unloaded.

"I still think someone should sweep out the bottom of the trailer," Kai-ling said. "I didn't know horses pooped so much. In China, a farmer who owned this much manure could fertilize his rice fields for a whole year."

"If we can find a shovel, I'll help," CC offered. The two went off toward the shanty in search of shovels. In the meantime, the others stretched their legs or rested on a stack of railroad ties alongside the corral. The horses, recovered now from their panic and free of the trailer, frisked about, leaping and making short runs around the arena. One by one, they approached the water tank and drank their fill.

Soon, CC returned waving a shovel. Kai-ling had a hoe. They worked away industriously pushing an enormous pile of horse manure from the trailer.

The afternoon seemed to be getting away from them. With the lengthening shadows, the women became uneasy. It was a long time before Jake came out of the house. When he did, the women noticed his walk was a little unsteady. They unconsciously stood at attention, wondering what was expected of them next. They were not pleased with giving Jake the upper hand, but they weren't about to cross him at this point.

"After you git the horses loaded, we'll git on to Albuquerque and find the horse motel," Jake said sourly. "So ya better foller me—and no funny business."

* * *

They reached Albuquerque after sundown. Jake had problems finding the truck stop with the "horse motel." He either couldn't remember or, the Foofwahs suspected, he was befuddled by the refreshments at the ranch house.

The Gypsy Spirit followed the horse trailer around the outskirts of town for half an hour before Jake recognized the motel and pulled into the parking lot. Jake yelled for them to follow him back to the corral. The women still smarted from his bossy attitude and the humiliating remarks he'd made in front of his friend at the ranch. Angie drove instead into the motel parking lot across the street and stopped at the office to check in.

They didn't find out whether the horses were unloaded, watered, fed, or even where Jake spent the night. They didn't see him again that night and supposed he slept in the pickup or in the corral with the horses. The first day had been long and stressful.

CHAPTER ELEVEN

A NEIGHBORLY CALL

After her evening with Chan, Lindsey awoke early, exhilarated partly by the thought that such an elegant, important man found her interesting enough to flirt with. Not that she would allow it to lead to anything, but still it made her feel good.

She showered quickly, running the fresh lemon-scented soap over her smooth, full breasts and the womanly curves of her belly and hips. She was pleased to notice her legs looked as firm and well shaped as when she was a teenager. Not bad for an old girl, she thought.

Stepping from the shower, she considered how long it had been since she'd thought about her figure. Cody used to admire it, but it had been a long time since he'd passed a compliment. She stood in front of the tiny bathroom mirror, and as she ran the comb through her damp curls, she was surprised to see that the touch of gray enhanced her dark hair with an almost glamorous frosting. She seldom wore lipstick, but today she studied her lips as she carefully applied a soft coral shade.

The sun-dappled green glade of her dream fluttered through her mind and she felt again the sensation of surrendering to Chan's deeply satisfying kiss. In the mirror, she saw her face redden, then she laughed aloud at the silliness of it all. She would never be unfaithful to Cody, so why was she letting this man dominate her thoughts? True, he was compellingly sexy, with eyes you could get lost in, but she'd noticed other attractive men since her marriage, and she'd never once wavered.

While dressing, she thought of things she needed to do today. Besides the phone calls to the landowners along the route, she needed permits for crossing public land. That meant a trip to La Cholla, but she needed to stop at the auction yard anyway, to nail down arrangements for the sale of the cattle once she got them there.

Before she could leave for La Cholla, she had to feed the horses, and she was in a hurry. During one trip into the tack room, she noticed the saddle and blankets Cody had used the afternoon he broke his leg. In all the excitement of getting Cody into the hospital emergency room, she had thrown the gear inside the tack room and was only now getting around to putting the saddle on its stand.

Lindsey picked up the saddle and mounted it on the wooden stand, then turned to pick up the Navajo blanket Cody preferred beneath his saddle. Something flicked out of the blanket and onto the floor. Her first thought was that it was a field mouse. Mice were a common sight around ranch stalls and feed rooms, but she didn't like to find one in the tack room for they chewed up the blankets and pulled wool from underneath saddles to line their nests. She looked again and was relieved to find that the object was only a large cocklebur, not a field mouse.

Lindsey picked up the cocklebur, a berry-like growth with long spikes that made the bur about the size of a small walnut. These spikes could cut through a horse's hide and drive him mad, she thought. Beneath a saddle, the pressure would be enough to make the gentlest horse wild. The cocklebur had been caught under the saddle blanket, the one on Ringo when the usually docile horse went crazy and threw Cody.

In her mind's eye, Lindsey revisited every second of that morning. She'd been washing dishes, cleaning up after breakfast, when she looked out the window over the sink and saw Cody, who was saddling up, talking with a man who was on horseback. She couldn't see who it was, because the rider was partially obscured by a tree, and the horse didn't look familiar, but she knew the men talked for ten minutes or so. A little later, she'd led her horse from the barn to where Cody was watering Ringo. They would ride together in the fresh morning air while checking the cattle pastured on the leased land.

Lindsey's back was turned to Cody as she reached beneath her horse's belly for the cinch. She heard Ringo's grunt rather than saw the horse buck as Cody lifted himself into the saddle.

She turned in time to see Cody flying over the horse's head and onto the hard-packed ground. He lay helpless, grimacing with pain, one leg twisted under his body. She knew at once that Cody's leg was broken.

Now, Lindsey placed the bur on the windowsill and stretched the blanket over the saddle to air out. She loaded the wheelbarrow with pellets to feed the horses. While they ate, she inspected Ringo's back and was not surprised to find a fresh sore the size of a quarter where the saddle exerted the most pressure. It was raw and festering, surrounded by flies. She wiped a fly-repellent rag over the area and put a disinfecting ointment on the wound.

How in the hell did that cocklebur get under the blanket? She couldn't get it out of her mind. She tried to call Cody to tell him what she'd found and to ask who he'd been speaking with just before his accident. Cody didn't answer, and the Taylors didn't possess an answering machine. Cody thought it would be a waste of money.

* * *

On her way into town, Lindsey decided to stop off at Chan's ranch to ask if he'd been talking with Cody shortly before the accident, while he was saddling up, or if he knew who might have been there. Maybe one of his men. He certainly hadn't mentioned it.

She came to an impressive wrought-iron archway proclaiming "Tres Alamos," Chan's ranch. Turning up the long driveway lined with tall, dark-green fir trees, she was awed by the sight of the large two-story Victorian house before her.

The house was misty-muted gray, its gingerbread latticework trimmed in white. A wide verandah encircled the house at ground level, and small balconies graced the two front rooms at the second level. A widow's walk crowned the slope of the black-shingled roof. Three enormous poplars at one side of the house stood guard against the icy blasts from the northern plains in the winter.

"It's magnificent," Lindsey breathed. She slowed the pickup, then thought stopping was maybe a bad idea. She started to accelerate when Chan opened the front door and gave her a friendly wave.

"Come on in," he called.

Lindsey smiled, realizing it was too late to back off. Chan quickly stepped around to help her from the pickup, and there it was again. The familiar touch, the little extra pressure to her upper arm, and now the brush of the back of his hand against the fullness of her breast.

"I was on my way into town," she began breathlessly, trying to remember why she'd come.

"And you decided to stop by for a neighborly cup of coffee," Chan finished her sentence.

"That's right," she said, grateful for any excuse that sounded reasonable.

He took her arm again and led her into the house. "First-time visitors must have a tour of my home," he said. "I'm very proud of it. For all her faults, Yvonne, my ex, was a helluva decorator."

Chan guided Lindsey through the house. It was solidly built with ornate walnut woodwork framing the doors and windows. Crossing the Italian marble of the foyer into the living room, she looked admiringly at the frescoed ceiling with delicate pastel floral panels inside gold baroque frames. The dark, pegged planks of the hardwood flooring were highly varnished, exhibiting to perfection oriental area rugs, with their deep red backgrounds and jewel-color patterns tying together the rich hues of the burgundy draperies at the sides of the tall windows and the velvet-upholstered furniture. Creamy, hand-made lace curtains elegantly covered the windows.

The dining room decor echoed that of the living room in colors and style. The antique Chippendale dining table and chairs were set to accommodate eighteen guests. The buffet at the side displayed an ornate silver tea service, and the built-in, lighted breakfront across the end wall invited attention to a magnificent collection of bone china, sterling, and cut crystal. It would have been the envy of princes, Lindsey guessed. She was too overwhelmed to speak.

The kitchen had been remodeled to include every modern convenience imaginable plus a brick fireplace to preserve the Victorian influence. The pale, lilac-colored wooden frames of the cupboards were inset with leaded glass, displaying neat stacks of dishes and glassware. Canned and dry goods were stored in their own walk-in pantry.

Lindsey thought of the dull, functional kitchen she had at home. She had always considered it adequate for its purpose, and it had been modernized to include a dishwasher in 1985. But this was a kitchen to die for! The spaciousness, the lovely colors. What wouldn't she give for surroundings like these?

Chan led her up the back stairway and through the four bedrooms, each with its own bathroom, individually decorated in a variety of colors, deep blue porcelain or petal pink, glacial blue or mahogany, depending on whether the room was designed for a woman's or a man's taste, but all with hand-painted florals. The brass and white porcelain fixtures were modern versions of Victorian hardware.

The enormous master bedroom sported a huge canopied waterbed with lacy white curtains tied back by gold tasseled cords, echoing the richness of the white velvet drapes and lace curtains at the windows. The pale blue of the carpeting was carried out in the grosgrain ribbon pattern of the wallpaper. The windows opened out onto a balcony overlooking a glorious rock garden of wildflowers at the back of the house.

Chan smiled with pride at the speechless, awestruck Lindsey. She and Cody would never be able to live like this in a zillion years.

She met Chan's eyes in the tall pier glass beside the bed that was obviously his. His eyes held hers and what passed between them told her that were she to give him the slightest encouragement, he would fulfill the passion she longed for ... dreamed of ... wrote poems about. For a long moment, Lindsey wanted more than anything she could remember to acquiesce to the invitation in Chan's eyes. Her body quivered imperceptibly, poised at the edge of a precipice. One step more and there would be no turning back. In possibly the most wrenching decision of her life, she broke the spell by looking away.

"Your home is lovely, Chan," she said lightly and walked through the doorway to the hall. "I'm afraid I've misjudged my time, though, and I'll have to take a rain check on the cup of coffee."

She stepped quickly down the stairs to the foyer, faking a casual air, but in truth fearing to risk further temptation.

"What a pity. I haven't shown you the swimming pool. I thought you might even have time for a swim this morning."

"Afraid not today, but thanks, anyway." With what she hoped was a dazzling smile to show her gratitude, she fled out the front door.

Behind the wheel of the pickup, she sensed that she'd forgotten to ask him something. Whatever it was, it could wait.

CHAPTER TWELVE

THE PIONEER WOMAN

The Gypsy Spirit circled the town square and stopped in front of a commemorative statue. A small crowd gathered, curious about the unusual contraption. Saturday afternoon spectacles on the town square were rare, but when nothing more exciting happened than a bunch of bedraggled women stepping forth, the crowd dispersed, disappointed with the poor showing.

"Our first priority is to call Lindsey," Angie said.

The women walked to the street corner and stood, braced against the wind blowing in from the high prairie. They eyed the buildings around the square skeptically. The town was small and typically western.

"Plainview may have been an important cog on the Santa Fe Trail a hundred and fifty years ago, but it obviously hasn't changed much," Gina said.

While they hesitated, unsure which direction to head, a fire truck pulled alongside the Gypsy Spirit. The firemen jumped down and prepared to hook up to a water main.

"Wait, wait," Angie cried, running back toward them. "What are you doing?"

"We'll just look around, ma'am," the captain said, tipping his hat.

Angie noticed a small amount of steam drifting from under the truck's hood. "It's all right. It does that sometimes. It's just a little overheated." She didn't want them inspecting the Gypsy Spirit too closely. They might find the box of fireworks she'd picked up in New Mexico. Fireworks were probably illegal in Colorado.

"We'll take a look anyway. Can't be too careful where gasoline's concerned." He popped the hood open and carefully loosened the radiator cap. "Better let it cool off, then get some more water, ma'am."

"I understand," Angie said.

The captain chuckled. "I'm the police chief too, ma'am, and when I heard about your arrival in this odd-looking vehicle, I was worried you might be plannin' on settin' up some kind of business or be a weird cult, maybe even runnin' dope from Mexico with that Arizona license plate. But you look like decent women. Where you headed?"

Angie told him they were friends of Simon Garland's niece and had come to help her move the cattle.

"Guess you've had experience along those lines?"

"No, but you gotta start sometime." She'd rather not start at all, if she could be honest about it.

The captain scratched his head and looked across the street at the Foofwahs huddled in front of the bank building. "Well, I wish you the best of luck." He gathered his crew and left.

The women returned, full of questions about what the fire captain had said. "Did he tell you how to get to Lindsey's? It's four o'clock, and we ought to be getting on out there," Gina fretted.

"No, darn, I forgot to ask him," Angie admitted. "We'll have to call."

"Hey, no worry," CC said. "I used my cell phone while we were waiting. Lindsey's on her way into town now. Said to meet her at Evelyn's diner down the street."

They stood in the shadow of the twenty-foot high stone statue. Chloë read aloud the inscription, "Madonna of the Trail."

"My God, she's everywhere," CC cried, "and carrying her kid."

This Madonna depicted the spirit of pioneer women who followed their men west. She held an infant in one arm and a rifle in the other. Her booted feet strode purposefully into the sunset. Granite eyes sought the distant mountains, chin set in determination. Her hair was tucked beneath a bonnet, and a small boy clung to her long, swirling skirt.

The women silently admired the statue, pondering their kinship to the spirit of the women pioneers, who had endured and triumphed over enormous hardships. They paused in respect for their older sisters, true heroines of the Old West and felt grateful that dodging starvation and flaming arrows was not on their agenda.

They found Evelyn's little cafe on a side street. Red-and-white checkered curtains in the front window and white plastic table coverings gave it a fresh country air. The cafe was deserted of its usual assortment of faithfuls, and the only waitress, Evelyn, looked as though she'd had her afternoon nap interrupted. Stifling a yawn, she took their orders for pie and coffee and disappeared around a corner without ever looking fully awake.

"Hope she finds the kitchen," Gina said, concerned that food might be delayed. "I don't know about the Gypsy Spirit, but my fuel is running low."

Penny observed more charitably, "Bet she walks in her sleep half the time. She's probably the whole act here, cook, waitress, and clean-up crew."

Evelyn staggered with a heavy-laden tray. Kai-ling jumped to her aid by handing out the plates of pie.

"Thanks, honey," Evelyn said, writing out individual checks. "Where're you all headed?"

Gina told her their destination without supplying details.

"I know'd old Simon Garland," Evelyn said, tearing off the tickets and handing them around. "Just keep an eye out for that scurvy sonofabitch Reed lives next ranch over. The man's all hat and no cattle."

Before she could finish, the door flew open, and Lindsey blew in. Evelyn stared, open-mouthed, at all the hugging, squeals of delight, and laughter Lindsey's arrival elicited. "You'd think they was a bunch of kids," she said to herself as she started back toward the kitchen, then remembered the newcomer might want something to eat.

"Say, you look kind of familiar, hon'," she said to Lindsey. "Ain't you the woman lookin' for someone to help you move your cattle?"

Lindsey smiled broadly and nodded. "I have all the help I need now."

She joined the Foofwahs at the round center table, and they began to make plans. In the morning, Chloë would drive the Gypsy Spirit, loaded with food and gear to the first camp. That way, the cattle drivers, "drovers," Lindsey called them, could expect a good hot meal cooked over an open fire at the first stop.

"An open fire?" Chloë felt a surge of panic. "I've never cooked anything other than a hot dog on a stick over an open fire in my life." She was beginning to wonder why she'd volunteered as cook. The whole project was taking on the aspects of an idiot-in-the-attic horror movie. Chloë wondered which course of action was worse, riding a horse six or seven hours a day or cooking two meals a day for eight people over an open fire plus fixing sandwiches in between. "Won't I be cooking over Angie's Coleman stove?" she asked.

"Partly," Lindsey said, "but it won't do for a group this large."

Chloë frowned as she considered her options. I'll get through this somehow, she told herself.

The other Foofwahs would head the cattle out by sun up the next morning. They would drive the cattle about fifteen miles and meet Chloë at Comanche Reservoir.

Lindsey told them Jake had already arrived with the horses and was at the ranch preparing dinner for them.

"I can imagine what kind of dinner to expect from Jake," CC groused.

"As a matter of fact, Jake is a good cook," Lindsey defended him. At first she started to say he was a wonderful cook but decided not to overplay her hand. "He used to be a camp cook back in the days when a chuck wagon was standard equipment on a ranch."

"Good," Chloë said, seeing a ray of hope. "Maybe he'd like to take over the cooking."

"I'm afraid not, Chloë," Lindsey smiled. She understood Chloë's anxiety but was equally certain a woman who had raised three children, returned to college in mid-life to earn teaching credentials, then taught for ten years, could manage to drive a truck and cook outdoors. "We need him working the herd."

As they lined up at the cash register, Lindsey added, "Jake's planning a special cowboy dish. He wouldn't tell me what it was. He stopped off at the meat market here in town before he drove on out to the ranch."

"Whatever it is, I'll bet the main ingredient is Jack Daniels," CC said under her breath, careful that Lindsey didn't hear. For some reason, Lindsey seemed to have a special regard for the old fart.

CHAPTER THIRTEEN

JAKE'S REVENGE

At Uncle Simon's ranch, Jake busied himself around the kitchen, chopping and slicing and popping things into pots. A sound bearing faint resemblance to "Home on the Range" issued from somewhere in the region of his beard.

J. Chandler Reed, elegant in his white western attire trimmed with silver and turquoise, stuck his head in the back door and called out, "Ho, Jake, you're making so much racket you couldn't hear me knock."

"Hullo, Reed," Jake said darkly. The two first met several years back at a cattle auction in Grand Junction where they spent an evening playing poker and getting drunk. Chan's far-flung reputation spiced many a cattleman's tale, so Jake knew considerable gossip about Chan. Neither was particular about their drinking and gambling companions as long as the liquor flowed and the game wasn't rigged.

Jake didn't mind the drinking and the gambling, but he'd never had much use for a man who spent too much time courting women and not enough running his ranch. He paused, put down his rolling pin, and wiped floury hands on a large, dirty chef's apron. "Lindsey ain't here. Whatcha want?"

"Now, Jake, that's not a friendly greeting after all this time, 'Whatcha want?'" Chan mimicked him perfectly. "I came over to see if the lovely lady needs any help. Just being neighborly."

Resuming his work with the rolling pin, Jake said, "The lovely lady's got a lovely husband, though some of his parts ain't workin' so good right now. But she's got me, I'm lovely, and she's got six of the loveliest old bats you ever saw arriving any minute to help her out. One thing about old bats, I 'spect they can even see in the dark ... hadn't thoughta that before ... that'll make 'em better out there on the range than any dudes you'd drum up."

Lindsey had told Jake of Chan's offer but not of their dinner together. Jake volunteered that the man was trying to skin her.

"I can't wait to meet them," Chan said.

"You won't have to," Jake said. "Take a look at that." He nodded toward the ranch yard where Lindsey was parking her pickup truck loaded with women. The Gypsy Spirit pulled alongside.

The Foofwahs chattered happily as they approached the ranch house.

"Jesus, they never stop talkin'," Jake said, dusting his hands after putting the final touches on lumps of biscuit dough. "That'll be good too. Keep the coyotes away, if it doesn't give the cattle nervous breakdowns."

"Or you, my friend." Chan put his hand on Jake's shoulder, but Jake shrugged him off. "You seem mighty fretted by these ladies. And they've got *you* in the kitchen. That's rich."

"They're okay. They just belong back in Arizona, is all. And don't you worry about me bein' in the kitchen. I know what I'm doin'." Jake motioned Chan toward the door. "Whyn't you go on out and greet 'em. They might need their hands kissed or somethin'."

Chan grinned and stepped outside, interested in seeing who these women were that Lindsey trusted to help her out of an impossible situation.

What he saw astonished him—six women of middling years and unbelievable shapes. If he had to describe them, he'd say they ranged from teapots to oak trees. Not that they looked so bad. What Nature left out in beauty, she'd obviously made up for in good spirits, for their faces were aglow with excitement, like teenagers on their way to a rock concert. They babbled happily as if they'd only now run into one another at a high school reunion.

"Amazing," he said, under his breath. "Poor Jake." He chuckled with the slightest hint of malice.

"Lindsey, my dear," Chan said, doffing his Stetson.

"Chan, what are you doing here?" Lindsey looked uncomfortable at his presence—and his magnificence. Why can't he just look ordinary, like most men? she thought. He truly looks like a movie star.

She was afraid her friends might mistake the relationship, not that there was one, between herself and this handsome neighbor. She'd decided beforehand to keep their meetings to herself. Even these good friends might misunderstand the intent, or the result.

"I'm on my way to head up a parade in town. Just stopped by to see if you might need anything." He smiled with his special knowing look. Surveying the Foofwahs at closer range only increased his wonderment. "But I see your troops have arrived and you have plenty of help."

He replaced his hat and stood aside for the Foofwahs to pass. His eyes were drawn to Angie's flame-red hair, and their eyes locked for a moment before she smiled and offered a friendly, "Hiyah."

Chan, ever the ladies' man, was instantly captivated by her exotic looks—and quick to assess her potential.

Returning her greeting, he bowed in a mock-courtly gesture, but before he could introduce himself, Lindsey headed him off.

"You can meet my friends later, Chan, if you don't mind. Right now, we have to get settled. And Jake's got dinner on," she lied to get rid of him.

"I understand. But remember, if you or these remarkable ladies need *anything*, you can call on me." Strolling to his Cadillac, Chan paused to look back and grin. He began to whistle as he drove away. Decommissioning *this* army will be a cinch!

* * *

Jake forbade any Foofwahs to enter the kitchen, except Lindsey. "It'll be a little while till dinner," he told her. "Just keep 'em outa here."

The women took advantage of the time to spread out their bedrolls on the floor in the two bedrooms, but naps were out of the question. The barn cat, Felon, strolled in and plunked himself down in the middle of Chloë's bedroll.

"Get out of here, you walking flea motel," Chloë screeched. "I never could stand to be around cats. Makes me itch just looking at one."

Hearing the commotion, Jake stuck his head in at the door. "Ain't that the ugliest creature you ever seen? Ears all tattered, rat bit probably, and he gets real mean looking when you cross him. He brought me a nice fat mouse fer your dinner, but I took pity on ya and told him to take it back." He snickered and carried the cat outdoors.

Lindsey insisted the women tour the ranch and look over the herd as it was time for the cattle to be fed. She oversaw the operation, driving the tractor while three Foofwahs shoveled feed from the tractor-trailer into cement troughs built into the side of the corral.

"My God, this is hard work," Gina complained.

"You think this is hard? Try doing it by yourself," Lindsey called from her seat on the tractor.

Afterward, Lindsey saddled her horse so she could check each cow to make sure all were in shape for the drive. She was particularly concerned about some of the late spring calves born less than three months ago. Her tour of inspection was thorough as she wandered back and forth among the herd.

Lindsey then called the women into the house where they gathered in Uncle Simon's office to study their route and plan overnight stops along the way.

"When you're herding cattle, you can't get in front of them and head them off. You have to ride alongside and gradually shift their direction," Lindsey told the women. "You do this by the rider on the right side crowding the cattle to the left or the left rider crowding them to the right. That means the riders opposite have to know what you're planning to do and give them room to shift direction.

"If you race to get ahead of the cattle, they'll stampede and, believe me, a stampeding herd can run faster than you. If you try to stop them, they'll merely feint a few times, then dodge around you, or run right over you.

"I'll ride on point. Cattle will follow a leader. Some of you will ride left or right flank. The worst job is bringing up the drags, the stragglers. We'll alternate so no one gets stuck with that job all the time. You eat a lot of dust, but your job is to make sure none of the cattle hang back too far or drift out of sight and get left behind. Cattle aren't smart, but don't make the mistake of thinking they're dumb. They try all the tricks, like getting behind a snag or a hillock, out of sight, and stand still until we go past. So keep your eyes open. Most of the time we'll be strung out over about a half mile. That's pretty normal."

The Foofwahs eyed one another uneasily.

Lindsey continued. "What we have to fear most is a thunder or electrical storm. Cattle stampede easily when startled, and sudden noises or flashes of lightning terrify them. If we have a storm, we'll round them up as tightly as we can. Then we'll have to stand guard and croon to them. We can walk among them if we do it quietly. Just make sure they don't get frightened and take off. We'll have two people standing watch at night all the time to make sure none of the cattle wander off.

"We're lucky to have had a wet summer early on, but that means grass is high. We haven't had rain for several weeks, and right now the grass is pretty dry. Our greatest danger is from a grass fire. We should have the advantage of being able to see the smoke in plenty of time, and we'd be able to smell it. Unfortunately, cattle have a keener sense of smell than we do, and they get terribly nervous when they smell fire. If that happens, our only hope is in starting a backflash fire or getting the cattle into an area where there's nothing to burn, like in the bottom of a creek bed, or better yet, in a creek with water in it. Let's hope that doesn't happen, or if it does that it happens when we're near enough to drive the cattle into the Arkansas River bed.

"I understand the Arkansas is quite low this side of the dam, but there's always the danger of quicksand. I don't anticipate this happening, but you need to be aware of all possibilities so you'll not be confused about our plan of action in an emergency.

"Any questions?"

Five struck-dumb stares returned Lindsey's bright finish. Oh, oh, Lindsey thought. The first stampede may be to the airport.

"Don't worry," she reassured the silent Foofwahs. "None of these things are apt to happen, but I wouldn't feel right if I didn't cover the worst-case scenarios."

Gina swallowed hard. "We're tough, Lindsey. You can count on us." The others murmured their agreement.

Kai-ling asked, "Will we each have our own cows to look after? Say sixty apiece?"

"Great idea!" CC exclaimed. "Then we could tie different-colored bows to their tails and everyone could keep track of her own."

Lindsey laughed. "Inventorying will be the least of our worries. No, we may lose one or two along the way, though that's doubtful in this short drive. We'll just stay around the outer edges, to keep them from straying."

Jake, still wearing his dirty white apron and a light sprinkling of flour, intervened with an announcement: "Dinner will be ready in half an hour." From a tray he carried, he handed out cans of cold beer or diet sodas.

"What are we having?" Penny teased. She was certain the answer would be grilled hamburgers or hot dogs, though the evidence of flour puzzled her.

"Jest your typical roundup bill of fare. If yer goin' to be cowboys, you might as well eat like cowboys. You know, durin' the Depression, cowboys was poorer than anyone, but we always et good. Steak every night. Cowboy biscuits and sausage or bacon gravy for breakfast. Cowboy beans, cowboy coffee."

"Sounds wonderful," Gina cried. "I'm hungry enough to eat a horse. No! Cancel that!"

"Can I help?" Angie asked.

"Nope, don't want to spoil the surprise," Jake replied.

The Foofwahs relaxed with their refreshments until Jake announced dinner, then they trooped into the large kitchen with its harvest-sized dinner table. The table was neatly set and sumptuously covered with fresh biscuits, big bowls of red beans, potatoes fried with onions, and gravy. Only after everyone was seated did they notice there were no steaks on the table. No one wanted to mention the fact, certain it was an oversight.

"Now for the piece of resistance," Jake announced with resounding pride. He lifted a large platter from the oven and carried it to the table. The platter was covered with what appeared to be deep-fried chicken livers. The ravings about the wonderful-looking dinner ceased. They had expected steak, and chicken livers wouldn't cut it!

Jake set it on the table, seated himself, and took a large serving before passing the platter on.

"What is it?" Penny asked, nibbling gingerly. "It doesn't taste like chicken livers."

Chloë entertained visions of the cat's mouse offering, thinking she wouldn't put it past Jake to pull a stunt like serving up mouse. "Yes, what is it?"

"Mountain oysters," Jake said. "Ain't they great?"

"In Taiwan, where I grew up," Kai-ling offered, "people ate only fish. It was our best source of protein, but I have never heard of 'mountain' oysters, only oysters from the sea." Though a vegetarian, she sometimes enjoyed fish.

"Oh, boy!" CC said, delighted at the prospect of oysters. These would no doubt be the small, eastern ones rather than the flabby, strong Pacific oysters. She took a large mouthful and smiled. "Good," she purred.

Penny, however, was skeptical. She sensed something here didn't make sense.

"Where do you get oysters in the middle of the high plains?" she asked, trying to keep her voice casual. The others were digging into the oysters, potatoes, beans, and biscuits with relish.

Angie by-passed the oysters when the platter reached her. She made no explanation, but her dark eyes watched the women heap their plates with the mountain oysters.

"Not ocean oysters, *mountain* oysters," Jake said, helping himself to another large serving.

By now, Gina's suspicions were aroused. "These don't taste like oysters we had in New England or Seattle," she said. "What's the difference between mountain oysters and ocean oysters?"

"Mountain oysters come from steers," Jake explained.

"How, from steers?" Penny persisted.

"Not from steers originally. They were steers afterwards. Before that, they were bulls." The women looked at each other, unable to fathom the relevance of this latest information.

Lindsey at this point was unable to keep her face straight. She burst out laughing. "What he means to say is that mountain oysters are the testicles of young bulls who have been castrated. Once castrated, they become steers. Cowboys consider this quite a delicacy."

A shock wave enveloped the room. Until now, most were eating the oysters with gusto. The chewing stopped, and several covered their mouths to keep from gagging. Lindsey alone among the women continued to enjoy the fare.

"My God!" Gina breathed, bolting from the table in the direction of the bathroom.

For the first time in her life, CC was speechless.

Penny began to laugh. Kai-ling hadn't truly understood what had transpired but instinct told her whatever it was, it was something dreadful.

"Did I understand you to say testicles?" Chloë asked.

"Try some more. You ain't et nothin' till you've et mountain oysters. Cowboys love 'em. 'Nother thing I used to fix for the boys was calves' brains. When we had leftover oatmeal, I'd scramble eggs up with the reheated oatmeal. Couldn't hardly tell the difference between them and calves' brains."

Penny, a world traveler, had experienced her share of unusual dishes. "Once during summer vacation when I was a foreign exchange student in Lebanon," she said, "at my first family-type dinner they served lamb. Since I was the guest of honor, I was served the best part, the eyes. Believe me, you've seen nothing until you've had a pair of lamb's eyes looking up from your dinner plate. I didn't want to insult my host, so I ate them."

CC, looking pale, excused herself from the table, followed by Chloë.

Lindsey decided they'd had enough fun. She rounded up the deserters by announcing that New York steaks had been prepared for those too squeamish to appreciate mountain oysters.

After the women returned to the table, Jake's face split with a snaggled-toothed smile. "Gotcha!" he said.

CHAPTER FOURTEEN

ROUNDUP

Satisfied that he had shocked the women sufficiently with his mountain oysters treat, Jake went to the barn to feed the horses and make sure the new arrivals were getting along well with the others. After taking care of the animals, he unloaded his bedroll from the pickup and headed for the bunkhouse. He was tired and ready to hit the hay.

Two cowboys stepped from the shadows of the farm buildings. Surprised, Jake looked around for a pickup but didn't see any sort of vehicle. They must have ridden in and tied their horses back of the building, he figured, out of sight of the main house. Why didn't they want Lindsey to know they were here?

As they drew closer, Jake realized he'd never seen the men before. He had known plenty of skullduggery in his lifetime, enough to make him chary of strangers. The sudden, quiet appearance of these men didn't add up.

The two men sauntered into the bright circle cast by the yard light. As Jake approached them, his purposeful stride slowed somewhat, but he continued toward the bunkhouse.

"Howdy, Jake," one of the men called out, his voice friendly. "We been waitin' fer ya."

"Hey," Jake responded, polite but unenthusiastic.

The larger man stepped forward. "My name's Jimbo Crawford. This here's Sam Saulie. Heard in town ol' man Simon's cattle was bein' moved out tomorrow. Thought we'd ride out and see for ourselves what kinda outfit was doin' the drivin'. Kinda curious about who would work for a woman ..." The cowboy let his sentence drift off suggestively as he turned his attention to lighting a cigarette, then flipped his Zippo lighter shut with authority and stared hard at Jake.

"I'm headin' the outfit that's doin' the drivin', but I ain't workin' for no woman. I'm takin' my orders from the woman's husband. Been workin' for Cody Taylor in Arizona off and on for ten years now." Jake continued toward the bunkhouse at a much slower pace. His animal instinct told him not to show fear. Two-legged bullies were wors'n a pack of hungry coyotes.

"Yeah? Where is this husband?" the second man taunted. "From where I been sittin', looks to me like about a dozen wimmen. I ain't seen hide nor hair of a man around anywhere."

"Don't need no boss around," Jake responded. "I been drivin' cattle long enough, and the boss—he knows he can depend on me to do him a good job. What concern is it of yers anyway?"

"Hey, we're just tryin' to be friendly. Ain't here to make trouble. Just thought we'd come out and see if a fellow cowboy needs anything, maybe a friend or two." The first cowboy waved his hand and screwed up his face as though insulted that his intent was misconstrued.

"Yeah," the second cowboy said. "We just thought one of our own might need some he-man company after being surrounded by all them wimmen. Ain't fit for a cowboy to have to take orders from wimmen. Thought maybe we'd bring you some luck or at least some liquid courage. Figured you might possibly be a drinkin' man, and you ain't been havin' much fun the past few days with all them wimmen orderin' you around." The cowboy brought out a bottle of Jack Daniels from his hip pocket and held it out to Jake. Jake stopped in his tracks and eyed the bottle.

"I got a big day ahead of me tomorrow. Some other time, I might 'preciate it." Jake moved on toward the bunkhouse.

"Come on," the second cowboy said to his buddy, motioning with his head that it was time to leave. "We ain't talkin' to no real cowboy here. We're talkin' to a lap dog. 'Here Fido, come to mama,'" he mimicked.

"Yeah, I reckon we know when we're not wanted. Just goes to show what happens when wimmen take over. Can't even drop by for a game of poker."

Jake had the foresight to replenish his supply of liquor on his way through Plainview, but it had been a long time since he'd talked to a cowboy, a man who understood the cowboy's life and hardships. It had been an even longer time since he'd had a good game of poker. He was tempted. But he was also wary.

Plainview was twenty-four miles away, and the nearest ranch house was five miles at least. A cowboy loves to ride, but he gets enough of that during the day. He wouldn't ride that distance without a good reason. If it was a social call, they'd come in a pickup. Something was not setting right with Jake.

What bothered him most was that the men seemed to know an awful lot about what was going on here. The old girls only arrived this afternoon, yet everybody in the county seemed to know about them and the fact that cattle were being moved out in the morning.

Them danged wimmen musta done a lot of talkin' in the short time they were in town! Probably the one with the danged phone in her ear half the time talking to Ace, whoever that is. What'll it hurt to spend a coupla hours playin' poker with these fellas? Jake convinced himself he'd be able to find out why these men were interested and who was concerned enough to keep tabs on everything that happened on the ranch.

"Waaall, since you put it that way ..." he hesitated. "C'mon in. Did you bring some cards?" He led the men into the bunkhouse and threw his bedroll on one of the empty beds.

Under a cracked yellow plastic lampshade, a hundred-watt bulb cast light on a small table at the far end of the room. Jake rounded up some chairs, and the three men settled in for a game of poker. Jimbo lit another cigarette and placed his Zippo on the table. "Jimbo" had been crudely etched in the metal.

"Guess you ain't lookin' to lose that lighter," Jake said, trying to sound friendlier than he felt. After all, these fellas is just tryin' to be neighborly, he told himself.

"That's right. An' I ain't goin' to lose this Swiss army knife my kid sent me from Germany neither," the man said proudly. He showed Jake the knife with "Jimbo" scratched into its hard red plastic. "He's a good kid an' he knowed I been wantin' one a' these for a long time. Look! It's got two knife blades, a corkscrew, can opener, bottle opener, tweezers, ballpoint pen, pair a' pliers, scissors, magnifyin' glass, four kinds a' screwdrivers, a wood saw, a file, a measurin' stick, an awl, and a needle for sewin' canvas and leather. A fish scaler and hook remover, a small chisel, and best all, a toothpick! It's a whiz. Don't know what I'd do without it."

"Well, I'll be doggoned," Jake said politely as he fanned the deck of cards across the table to cut for dealer. "Let's play cards!"

* * *

When Angie staggered into the kitchen before daybreak the next morning, Lindsey already had a fire going in the woodburning stove. She wasn't too groggy to notice that Lindsey looked worried about something. Angie supposed she'd be fretting too if she was responsible for something the magnitude of this cattle drive.

Angie started to set the table, but Lindsey interrupted her. "No, leave that, please. I'm surprised Jake isn't here by now. Would you mind going out to the bunkhouse to see what's keeping him?"

Grabbing her jacket and a fat, brown link sausage from the skillet, Angie took off at a brisker pace than she'd used setting the table. It was still dark outside, but the light of dawn was turning the eastern sky the color of pink pearls.

Angie searched in the half-light, looking for Jake among the cattle and horses but saw no sign of him. She continued toward the bunkhouse. It didn't look like the lights were on inside. The cold morning air gripped her, and she wrapped her arms tighter across her chest. Spooky, she thought.

She banged on the door of the bunkhouse but received no response. Opening the door, she stepped timidly into the darkened room. The room smelled musty—and boozy. Her eyes slowly adjusted to the darkness. Finally, she saw the shapes of several bunks at the far end of the room. She groped for a light switch but found none.

"Jake!" she called several times. No answer. Angie was reluctant to venture too far into the room, but as her eyes became better adjusted, she could see a lamp hanging over a table nearby. She groped around until she found a chain to pull on the switch. The lamp cast dim light into the far corners of the room.

Only one bunk was occupied. Jake was lying on top of the thin mattress with his unzipped bedroll spread on top of him. He was fully dressed but motionless.

Angie let out a whimper, "My God, he's dead! Oh, poor Jake."

She approached the inert body cautiously, afraid of what she might find. The stench of stale liquor assaulted her senses, making her eyes sting, but she could see his chest moving up and down. "The little shit is dead all right. He's dead drunk!"

Furious that the one person Lindsey relied on most could let her down this way, Angie shook Jake vigorously. At first he didn't respond, then with her increased roughness, he groaned and flopped over.

"Sit up, you stupid old fool!" Angie screamed in his ear. "How dare you get yourself in this condition when Lindsey is counting on you!"

Jake opened his bleary eyes. Angie shook him harder.

"I'm going to the house to get some coffee. When I get back, you'd better be outta that sack and moving around, or I'll kill you with my bare hands! Do you hear me?" She shook him again. Jake nodded like a rag doll and made a futile effort to get up. "If you value your life, you'd better get a move on!" Angie threatened as she headed for the door.

Lindsey wasn't in the kitchen when Angie returned, but the other Foofwahs huddled around the stove in their flannel pajamas and nightgowns, hands extended to the fire to gather in some warmth.

Angie filled a thermos with hot coffee and fled back to the bunkhouse. Jake was sitting up but his motions were slow and cautious. Angie forced him to drink the strong black coffee, then helped him to his feet and walked him back and forth until he showed signs of comprehension. Her anger simmered down with a consoling thought, At least, I won't have to dress him.

* * *

"We'd better get breakfast out of the way and get going," Lindsey urged the women, concerned with the wide-spread lethargy she observed, especially in Jake. He looked like the walking dead. She detected signs of a first-class hangover and was annoyed that he would drink heavily the night before the big drive when she needed him to back her up. She had been half-dressed and on the run when her feet hit the floor that morning. "Jake, sit down and have a cup of coffee. Everyone else, time to get dressed so we can get out of here. This is our big day!"

The women made a beeline to shower and dress. "Who can tell when we'll have another chance to bathe?" CC muttered.

Gina returned first, striding into the room attired like a *Town and Country* equestrienne with designer jeans and jacket, red-checkered shirt, and polished, smooth leather boots. Her blonde hair, brushed and gleaming, cupped smoothly beneath her precious brown felt Revenuer Stetson.

"You look pretty fancy," Lindsey said. "Nice outfit, but aren't you worried you'll ruin your good clothes on the trail?"

"I'm almost certain of it," Gina replied, "but I want pictures to take back to Ted, something to show him how wonderful we all look as we set off on this monumental event." She busied herself helping Lindsey put the breakfast on the table.

Other than the clunking of boots back and forth across the linoleum floor and the rattle of dishes and silverware, the only sounds were the crackling fire and the perking coffee.

"Smells good," Jake said from where he'd seated himself at the head of the table. His soft voice conveyed a forced heartiness.

Lindsey wondered how he could stand the thought of food but knew him to be a veteran hard-drinker and supposed his system had long ago adapted to binges. Jake pulled platters of hotcakes, sausages, and scrambled eggs toward himself and heaped his plate with the food. To her annoyance, he sent the empties back to Lindsey for refills.

"I guess you might as well load up," she said, trying to remain unruffled. "No telling what we'll have the next few days. Chloë didn't look too enthusiastic about cooking over a campfire."

"Yeah, but you always got me for back up. I'm a Class A camp cook," Jake bragged.

"'Yeah but' yourself," Gina said, still piqued over last night's lousy meal but helping herself to a plateful of the inviting hotcakes. "I wouldn't trust anything you'd turn up to cook out on the trail." She carefully placed the refilled sausage platter at the opposite end of the table, out of Jake's reach.

"Where's the gravy?" Jake asked.

Lindsey bit her tongue to hold back her temper. "I didn't make any."

"You know I like sausage gravy. Couldn't you just whip up a little?"

"Jake, you truly try my patience," Lindsey said, throwing some flour in the sausage drippings and furiously stirring in milk. "Nobody, *nobody* but you puts gravy on their hotcakes."

"That's 'cause every breakfast should start with biscuits. Now don't git mad," he waved his fork in Lindsey's direction after correctly reading an expression verging on the flash point. "I'm just as happy with it on my hotcakes."

Kai-ling entered the kitchen dressed in denims, looking the proper cowgirl except for the coolie-type straw hat she wore and the white sneakers. Penny followed, clutching her black guitar case with its waterproof covering. She carefully stowed the instrument in a corner, fearing someone would trip over it in the crowded room. On her head was a blue straw sombrero with red tassels trimming the wide brim. The color of the hat accentuated the china-blue of her eyes.

Penny's ready smile cheered the others, who were mired in second thoughts about the trial ahead. Today would be the test of whether the Foofwahs could meet the challenge of a lifetime. Six hours in the saddle on the first day out was a grim prospect.

Chloë's green eyes, bright after a good night's sleep, scrutinized the condition of the individuals at the table. Not a hopeful sight at the beginning of what promised to be a demanding tour of God knows what, she thought. She worried about finding Comanche Reservoir, though Jake assured her it was an easy drive from the ranch. But look at Jake. He looked like he was still half in the bag, so how could she trust him?

Jake, noting Chloë's attention, growled, "We'll git yer gear stowed, so quit fussin'."

"I wasn't 'fussing,'" Chloë protested. "I was just thinking about how much fun this is going to be."

CC was the last to enter. She'd slipped back into bed for a few more winks while awaiting her turn for the bathroom. She still looked sleepy, and her eyelids drooped. She sat heavily in the only empty seat, next to Jake. "Pass me something, please, then feed it to me."

Jake sniffed and frowned. CC's face and all exposed parts of her body were smeared with a pungent sunscreen.

"Dang near ruins my appetite," Jake complained. "Good thing I already et."

CC ignored him. She wore her straw cowgirl hat, loose jeans, and, over a plaid western shirt, a pink sweatshirt with kittens romping across the front.

After a few minutes, Jake stood up and offered a profoundly resonant belch. "C'mon. Time to go!"

Over her steaming coffee mug, CC pinned eyes on Jake that transmitted a glare just short of incineration.

Jake tipped his hat forward. "You too, missy." He headed for the door. "I'll git the cattle rounded up. You folks look to roundin' up yerselves and in damned short order. The day's half over."

Gina growled, "The good thing about Jake is, he gets our hackles up. By the time you've figured how to murder the sonofabitch as an act of justifiable homicide, your motor's running. Let's get this stuff washed and put away so we can get out of here."

"Listen up, everyone." Lindsey raised her voice to be heard above the clatter of dishes and conversation. "We won't be stopping for lunch. There are sandwich makings, but you'll have to fix your own. And fill your canteens, because we won't have water or soft drinks until we meet Chloë at Comanche campground."

Lindsey was certain the one weak point in her plan was allowing herself to be talked into Chloë's driving the Gypsy Spirit the seventeen miles north to Comanche reservoir. She'd been a passenger in Chloë's car at times and knew how easily she became lost. But it was too late to worry about that now.

While Jake loaded the Gypsy Spirit with tether ropes, spare horseshoes and tack, skillets and pots, the women quickly set about making sandwiches. Kai-ling, the vegetarian, preferred oatmeal to sausage and scrambled eggs and had only nibbled at a piece of toast. No time to cook cereal now, so she filled the pockets of her denim pants and jacket with plastic bags of bite-size cereal. While others made ham and cheese sandwiches, Kai-ling spread two slices of bread with peanut butter and jam and slipped the wrapped sandwich in her pocket.

Finished with the cleanup and dishwashing, the women grabbed their jackets and bedrolls.

"How can you be so happy?" Kai-ling asked Penny. "I was so worried, I didn't sleep well last night. I keep thinking I will do something stupid because I know so little about cows and cowboys."

"Not to worry. You'll do just fine," Penny reassured her. Penny's smile masked her own deep concern about the less experienced riders among the Foofwahs.

"But I feel so uneasy ..." Kai-ling fretted, as they headed outdoors.

"You're not alone there," CC chimed in. "However, God looks after fools and children. We're not children, but we won't have any trouble qualifying as fools."

CHAPTER FIFTEEN

"HEAD 'EM OUT!"

At the corral, Romancer pranced impatiently, appearing eager to be saddled. The mare sensed the excitement and frisked about in the cool morning air. Her playfulness didn't make it easy for Kai-ling to saddle the horse, as she was afraid to reach underneath Romancer's belly, placing her head within easy reach of the menacing hooves.

While Kai-ling was putting the halter on her, the mare snuggled up for hugs, and Kai-ling was sure the horse would climb in her lap were she to sit down. "You're well named, Romancer," Kai-ling smiled. She patted the horse affectionately and gave her a handful of cereal.

Kai-ling expected mass confusion, but the business of saddling and mounting their horses so early silenced the chatter that had begun indoors.

Penny brought a wooden chair from the kitchen and helped each Foofwah mount.

"I think I'm getting the hang of this," Gina said, after Penny adjusted the stirrups so Gina's long legs didn't dangle awkwardly.

Gina snapped a picture of CC accepting Penny's assistance. "No fair," CC called. "Wait till I get my hands on that film," she whispered to Penny. "The last thing we need is documentation of our ineptitude."

"Be glad she left the video camera at home," Penny observed. "We could all end up on "Funniest Home Videos."

Angie, by nature more athletic and in better physical shape than most of the other women, took to the situation with little difficulty and a great deal of relief. Astride Uncle Simon's favorite horse, Twinkle, Angie sat her horse like a veteran and prayed that once it started to move she'd retain her poise in the saddle.

Lindsey's horse stood at attention, head up, eyes alert. She elected to ride Ringo, an experienced drover's horse, nimble and intelligent. Ringo was the horse that had thrown Cody, but she'd made sure no cocklebur was under his blanket today.

When she'd finally reached Cody and told him about finding the bur, he wasn't sure what to make of it. The man she'd seen talking to Cody the morning of the accident *was* Chan Reed, but Cody felt sure Chan hadn't had the opportunity to do anything so malicious.

"He may be a snake," Cody said, "but I don't think even he would stoop to such a low act. Now, if it'd been that lawyer of his, that Lerner, I might be suspicious, but not Chan. That bur must have come from the ground when I set the blanket down."

"I suppose," Lindsey said, but she wasn't so sure. There wasn't a tree on the ranch that dropped burs like that. Nevertheless, she let the subject drop. At any rate, there wasn't much she could do about it now, but she'd keep her eyes open.

Lindsey waited until all her troops gathered at the gate, their horses saddled and mounted. She threw open the gate and yelled, in her best western-movie drawl, "Head 'em out!"

Lindsey took her place riding on point with the cattle and the Foofwahs following. The women had been given their first day's position along the line at the briefing the night before.

* * *

With the exception of Penny's mount, the horses acted like they knew what they were doing. Old Bushmills's staggering gait quickly turned into a stiff-legged little dance, like a mad ostrich. The guitar case and bag of clanking percussion equipment for the singalongs frightened him when they bounced around on his rump. He settled down after Penny dismounted and adjusted the offending instruments.

Romancer was a dream for Kai-ling to ride, smooth-gaited and gentle-tempered. She was pleased with how simple this was turning out. Whenever the caravan paused long enough for her to break into a packet of cereal, Kai-ling offered a handful to her mare, who strained her neck reaching back for more.

Gina looked uncomfortable, bobbing along on Mouse, the horse that had originally been picked by Chloë. Mouse's tendency to shy nervously at unexpected sights and sounds was offset by his sure-footedness. Gina's greatest difficulty lay in trying to snap pictures of the scenery without including the rear ends of cattle, horses, and Foofwahs. Too preoccupied trying to stay in the saddle to capture the precise photo-op, she relied on her new digital camera to pick up enough scenery shots for her to edit out rumps when she returned home to her computer.

"It looks like you're as fond of cereal as I am," Kai-ling said, patting Romancer on the neck. She conversed steadily with the horse in Chinese. "All right, now. Time to go. Pretty Romancer! Dear Romancer! A wee bit faster now ... No, not so fast ... That's my girl, go around that scratchy old barbed wire ..."

CC had tried to teach Kai-ling the horse language cowboys used, but it sounded even more foreign than English, and Kai-ling felt Chinese suited the horse as well or better than cowboy slang or formal English words.

The first few miles were over dusty dirt roads used primarily by farmers to reach the paved farm-to-market roads. They had not gone far before Kai-ling noticed an ominous-looking gathering at the intersection ahead. A dusty, battered pickup had pulled off to the side of the intersecting road. A cowboy sat on each of the front fenders, another stood in the bed of the pickup. They appeared to be waiting for a parade to pass by.

Kai-ling grew uneasy, wondering what the men were expecting. She glanced nervously around at her friends. The other women didn't seem disturbed, but Kai-ling's sixth sense warned her that the men were up to no good. As their group drew abreast of the men, she was not reassured when Jake, who rode slightly ahead of her on the left flank, exchanged scornful banter with them. Jake seemed to recognize the men. He called one "Jimbo."

Jimbo hooted, "I heard the Ol' West was dyin', but I didn't believe it till now. Looks like it's true. Here comes the funeral procession." All three stood at attention, taking off their hats and holding them over their hearts in mock respect, but their grinning faces were unkind, even cruel.

"Don't look like no funeral to me," a second man called out. "Looks to me like one of them old broke-down rhinestone cowboys goin' to a knittin' bee. Howdy, Jake! How's your head this mornin'?"

Jake kept his eyes pinned straight ahead, doing his best to ignore the taunts.

"Musta been hard-wintered from the looks of this outfit," the third man jeered, slapping his knee at his own joke.

Jake turned in his saddle and called back to Gina and Kai-ling, riding right and left flank and the only Foofwahs close enough to hear, "Pay no attention to these sheep herders. Why, these dudes ain't been no closer to a cow than a milk truck."

Jake turned to the men. "I understood all the real cowboys are at a ropin'. Guess you three couldn't pass muster 'cause you couldn't rope a balky burro."

As Kai-ling approached the spectators, they noticed her pointed coolie hat and doubled over, choking on their laughter.

"Hey, Jake," the man in the truck bed yelled. "Didja git yerself a mail-order bride?"

Kai-ling's face flamed with humiliation. She understood the implication only too well. Raised in Taiwan, she had seen many of her elementary school friends sold into virtual slavery in the brothels because their parents were desperately poor. She had friends who had offered themselves as mail-order brides to escape the stark poverty and hunger, the constant turmoil war inflicted on her country. Kai-ling had been one of the more fortunate. Her parents had worked tirelessly to give their five children the best education offered by Taiwan's university. Through her own efforts, Kai-ling had won a scholarship to the States and earned degrees in genetics and chemistry. Now, in mid-life, she pursued her first love, literature, and worked toward a master's degree in English with the goal of teaching college literature classes.

"Tighten the latigo on that jaw of yours," Jake was no longer tossing harmless repartee. He was angry. "You can't express yerself unless yer scratchin' in the dirt like a chicken in a dung heap."

Appalled at what she was hearing, Gina had escaped the barbed comments but was helpless to interfere. All she could do was yell across the cattle separating her from Kai-ling, "Pay no attention to them, Kai-ling. We've interrupted a class studying to be half-wits."

Soon the men were out of earshot, but Kai-ling could tell that first Angie then CC and Penny who brought up the drags were being hassled as they passed by the cowboys' reviewing stand. She wished she could hear them because she knew both Angie and CC would give the men as good as they got. Kai-ling wished her English language classes had included lessons in scathing remarks so she could knock them dead with a humiliating comeback.

After the herd filed past, the cowboys got into their pickup and drove off.

CC caught up with Kai-ling whose head hung in shame. "I don't know what that was all about, but don't let whatever they said bother you. They're only a bunch of cowboys with nothing better to do than show their ignorance." CC patted Kai-ling's knee, then turned her horse and went back to the end of the line.

She placed a quick phone call to Ace using his cell phone. Keeping in touch had become a daily ritual, so Ace could network with the other husbands, reporting that all was well.

"As if we'd report anything that *wasn't* well," CC quipped to Penny. "Then they'd be upset."

The Foofwahs' lack of experience handling horses and cattle became troublesome the moment they left the roadways and entered the high plains. The animals wanted to graze in the tall grass, and the women couldn't keep their horses from stopping to grab mouthfuls of the delectable stalks. The riders felt mean when they were forced to jerk on the reins and pull the horses' heads up, but Jake kept making the rounds, yelling, "Keep their heads up. Take control! Don't let 'em stop. We'll make no time at all if we let 'em graze. Keep the cattle moving!"

If the riders allowed their attention to wander for only a moment, the horses and cattle took the opportunity to munch on another clump of the abundant grass, delaying the already agonizingly slow movement.

It didn't take Kai-ling long to find out what it meant to be a tenderfoot. Unable to fit into her boots comfortably, she had decided, against Lindsey's advice, to wear her sneakers. After the first hour, her ankles became raw from rubbing against the stirrup straps. She tried to hold her long legs away from the horse at an unnatural angle to avoid the rough straps, but she could only do that for a few minutes at a time. By the end of the second hour, she felt as though her legs had been welded to the flank of her horse. The pace was slow and leisurely, so there was no bouncing up and down in the saddle, but she had to hold her legs tense all the time, and her muscles were beginning to ache painfully.

Kai-ling hadn't really thought much about bathrooms before she started on the trip. Now, growing uncomfortable, she began to look for a tree or a bush. All she could see ahead or around her were miles and miles of grassland. The stands of trees in the distance were much too far away to wait that long.

She dropped back to ask CC's advice.

"The only one you need to shield yourself from is Jake," CC told her. "Why don't you look for a stalled cow and squat real fast. The grass is tall enough to hide you."

"I don't know ..." Kai-ling looked dubious. "What if I'm hanging my bare bottom out and a toad jumps up or, worse, a snake slithers by. I might embarrass myself."

CC laughed. "Well, you don't have many choices."

Kai-ling decided CC was right and rode a little way off from the others, looking for a standing cow, though she wasn't convinced that a cow with its long, skinny legs offered that much protection. Painfully modest, Kai-ling wasn't happy about having anyone, even the Foofwahs, observe her act of relieving herself. But she was desperate.

Her legs were so stiff she could hardly lift her right leg over the saddle to dismount. When her feet touched the ground and she put her full weight on her legs, she would have fallen without the saddle horn to cling to.

Now, what should I do about Romancer? she worried. Kai-ling assumed all horses ran off given any opportunity. There was no place to tie the reins. She would need both hands so she held the reins securely in her teeth as she walked behind a large cow that had defied the rules and paused to graze. Romancer followed docilely, no doubt hoping for another bite of cereal. Kai-ling lowered her trousers, looking around to make sure she was unobserved. As she did so, Romancer nuzzled her bare backside.

"No! Go away!" she shrieked. Dropping the reins, she pushed the horse away. Too late, she realized she had drawn the attention of all the Foofwahs and cattle within earshot. "It's okay," she called, waving with one hand and holding her pants up with the other. The reins were out of reach. To her surprise, Romancer merely stepped aside, patiently cropping a few mouthfuls of grass.

"What a nice horse you are, Romancer, my girl." Kai-ling patted the mare gratefully after she concluded her business. "I'm sorry I yelled at you. Next time, I'll trust you not to run off."

Kai-ling checked her watch. They'd started shortly after sun up and had been on the trail for two hours. Four more hours in the saddle seemed like a sentence of death. She wondered if she'd be able to get on the horse without help but was surprised to find that in spite of her stiffness her leg muscles—and her new jeans—had stretched enough to allow her to mount without a struggle.

* * *

To everyone's surprise and immense relief, the first morning's drive was uneventful. Though the Foofwahs found the pace boring after the first couple of hours, there was one exception. CC discovered that Shitears had a phobia about letting another horse come up from behind and get ahead of him. He had to lead the parade. He didn't mind cows getting ahead, no doubt recognizing them as inferior creatures. But the instant another horse approached from the rear, Shitears went into a frenzy of out-walking, out-trotting, or out-galloping the interloper. No matter what it took, Shitears was determined to stay ahead.

All morning, Jake circled the herd to give the Foofwahs pointers where needed. He was unfamiliar with Shitears and thus unaware of the horse's phobia. Coming from the rear and slowing his horse, Tonto, to a walk beside CC, Jake conferred with her a few minutes, then signaled to his horse to speed up so he could return to his station along the line. Shitears took off like an F-16 fighter jet. CC nearly did a back-flip over the horse's rump but managed to hang on through sheer grit and terror.

At first, believing the horse to be running away, as indeed he was, Jake attempted to catch up so he could grab the reins and stop him. He soon realized that the faster Tonto ran, the faster Shitears ran.

Shitears raced ahead with CC bouncing high into the air, her bottom flopping back into the saddle only long enough to gather momentum before being propelled into the air again. From the rear, she looked like a jumping jack in the hands of a diabolical child. All the while, she screamed bloody murder. She was afraid to pull too hard on the reins for fear the horse would stop suddenly, and she would either sail over its head or be squashed flat when he rolled over and played dead.

By nature a slow, methodical thinker, Jake's only thought was to try to catch up with Shitears, but the woman's screaming was unnerving to him and his horse.

"If only she'd shut up so I can think!" he grumbled.

Something he'd learned long ago struggled to break through his subconscious.

If I ever get the blasted horse stopped, I'll strangle the goddam woman, he told himself.

The idea finally percolated through his mind. Hoping he was right, Jake reined Tonto to a walk and yelled, "Turn that damned horse in a large circle. A helluva wide circle!"

Jake watched anxiously as Shitears galloped on. Deep inside, he didn't care if CC broke her damn fool neck. It would serve her right. But he had been hired to do a job, and Jake was a man who believed when you worked for another man, you busted your butt and owed him your loyalty. If you couldn't give him that, then it was time to get on down the road.

Jake made up his mind that he'd put up with this and whatever else he had to do for the next four days. After that, he didn't care what happened to these god-danged women. Four more days! Just as soon as this nightmarish drive was over, he'd knock the Colorado caliche from his boots and be on his way back to Arizona. After that, he hoped they'd all croak from their own stupidity.

Nevertheless, Jake was relieved when he saw CC begin to turn her horse to the right, make a wide circle, and finally bring the lathered horse around to his side.

CC was furious. "Why the hell didn't you stop this crazy beast?" she demanded. "You abandoned me, you God damned flea-bitten bent prick! I could have been killed!"

Jake waited for her to calm down before he attempted to explain. "It took me a while to recognize the problem," he said. "You gotta put yerself in the horse's place. Horses is just like people. Every once in a while you run across a horse that has to stay ahead of the pack or bust his gut tryin'. From now on, just don't let no horse try to pass you. If he tries to pull a stunt like that agin, just turn him away from the other horses. He's a quarter horse. He'll soon run outa steam if there's no one to race him."

"First they tell me this is a circus horse. Now you're telling me he's a race horse." CC exploded. "Next you'll be telling me he's a *dancing* horse!"

Jake wheeled Tonto around and rode back toward the line of cattle. He sat straight in his saddle, head held high, too angry even to spit. He wasn't used to being cussed out, especially by a woman. Throughout his working life, he'd pulled his weight and earned the respect of his fellow cowboys. But to be cussed out by a woman in front of other women was more than any man should have to endure. His face burned with anger.

After he regained his temper, Jake sent CC back to her position riding at the tail of the herd. As long as Shitears could see the other horses and none tried to pass him everything went fine.

CC sulked as she rejoined the slow-moving herd. This demon horse from hell would kill her out here on the prairie, and Ace wouldn't even know what a good job she'd been doing. He'd probably think it was her own incompetence at horsemanship that got her killed.

I hope the Foofwahs, or at least Jake, will explain to him that it wasn't my fault, she thought, envisioning her funeral and all the sad Foofwahs, gathered around the open grave. At least *they'll* miss me.

Kai-ling and Jake rode left flank while Angie and Gina rode on the right. Their job was to make sure the cows stayed together and that some calf didn't wander off into the tall grass causing the mother cow to bellow with anxiety and go charging off in search of it.

The mother cows' anxiety concerned Kai-ling the most. Jake had told them a sudden movement of one cow could excite the entire herd and start a stampede. They'd been told to avoid yelling to each other or sudden screams under any circumstance. Kai-ling had already disobeyed this order when Romancer nuzzled her exposed bottom, but luckily the only cow near enough to be frightened had been the one she was hiding behind, and it had munched on unperturbed.

Jake repeated what Lindsey had already told them, that there was little cause for anxiety about a stampede unless a thunderstorm with lightning came up or something spooked them—like a piece of paper blowing across the road. A rattlesnake could make a horse try to "chin the moon," Jake told her.

* * *

Chloë's exodus had gone far better than she expected. She got the hang of driving the Gypsy Spirit fairly quickly. Her biggest concern was that she would misjudge the distance on the right side of the road because her spatial perception was never very good. She'd scraped more than one of Ray's new cars along things sticking out on parked cars when she tried to parallel park, so she knew she had a problem.

On one narrow road, she took a wrong turn and had to maneuver the cumbersome truck around, seesawing back and forth while scared to death that she'd end up in the ditch.

After she found Comanche Reservoir, Chloë selected a spot for their campground. She had plenty of time to organize her supplies and prepare for dinner.

While she was setting out pots and pans, she saw movement in a corner of the Gypsy Spirit's cottage. She grabbed a broom, thinking a mouse had sneaked in while they were loading supplies. Chloë whacked in the direction of the noise and was almost knocked off her feet when Felon dashed past her to safety.

"You g.d. cat," Chloë yelled. "I ought to beat you to death with this broom." She knew she couldn't do it, but she'd like to. "You nearly scared the liver out of me!"

Felon, from the safety of a shrub, stared impassively. Suddenly, his scruffy hair raised and he looked under the bed of the truck where Chloë heard a rustling sound. She quickly jumped inside the cottage. Could it be a snake or a javelina or some other wild creature that would tear her to shreds? Why, oh why, had she allowed herself to be talked into coming out to this God-forsaken place alone?

Peeking out from behind the curtains of the tiny cottage window, she saw a large yellow dog scarfing down the hamburger she'd set out for tonight's dinner. Felon had disappeared, which was one consolation.

Chloë threw open the door and screamed, "Bad dog. Get out of here!" She waved the broom to frighten the beast away.

The dog glanced up but continued eating. When he'd finished the two pounds of hamburger, he stretched out, belched, and licked his paws. The grin on his face told him the meal had been more than satisfying.

"You startled me!" Chloë said.

The dog thumped his tail, his eyes sad and pleading. "Let's be friends," his expression begged. With his chin on his crossed paws, his eyes soulfully searched her own. He looked tired and skinny.

The dog's eyes remained fixed on Chloë's face. He was a large, German shepherd mix, with a thick yellowish-brown coat tipped with black. Chloë wondered if he had a collar but couldn't tell without getting too close. As it was, she'd need to beat a quick retreat if he decided to attack. She concentrated on returning "Let's be friends" vibes, hoping she wouldn't give out any scent of fear. Then she noticed that he wasn't just thin. His sides were sunken in as if he hadn't eaten for a long time.

"You poor thing," she said. "You look more like a skinny coyote than a dog. And I'll bet you're thirsty, too." She found a pie tin and filled it with bottled water.

The dog lapped greedily, looked up with a grin, and let out another polite belch.

"Watch it pal, you're beginning to sound like Jake. Come to think of it, you smell a little like Jake. Only better. You just smell like a dog, not a skunk," Chloë told him. The idea of having the dog for the next few days was the most comforting thought she'd had for some time. The dog didn't appear to be aggressive, just the opposite. He needed her, and she needed him.

"Now that you've finished the fresh meat we were going to have for dinner, friend, what am I to do?" They had tinned meat, cans of chili con carne, eggs and bacon, but everyone expected and deserved hamburgers.

Chloë thought of the fishing tackle Lindsey had stowed in the truck. "Why not? We're camped beside a reservoir," she said to the dog. "Let's go fishing."

She'd accompanied Ray many times on fishing trips, but had never caught anything herself. And Ray had always baited her hook. This would be a desperate try, but she wouldn't deal with worms. She would use bacon for bait.

Chloë and her new companion walked to the edge of the reservoir as if they'd been friends forever. She talked to him, while he cocked his ears attentively, wagging his tail.

After casting her line, Chloë settled into a camp chair and waited for a strike. She watched the dog sitting as still as a statue, his nose in the air, catching the breeze, his eyes closed in ecstasy. What a proud dog, she thought. He sits there like King Tut. That's what I'll name him. King Tut. We can call him Tut, for short.

Felon reappeared and gingerly walked up to the sated dog. They touched noses briefly, then Felon returned to his rightful place inside the cottage.

After two hours of fishing without success, Chloë decided to give up the idea of a fish fry for dinner. Midday was no time for fishing, anyway, or so Ray had always said. Maybe they could catch some this evening or tomorrow morning early.

Back at the campsite, she gently washed Tut's torn, rough paws and rubbed them with bag balm Jake had brought to keep the cow's udders from becoming chapped. Tut stretched contentedly and fell asleep beside her chair.

With a long afternoon still ahead, Chloë dug out her lap desk and yellow-ruled pad, sharpened a couple of number two pencils, and set to work. Within minutes, she was deeply engrossed with the characters in her novel, transported to another time and place. She was comforted by the dog's snores, and looked fondly at him from time to time. "Reminds me of Ray," she said, with a sad, sweet smile, wishing her husband could join their domestic little scene.

* * *

Around four o'clock, Chloë saw the dust of the approaching cattle herd and its hungry drovers coming over the crest of the hill to the east, still some distance away. She had a kettle of chili simmering on Angie's Coleman stove and would make cornbread in a skillet after everyone arrived.

She sat by the creek and threw sticks for Tut to fetch. She'd handled her job so far with only a minor hitch or two. Chloë felt good about herself.

CHAPTER SIXTEEN

NIGHT WATCH

By mid-afternoon, Lindsey's crew of drovers paused on the crest of a hill where they could see directly west to Comanche Reservoir nestled in a low area. The lake looked fully two miles long and a half-mile across, treeless around its edge. The sparkling clear water glistened like an enchanted sea. The surrounding grassland was anything but park-like, and though the lake had a boat-launching ramp and a road approaching it, no holiday boaters or water skiers skimmed over the lake, no campers or hikers picnicked alongside. A flock of white geese bobbed on the choppy waves kicked up by the strong breeze. Little white-capped breakers formed along a shallow, sandy beach, giving the lake the appearance of a miniature ocean set in a cow pasture.

As the riders drew nearer, they passed among young poplar and sycamore trees bordering an overflow creek.

Jake rode ahead of the herd to inspect the camping spot. Plenty of room lay east of the creek and the reservoir to bed down the herd. Satisfied with the selection, he rode back and proceeded to travel up and down the line, giving instructions to the Foofwahs on how to keep the cattle together in a large circle.

"You droverettes," he began, ignoring their hostile looks, "try to keep these animals east of the creek."

Kai-ling was famished. With little breakfast, she'd eaten her sandwich early. The day's ride, supposed to take six hours, had stretched out to eight as they'd paced alongside the slow-moving cattle. Lindsey had reminded them of Cody's instructions that the herd must not be "run," if they were to reach the auction in prime condition. Kai-ling thought watching cattle graze across the land must be the most boring job in the world, so she entertained herself by thinking up stories to be written later. She wanted to indelibly imprint on her memory the deep blue color of the sky, dotted with fleecy clouds, and the clean scent of the grasses blowing in the warm wind.

She could smell the wood fire and food long before they arrived. Kai-ling looked forward to dismounting, though she was uncertain her aching, stiff joints would unlock. And I'm one of the younger ones, she thought. What about the older ones? How do they feel? If I can still walk when I get off this horse, I will eat and fall into bed.

She watched, fascinated, as Lindsey approached the little creek between the herd and the campgrounds, dashing ahead to patrol the near side of the creek and keep the cattle east of the lake and the small stream.

The cattle began to hurry when they smelled the water, crossing the sandy beach to splash in up to their bellies. The reservoir was shallower than usual after the recent dry spell. The cattle drank, then began to mill around, looking uncertain. Movement forward was impossible; Lindsey blocked the trail. The early arrivals moved about keeping the latecomers from entering the cool, clear water, but they were soon pushed aside.

Jake raced up and down the line, giving instructions to the Foofwahs bringing up the drags to go easy but to keep pushing. The ones who'd ridden flank were instructed to spread out and allow newcomers to get to the water, letting the cattle form a large circle.

"Give 'em room. Spread out wider," he kept yelling.

Lindsey continued to patrol back and forth to keep the cattle from moving beyond the creek, but in the pushing and shoving to get to the water, fifteen or twenty managed to cross over. When the drags joined the rest of the herd, the Foofwahs made a wide swath around the perimeter of the milling circle.

For a moment, Kai-ling forgot her aching muscles. The herd covered a very large area, she guessed maybe twenty acres, but they were together. As soon as the cattle had drunk their fill, they began to graze peaceably.

Jake passed the word among the women that they were to continue circling but not to tighten the circle. The cattle needed plenty of space to graze. Kai-ling wondered when she would be allowed off the horse. By now, she felt as though someone had welded her to the saddle, that she was doomed to sit there forever.

In the distance, Kai-ling heard a dog barking. She was surprised because there had been no ranches in sight for miles. Then she saw Chloë waving at them. Apparently, she had picked up a friend. It stood, barking protectively, in front of the Gypsy Spirit parked alongside the gravel road skirting the reservoir. Where, and why, would Chloë have found a dog?

Finally, Jake came around and told her they'd take turns "chowing down." As soon as Lindsey and Gina returned from eating, Kai-ling could dismount and go to eat. "I'll take care of yer horse tonight, but from now on you water, unsaddle yer horse, and tether her so she can find plenty of fresh green grass. You care fer yer horse before you do anything else," he said sternly.

Every muscle in Kai-ling's body screamed in protest when she tried to lift her leg over the saddle. She was afraid she would cry. When Jake realized she was having a problem, he dismounted and helped keep her wobbly legs beneath her while she took the first few steps. She laughed nervously to avoid crying out. It didn't help that the other riders, still mounted, yelled encouragement. She'd never felt such excruciating pain in her life.

Kai-ling began to worry that she'd be permanently crippled from this experience but didn't want to voice her fears. She thought if she could just lie down to die, she'd never need another prayer to be answered. When she could take her first steps without help, Jake led Romancer to an area on the far side of the Gypsy Spirit where he picketed the mare with a long rope tied to a fourteen-inch wooden stake he hammered into the soft earth.

By will power alone, Kai-ling hobbled into camp where Chloë had a cup of steaming hot tea waiting for her. The strange dog sniffed everyone who approached Chloë, seeming to pass approval by not growling or biting anyone.

"I thought chamomile tea might ease stiff muscles better than coffee," Chloë said, in her comforting fashion. "I've been there, you know. I've had every single molecule in my body revolt after riding horseback the first few hours. I've been sure that even my eyelashes were broken."

Kai-ling took one look at the bowl of chili Chloë thrust in her hands and decided food no longer had any appeal. She was too tired to "chow down."

"You'd better eat somethin'," Jake warned, not unkindly. "We're going to have to take turns standin' watch all night, and I've got you scheduled for the nine-to-one watch. I'll be standin' watch with you."

"Standing ... Does that mean we don't have to get back on the horses?" A ray of hope illuminated Kai-ling's face.

"Sorry, figger of speech," Jake apologized. "Our horses will be standin'. We'll be sittin' in the saddles."

"Ohhh." Kai-ling couldn't suppress a moan. "You mean I'll be on that horse for another four hours? I can't believe it. Please tell me it isn't true."

"Well, ordinarily we'd have enough hands and enough fresh horses to see that the night watch doesn't create much of a hardship. To an experienced hand, six or ten hours in the saddle ain't no problem. But yer a greenhorn and yer horse ain't no yearling. She's probably tired, so I'll let you have the spare horse. It ain't worked much today so it oughta be fresh enough for a stint."

Kai-ling had been sitting cross-legged on the ground. Now she lay back, stretched out her legs, and closed her eyes. I am feeling like death would be a friend, she thought, and he is worried because the horse is tired? I am so tired I think I will be sick.

Jake went to his horse and ransacked a saddlebag. He returned with a pint of Jack Daniels and offered the bottle to Kai-ling.

"Take a swig."

"Thank you, but I do not drink alcohol," Kai-ling said weakly.

"It'll help the muscles ease up some. I ain't trying to lead you into no bad habits. I just know them muscles ain't goin' to feel any better for a day or two without help. Believe me, this'll give you some comfort—better than any dang tea."

Desperate for relief, Kai-ling took a swallow, choked, and felt the strong liquor burn all the way down. A flush crept from her jaws to her hairline. "Wait a minute," she said, holding onto the bottle. "If one little bit helps, two will be better." She took a third before handing the bottle back to Jake.

Jake took a swig himself before screwing the top back on the bottle. "Nuthin' wrong with a hair 'a the dog, neither," he said with a satisfied expression. "Best medicine God ever made!"

"I laid out your bedroll in the cottage," Chloë said, helping Kai-ling to her feet. "Go crawl into it, and I'll waken you for the first watch."

Kai-ling needed no second invitation. She barely made it to the Gypsy Spirit before she collapsed, sound asleep, fully clothed down to her sneakers.

* * *

Almost immediately, it seemed to Kai-ling, Chloë was shaking her awake. Kai-ling groaned, "Oh, better to let me die ..." and rolled over. Usually, Kai-ling awoke with a smile of anticipation for whatever the day promised. But this was not morning, and she still ached all over. Not quite as bad, but now a new little pain throbbed in her head, and her stomach felt queasy. She remembered that she had not eaten, but she had drunk some of Jake's "medicine."

Painfully, Kai-ling crawled out of her bedroll. Good heavens! she thought, I slept very hard! The thought cheered her. Someone had taken off her sneakers. She searched around in the dark for a few minutes before she found and pulled them on.

She wished she had some ointment to rub onto her raw ankles. If she knew where her duffel was, she could doctor her ankles and wear a second pair of socks, but she couldn't distinguish her duffel from the pile of bags and supplies jumbled at the rear. All she could see were sleeping forms rolled up in bedrolls crowded together on the floor. She had to step over someone to get out of the bus.

Amazingly, when she stood up she didn't feel quite as bad as she had when she fell into her bedroll four hours earlier. She didn't exactly want to kick up her heels, but she could at least walk with less pain.

Outside the cottage, the wind had ceased with nightfall. Chloë sat in a folding chair beside the campfire, while Jake squatted down on his heels to poke at the fire. The dog lay beside Chloë's chair on the right, his short ears alert and his amber eyes scanning the darkness. The big cat hunkered beside her on the left. Chloë and Jake spoke quietly, obviously enjoying the warmth of the campfire for the night air had turned chilly.

Kai-ling limped her way over to the campfire. She wished she'd eaten something before going to bed.

"Are we ready to stand watch?" she asked Jake. She put as much enthusiasm into her voice as she could. "Sorry to poop out on you like that." Kai-ling looked around for her horse.

"The horses are picketed a little to the north and west of here. Remember, you won't be riding Romancer. You'll be riding the spare horse. Come along."

Before Kai-ling could follow him, Chloë shoved a plate of hot food in her hands. "I saved this for you. It's going to be a long night for someone with no supper."

Feeding a vegetarian on a drive like this was a challenge for the cook, but Chloë anticipated the problem by stirring up beans mixed with rice and a healthy dash of chili powder.

The meal proved delicious. Kai-ling ate as fast as she could, knowing Jake would turn back for her any minute. "Chloë, you are wonderful," she said. "I think I am going to live."

Jake discovered her absence and whistled for her to join him. She stumbled along in the darkness over the unfamiliar, rough terrain toward the direction of Jake's whistle. Her eyes became accustomed to the darkness by the time she reached him.

"Lindsey and Gina are finishin' up the first watch right now." What you and I gotta do is ride slowly and quietly around the herd. Actually, you won't be makin' a complete circle because the lake will back the cattle on the west. Don't crowd 'em. It comforts 'em to know we're here, but you git too close and they git the urge to stand up and move someplace else. They're coverin' about twenty to thirty acres, so each round will take some amount of time. The cattle git restless, so if you can, sing to 'em."

"Whaa-at?"

"That's right. Sing to 'em. Tonto is tired too, so we want to do ever'thing possible to make sure they don't spook and take off on a stampede. Cattle, like people, always want to be where they ain't wanted.

"Around midnight, the cattle do a lot of shiftin' and decidin' whether they're going to stay put or take off for parts unknown. If we're lucky, they'll mostly just stand up and turn around and then settle back down. The weather is clear, so ain't no danger of 'em being spooked by thunder or lightnin', but if some stupid leader gits up and starts off, they'll all take off behind him. If that happens, I'll try to git ahead of 'em and turn 'em back, but with a tired horse, I got about as much chance of turnin' them as a June bug herdin' a flock of ducks.

He lit a gas lantern. "Yer job will be to stay with 'em but give 'em plenty of space. Cows can get meaner'n rattlesnakes when they're frightened. And, for God's sake, don't cut in front of 'em, and don't take no leaps in the dark. If you fall or your horse stumbles, you'll be trampled to death, unless you kin git behind a big rock or a tree. Spooked cattle ain't got no more sense than jackrabbits. They'll run right off a cliff or into a lake and drown. Yer not an experienced rider, and yer horse ain't as fast or as range busted as it oughta be, so yer best bet is to try to stick with 'em and let 'em run theirselves out. We'll be relieved by CC and Penny some time around one o'clock."

Jake picked up her saddle from a pile and with the aid of the lantern located a gray horse, the spare brought from Uncle Simon's ranch. Jake left Kai-ling to saddle and mount by herself. "Extinguish the lantern when you git saddled up. Got to preserve the fuel."

She followed Jake's orders. Miraculously, she was able to mount in the dark and followed the direction Jake had taken.

The night was dark, but she could still see the outline of the cattle against the lighter horizon. A few cattle had crossed the creek and were on the camp side, which meant the herders crossed the creek twice.

She found Jake who took off counter-clockwise, telling her to go clockwise. "Give 'em wide latitude, and don't crowd 'em," he called as he disappeared into the darkness.

Kai-ling wondered why she wasn't frightened after the dire warnings of being trampled to death. The sliver of a moon rose to cast a little light, but the starry heavens seemed friendly, comforting. Here I am, she thought, riding a strange horse in unfamiliar territory, and I'm not afraid. I wish Hanchen could see me.

Every muscle was still sore, but not nearly as much as when she got off her horse before dinner. She grimaced ruefully when she remembered taking a swig or two of Jake's Jack Daniels. At home, she didn't even drink wine.

But it had helped. When she first learned she would have to ride herd for four more hours feeling as she did, the thought was more than she could bear. Other than stiff, sore muscles, she felt pretty good. Resting and hot food had made a difference.

In the distance, she could hear Jake crooning to the cows, though it sounded more like the croaking of a bullfrog. She couldn't hear the words, and the tune was unrecognizable. She hoped the cows felt more comfort from it than she did, though she smiled thinking of gruff old Jake actually singing to cattle.

Kai-ling began to sing in Chinese, lullabies she remembered her mother singing to her as a child. She advanced to love songs, sad and beautiful tales of Chinese lovers, then college songs she remembered singing with her friends in Taiwan. In the still, cool night air, her clear voice soothed her as much as it did the cattle.

Proving Jake's prediction true, at what must have been around midnight, one by one, the cattle stood up, stretched, and moved about a little before settling back down on their other sides.

Kai-ling always felt safer when she saw the creek that signaled she was now at the point nearest the campsite. She tried to see her wristwatch in the dark, then remembered her flashlight. When she reached for it in the saddlebag, it wasn't there.

"Oh!" she cried aloud, annoyed that she had failed to pack the flashlight after CC had so thoughtfully and thoroughly provisioned them with such necessities. But Kai-ling hadn't anticipated being separated from the other women, nor riding around on a horse in the dark. Now, she had no sure way of knowing the time, only that it seemed to pass very slowly. All she could do was keep her eye on the cattle to make sure a restless leader didn't become frightened or decide to move to a more desirable spot. Most of them seemed too tired to wander or straggle.

Several times, Kai-ling saw a shooting star. At another time, she saw a light far off on the north shore, like someone lighting a cigarette. Surely it was her imagination. She'd seen no campers or cars anywhere along the two-mile-long reservoir when they'd arrived. She thought perhaps she should befriend the dog, so it would accompany her the next time she had night watch. He ought to be good for something. He looked like a shepherd type. But I doubt if any of us can pry him away from Chloë's side.

The crisp night air was beginning to feel damp, and Kai-ling was glad she'd remembered to wear a jacket. Even so, it could be quite chilly by the time she was relieved at one o'clock.

Once, after she lost count of the times she'd made a half circle around the herd, she caught herself on the verge of falling asleep. She pinched her cheeks to stay awake.

The only time Kai-ling felt uncomfortable was when she approached the creek. It was not more than eight or ten feet wide, and the water was only a couple of feet deep at most, but she was afraid of water and it seemed her horse suffered from the same phobia.

"I don't even know your name," she said to the horse, but she urged him down the shallow bank, into the water, and up the other side.

When horse and rider neared the creek, they were about a half-mile east and south of the camp, and she could see the cheery campfire in the distance.

Kai-ling's route took her across the creek, around the twenty or so head of cattle that had crossed over. By heading north and gradually shifting to the northeast, she arrived at the edge of the lake, turned around, and retraced her steps past the stragglers under the sycamore trees bordering the creek. Then she forced her horse into the creek again. Continuing east and gradually shifting northeast then north then northwest and west, she again arrived at the lake. The cattle had the lake on their west side.

She'd lost count of the number of laps she'd made when she felt the call of nature and took advantage of the darkness under the sycamore trees. She dismounted before crossing the creek and was still struggling with the belt to her jeans when she was shocked by the sound of a horse nickering so close she could almost feel its warm breath. Her own horse stood silently on her right, but the sound came from her left.

"Jake," she called softly, but no answer came.

Kai-ling's mind raced. Maybe one of our horses got loose, she thought. She took a quick mental measurement of the distance between herself and their stakeout horses. The camp was fully half a mile to the south, and although she could not see them, she knew the horses were staked out west of the camp, which meant they were even further away. This horse was still quite close, and the thought that it might also have a rider terrified her.

The last time she'd passed Jake, he was headed in the other direction and now should be due east of her, at least a mile away. She could tell her horse was alert to something for she could hear him snort and nervously paw the ground.

Kai-ling stood on tiptoe, taking care to stay behind the bush without brushing against the foliage. She strained her eyes but could see nothing other than the black night. She knew she should remount and quickly cross the creek, get out from under the canopy of the trees, but panic paralyzed her. Something or somebody was near, and whoever it was had no business being out there.

After what seemed an eternity of silence, Kai-ling heard a rustling in the underbrush. Apparently, the horse had the freedom to move about. She stretched on her toes again, straining to see how near or how far this horse was and if it had a rider. Now she could see the dark shape of a horse silhouetted against the starry sky, not more than ten yards away. She couldn't tell whether it was saddled. She was almost certain it was riderless. But where was the rider? Behind her? She turned around quickly but could make out no human form among the trees. What was this horse waiting for in the dark?

A new terror enveloped Kai-ling. She smelled cigarette smoke. No one in their group smoked, not even Jake. She had no idea how close the smoker was, and she could see no glowing cigarette, which meant whoever was near was hiding behind brush or a tree, probably watching her this very minute.

She was afraid to scream to get Jake's attention for fear of spooking the cattle and starting a stampede. She had to get out of there, and fast. As she put her foot in the stirrup and her hand on the saddle horn, ready to lift herself up, she felt something soft and moist nuzzling her leg. "Ahhh," she cried out. It must have been the horse, but she didn't want to stick around to find out. If that horse had a rider, and that rider had a knife or a gun ...

Quickly, she scrambled into the saddle and forced her horse out from beneath the dark trees. Crossing the creek, she could hear the other horse's hooves striking the rocks in the water and knew the phantom horse was following her. The sky was lighter here, even though there was only a tip of the crescent moon adding brightness from behind a cloud. Turning in her saddle, she was astonished to see Romancer!

While she waited, pondering this strange development, Romancer approached and nuzzled her pocket. She had not forgotten where the cereal treats were.

"How come you're loose?" Kai-ling demanded softly. "I should be cross with you. You nearly scared me to death." Nevertheless, she searched her pockets and found a scant handful of cereal. She held it out for the horse she had become so fond of. Kai-ling reached over to pat the mare on the side of the head and noticed the halter was still in place, but the picket rope dangled from the halter. She pulled up the rope and saw it was only a few feet long. She knew Jake had tethered the horses on very long ropes. The rope must have had a weak spot in it, and the horse simply pulled free.

As she led Romancer back to the camp, she passed Penny and CC coming on watch duty.

"I found Romancer out there in the dark, following me around," Kai-ling laughed wearily.

"That's odd," Penny said. "Our horses were loose too, but we found them grazing nearby. I'd think their tethers had been cut, but I suppose Jake was careless and used rotted old rope or tied the horses poorly."

"You'd think the old fart would be good for something," CC added. "A cowboy who can't tether a horse ought to be sent to the knackers himself. And I'd like to be the one to do it."

Kai-ling was so relieved to be headed back to bed that she didn't think to mention her fears to anyone, even Jake.

The other horses all seemed to be properly tied down. After she retethered Romancer and picketed her nameless horse, she stumbled back toward the bus. She saw Jake riding in from the watch but was too tired to wait. She'd tell him tomorrow that the ropes should be checked.

She quickly slipped off her shoes and crawled into her bedroll. As sleep overtook her, one stray thought drifted across her mind ... cigarette smoke ... I'll tell Jake tomorrow.

CHAPTER SEVENTEEN

THE MAN IN THE WHITE HAT

Once Kai-ling snuggled down in the warm comfort of her bedroll, she slept the dreamless sleep of the totally exhausted.

In the morning, she looked around for Jake to tell him about finding Romancer roaming free—or Romancer finding her—but Jake was off checking the cattle. She decided to grab a quick breakfast of hot oatmeal, expecting him to show up any minute. When Kai-ling finished eating, it was time to saddle her horse, and Jake was still nowhere in sight.

"Romancer, you seem none the worse for your night's adventures, and I guess I'm not either," she spoke soothingly to the horse. Deciding to push her fears from her mind, Kai-ling felt a little silly in the morning light to think that perhaps, just perhaps, it was her overactive imagination that saw the glow of the cigarette. Perhaps it was only a firefly. And the smoke? Probably drifting from the campfire. Obviously, no harm had resulted. Yes, it was only her imagination.

* * *

CC was no more eager to mount Trickster, now known as "Shitears," than any of the other Foofwahs were to get back on their horses. She found the simple acts of standing up, getting dressed, and walking required will power beyond comprehension in the life of ease and luxury she had so gaily abandoned. What had she done, committing herself to this insane project? Struggling into the saddle was an undertaking of unbearable agony.

She had an added reason for dread. Fear of her horse. She could not use the same signals everyone else used when they wanted their horses to go forward or stop—simple, everyday horse activities. In fact, she was afraid to use any signals at all for fear she would trigger some circus button that would set the horse off on another idiot trick.

"It's like having a computer that runs on an entirely different system from everyone else's," CC explained to Penny at breakfast. "Whenever you click your tongue, your horse starts walking. Whenever I click *my* tongue, the g.d. horse kneels down and rolls over. Whenever you say 'giddup,' your horse puts on a little speed. My horse interprets it to mean 'Go to the head of the class.'"

"He must have been the lead horse in a circus," Penny said. "Why don't you ask Jake or Lindsey for one of the extra horses?"

"I thought about that, but Angie's riding one called Twinkle. Now there's a good horsy name. And Kai-ling rode the other one until late last night, so he's resting."

"Horses don't need as much rest as people. He's probably okay by now."

"Hmmm," CC said. "You know what they say, sometimes the devil you know is better than the devil you don't know."

"Maybe, but I doubt the other one is the same kind of devil as Shitears."

They sat sipping the hot coffee and enjoying the absence of pain for a several minutes.

Penny's thoughts digressed to an inspiration that came to her the night before. She would write a children's book about a horse trained for the circus but mistakenly entered in a horse race.

"I could call the book 'Mixed Signals,' and the horse could be symbolic of our mixed-up society. Imagine how it could be used to tell the story of a kid who has to learn two different sets of rules when he goes from one set of parents to another—"

"Oh, flush it!" CC snapped. Her temper flared with the realization that Penny wasn't really concerned about the risk she was taking. She scraped the remains of her breakfast onto Tut's plate and stormed off to saddle Shitears.

CC eyed her horse malevolently as she threw the saddle over his back. "You try any cute tricks today, Shitears, and I'll turn you over to the glue factory the minute we get to La Cholla." With no chairs or stumps to help her mount, CC gingerly placed her left foot into the stirrup to lift herself into the saddle. She found to her surprise that her thigh muscles were strong enough to get her over the top on the first try.

As she began the morning ride, CC ached so much, she wanted nothing more than to sit down and cry. Better yet would be to get the hell out and take the first flight home where she could count on Ace to give her plenty of sympathy and a good rubdown with sweet-smelling emollients. CC wanted to look and act and smell like a lady again, not like a grubby, smelly cowhand, breathing dust and dodging cowflops.

But CC had never been a quitter. Everyone else was hanging in, so what could she do but grit her teeth and pretend everything was just wonderful?

Getting the herd moving on the open range wasn't quite so easy this morning. The cattle had to be rounded up and blocked from taking off in every direction. Finally, the smarter cows got the idea that Lindsey and Jake were their leaders. One bull, Fernando they named him, elected himself the herd leader, and the rest fell in line.

After forty minutes of organization, the herd settled down. Amid clouds of dust, the mama cows bawled for their babies, and the bulls took a while to discover that this wasn't an ordinary working day for them. The Foofwahs were afraid of the bulls and kept at a respectable distance from them.

The second morning was as uneventful as the first. The pace of the animals was agonizingly slow, and by noon the sun beat down relentlessly. The Foofwahs dressed in flannel shirts over T-shirts for the cold mornings, but by midday they were uncomfortably warm and stripped down to their T-shirts.

CC's muscles and joints continued to scream for relief. She was hot, tired, and hungry. The peanut butter sandwich she'd slipped into her saddlebag wasn't particularly satisfying. She would have given any one of her precious antiques back home for a hot bath and massage.

She'd reached a dismal low when Penny hailed her, directing her attention northward. In the distance she could see a beautiful shimmering lake nestled in a shallow valley. CC paused to take in the pleasing sight, so reminiscent, on a grander scale of course, of her swimming pool at home. She longed to ride at breakneck speed and plunge into the crystal clear water.

She and Penny marveled at the lakes they had seen since the drive began, lakes without rivers or streams feeding them, but possibly fed by artesian wells. Like Comanche Reservoir, this lake was barren of trees and shrubs, with only grasses and wildflowers running up to the edge.

"What I wouldn't give to be able to dive in for a swim," CC said. "To wash my hair. I wouldn't care how cold the water is."

"Go ahead. Everything is going well, and we're moving so slowly you could soon catch up. I'll cover for you." Penny was glad to be able to offer some relief for her friend. She knew CC was suffering far more than she let on.

CC knew they would be in camp within a couple of hours. She could easily catch up with the herd before they reached the campsite. She carried soap and a towel in her saddlebag. Still, she hesitated. Taking her responsibilities seriously, she weighed the temptation.

"I wonder what the name of the lake is?" she asked Penny.

"The map shows it as Apache Reservoir."

"Are you sure you won't mind?"

"Do it! Just don't take any unnecessary chances in the water. It's dangerous to swim alone."

"I'm a good swimmer. Don't worry. I'll catch up in less than an hour."

CC spurred her horse forward to a gallop. It was great to be riding faster than a snail's pace—and in control. The lake was closer than it looked from the knoll where she and Penny had first viewed it.

Drawing near, she could see a sandy beach. The water line was low, and the overflow stream was completely dry but lined with tall grasses and cattails. A few young poplars followed its edge.

She dismounted, painfully, and stood for some time appreciating the blueness of the sky and water and the small explosions of light among the reflected clouds floating serenely on the pond.

After Shitears satisfied himself with a long, cool drink, she led him down the dry streambed and tied him loosely to a poplar sapling. She took out her soap and towel and looked carefully around before undressing. No one in sight.

Before she could lose her nerve, CC jumped into the chilly water, determined to have her bath. The shock of the cold water paralyzed her for an instant but served to mask her pain briefly. When she recovered, she swam briskly to rid herself of goose flesh. Then she shampooed her hair, lathered, rinsed off, and swam again. The water felt warmer now and acted as a balm to her aching muscles and cramped spirit.

Feeling refreshed and renewed, she stepped out of the water, dried herself quickly, and dressed in a clean T-shirt and Levi's. She couldn't find a comb, but her short, pixie-cut hair would dry quickly with just a few fluffings from her fingers.

Shitears appeared to have enjoyed the rest and looked almost benign when she approached the poplar sapling through the tall grass. She mounted and loped across the plain, feeling better than she had since the drive began. The herd had progressed further than she'd anticipated, and before she caught up she noticed another horse and rider ahead of her. From the hat and the jaunty posture, she could tell it was a man. She assumed he was trying to catch up with the herd too since he was traveling the same trampled path as she. Upon hearing the clippity clop of her horse's hooves behind him, the rider stopped and waited for her.

CC recognized the man as J. Chandler Reed, the man she'd seen briefly at Uncle Simon's ranch the evening the Foofwahs arrived—and the person pressuring Lindsey to sell her cattle. CC hadn't remembered that he was so handsome but thought maybe it was because the white Stetson looked as though it was made especially for him, plus he rode like he and the horse were one. Regardless of his impressive appearance, she asked herself what kind of a pompous ass calls himself "J. Chandler?"

"Howdy," the man called as soon as she was within earshot.

"Howdy yourself." CC decided to play it casual. Realizing that J. Chandler Reed owned half of the county and very possibly this property as well, CC thought she should identify herself.

"I'm one of the hands helping Lindsey move her cattle. I understand she was granted permission to cross your land. I hope you don't mind, but I took a swim in your lake."

"Well, now, isn't that interesting? I thought I recognized you," the man said. He smiled and his voice was friendly. "I saw the herd from the road and thought I'd come over and see what I could do to help. Lindsey didn't get around to introducing us at Simon's place. I'm Chan Reed. I don't own this land, but my good friend Victor Pelletier does, and it's okay. He gave Lindsey permission to come through."

The man didn't take his eyes from her as he casually removed his riding gloves, dismounted easily, and reached for Shitears's bridle. He looked like a man intent on doing some horse-trading. CC grew uneasy. She wanted to return to her friends and the herd, but she couldn't just ride off while "Chan" held her horse's bridle.

"If you don't mind, I've been away from the cattle drive longer than I should. I must get back." CC's discomfort increased. She never trusted men who were blessed with excessive beauty.

Chan's good will seemed a little slick, triggering an alarm in her. Why was he so interested in this trail drive? He was slated to get Lindsey's cattle if she failed to pay the lease money three days from now, but the herd was worth a small fortune at the sale. There was something about him that didn't ring true.

"Nice horse you've got there," Chan said. He patted the horse on the neck as though he hadn't heard her plea to be allowed to leave.

"He suits me fine." CC didn't know what else to say. The idea of being so far away from her friends increased her nervousness. The silence became strained, but still the man held onto the bridle.

"I see you have a cellular phone," he said. "How smart and modern of you. May I look at it? I've been thinking of getting one of these."

"It's my husband's. He insisted I bring it on the trip." CC wanted to back away, but he'd already unbuckled the phone case from the saddle.

Chan examined the phone and asked a few vague questions about adequate reception before returning it to the case and rebuckling the case to the saddle.

"If you don't mind, I think I'll mosey along with you," he said.

"I'd be delighted with the company." She tried to keep her politeness from sounding forced.

"I'm afraid I didn't get your name."

"My friends call me CC." She didn't care to give him her last name.

As he walked behind her horse, Chan gave Shitears what CC assumed was intended as a pat on the rump, the kind a horseman gives a favored horse. But instead of using his hand, he snapped Shitears with his gloves, the sound like a rifle shot. Shitears, née Trickster, rose on his hind legs and pawed the air. Chan leapt aside instantly with an agility born of long association with fractious horses.

"Eyyyyeee," CC screamed. She hung onto the saddle horn for dear life. In thirty seconds, it was over. Shitears had all four feet back on the ground and was standing still as though nothing had happened. He dipped his head and munched on a mouthful of grama grass.

On the ground lay the cellular phone, smashed beyond any hope of repair. "Oh, no!" CC cried.

Chan stooped to retrieve his white Stetson that had fallen in the dust during his frantic scramble. Seeing the phone, he apologized. "I'm afraid it was my fault. I must not have fastened it securely. You are brave to ride such a high-strung horse."

CC, though still unnerved, was more upset over the loss of Ace's phone than the risk of injury. "All I know," she gasped, "is that this horse used to be a circus horse, and I was told to be careful. You must have hit one of his buttons."

"It appears so. Tell you what, I feel responsible, and I'll be glad to replace your phone."

"You needn't do that." CC didn't know what to think. One moment she was suspicious of him, the next he seemed like the nicest guy on earth, in spite of his good looks. She desperately wanted to get away without sounding rude. "I would settle for you calling my husband with a daily report that all is going well with us on the trail."

"How will I know? I might not see you every day."

"You don't need to. Just call him with the report to give him peace of mind. I definitely wouldn't want you to call with bad news, anything that would stir him up."

"It's a deal," Chan laughed. "Any particular time of day?"

"After eight a.m. would be best. He hasn't been too happy with my sunrise calls since he's in an earlier time zone. It's very nice of you to do this."

"It's the least I can do."

CC was eager to get back to the herd. She'd been gone far too long. "I'll race you. No, better not. This horse may be able to fly, and I'm not ready for flying lessons. But, please, just stay behind me."

Together, they loped toward the herd, now several miles distant. With CC riding slightly ahead, Shitears accepted the fact that his leadership wasn't in contention, and the pair settled to a steady, easy gait, close enough to make casual conversation.

Chan seemed interested in everything CC said and drew her into telling how and why she and her friends had come to Lindsey's rescue. He complimented them for courage, saying, "Lindsey is fortunate to have such fine friends." CC found Chan to be a most congenial companion.

When they caught up with the herd, CC hailed her partner Penny to let her know she had rejoined the drovers. After her warning to Chan about Shitears's phobias, he rode around the back of the herd and up the other side to reach Lindsey who still led the line.

As CC watched Chan riding alongside Lindsey, their heads bent toward one another in a posture of familiarity, she was joined by Angie, astride Twinkle, named for the star-shaped white patch in the middle of his chestnut forehead.

"Who's that?" Angie asked, nodding toward Chan. She was careful to keep Twinkle slightly behind Shitears.

"That, my dear, is J. Chandler Reed," CC replied. "Don't you love the name? It sounds so wealthy, so pompous, though the man actually seems genuinely decent. Didn't you see him at Uncle Simon's when we got there?"

"Oh, yeah, what a hunk. I didn't recognize him," Angie said. "I saw you ride up with him." Her dark eyes sparkled with interest, her small body tensed with excitement. A handsome man on the scene never failed to put her senses on alert. "I thought he looked good when I first saw him, but wow! Does he ever look great on a horse. How'd you meet him?"

CC described her meeting with Chan and elaborated on the story of Shitears's reaction to Chan's slap on the rear. Angie laughed, though she commiserated over the loss of the cell phone. She and CC, always trying to outdo each other as storytellers, embroidered and polished their tales for humorous effect, seldom hesitating to steer the narration into the realm of fantasy. They recognized each other's styles and the challenge for them was to try to figure out where reality ended and invention began.

Angie turned her attention back to J. Chandler Reed, asking what they talked about, whether Chan tried to come on to her, had he swum with her, and wasn't he possibly the sexiest man she'd ever seen?

"He said he's divorced, and his ex-wife lives in Oklahoma. He's obviously very wealthy and owns a lot of the land around here."

"Lindsey said he has the reputation of being a ladies' man," Angie mused. "What else did you learn from him?"

"He wants to help Lindsey get the cattle to the auction sale. He supports Little League and Boy Scouts and the football team. He's on the school board, and he's president of the local cattle growers association. He lives alone and has a bunch of full-time workers on his ranch payroll. I got the distinct impression he was working very hard to make sure I knew he was one of the good guys. You know, the one who wears the white hat," CC laughed.

"I think I'll just sorta casually ride up, and maybe I can meet him," Angie's eagerness betrayed her motives. She was glad she was the only single woman in their outfit. She wouldn't have any competition from the Foofwahs. Besides, she was the youngest of them, and her figure was still pretty good. He couldn't help but notice her, and maybe if she got to know him he'd ask her out when all this was over.

Reading her fortune-teller friend's mind, CC had an inspiration. She would play cupid. She thought of the many conversations she'd had with Angie, exploring the prospects for her future happiness. Maybe she could contribute to Angie's dream. Angie was savvy enough to size up a man if he didn't ring true. She'd put aside her own doubts about Chan's ingratiating manner. After all, one woman's nightmare could be another woman's paradise. She'd do it.

"I have an idea," she chuckled. "Trade horses with me." CC dismounted Shitears with the appearance of more agility than she felt.

"Why?" Angie asked, eyeing CC with suspicion.

"Don't ask questions. You want to meet Chan? Just trade horses with me."

Angie moaned at the thought of dismounting one horse and climbing on another. She managed the feat, gingerly climbing aboard Shitears. CC mounted Twinkle while she gave Angie instructions.

"You're going to meet J. Chandler Reed, but it won't be all that obvious. You've got to use finesse."

"You mean deviousness."

"You bet your sweet ass. Now, keep your horse headed at an angle away from the herd so you don't spook them, but pass close enough to Chan so he'll see you need rescuing. Give old Shitears the spurs. Make him run. When you're far enough away from the herd, scream like the devil himself is after you. Pretend you're in that old silent movie, 'The Perils of Pauline,' and you're Pauline. Lots of body language but keep down the yelling. You're terrified, see? That's the quickest way I know to meet a handsome, rich cowboy."

Angie was intrigued but hesitant. The idea of encouraging Shitears to run away with her was not a comforting one. She'd been terrified for CC when the crazy horse took off. But, what the hell? The actress in her emerged, liking the thrill and the drama of the chase. "You think it will it work?"

"Trust me. A kick in the ribs will make him fly like a bat. You saw him yesterday. Just to make sure it looks legit, I'll pretend to be trying to catch your runaway horse. You know Shitears wouldn't let Tonto get ahead of him, so he sure won't let Twinkle or any other horse pass him. Let's see how good J. Chandler Reed is at rescuing a damsel in distress."

"What if he can't?" She had second thoughts, envisioning herself being thrown from the out-of-control horse, her body lying still and broken.

"Then, God help you, you're on your own. Keep in mind the only way to stop that horse is to turn him in a circle. And don't pull up on the reins. Use knee signals."

Angie grinned. They sat side by side like two teenagers at a stop light, revving their engines.

"Okay. Go!" CC yelled. She slapped Twinkle across the rump with her reins and took off ahead of Shitears.

Shitears bolted forward with such a sudden lurch, Angie nearly tumbled backward from the saddle. She screamed, and it wasn't play-acting, it was for real. Shitears flew like an arrow, passing Twinkle and CC and heading straight across the prairie.

CC on Twinkle shot forward being careful to stay a few feet behind. Every time CC and Twinkle approached Shitears's rump, the domineering horse put on an extra burst of speed.

When Angie and Shitears passed Jake, he was alarmed. He stood up in his stirrups to get a better view of the galloping horse and rider. His first instinct was to join the rescue effort, but then he realized Angie was riding Shitears and CC was on Angie's horse. He reined in his horse to watch with a combination of wonder and disgust. He spit a long stream of tobacco juice. "Aw, hell. Wimmen!" He turned his attention back to a worthier pursuit, keeping the cattle in line. But he kept a wary eye on the Wild West show taking place not far from the herd.

Angie recovered her balance and played the role of the imperiled damsel convincingly. She managed to keep her scream down to a stifled shrill whine until she got far enough away from the herd. When she passed Chan, she managed to get a few frantic arm motions into her act.

Chan took out after her. This was CC's signal to drop back, leaving the field free for Chan to be a hero.

CC grinned to herself, but she was still a little worried about Angie and curious to see how Chan would handle the rescue. After all, Shitears was highly unpredictable. She suppressed fears that the scene could end in tragedy, and she would be responsible. Remaining on the sidelines, she and Twinkle kept within hailing distance in case things went wrong.

As soon as Shitears realized the competition had dropped back, he slowed down. The challenge had gone out of the race. He was no longer young and became winded easily. Shitears slowed, and Angie began to rein him into a circle just as Chan caught up with them. With the surprise of another contestant to defeat, Shitears poised to take off again. But Chan quickly reached over and wrapped his arm around Angie's waist, pulling her from the saddle and into his arms.

Angie had no trouble playing a terrified victim to the hilt. She was so weak from fright when Chan set her onto the front of his saddle that she collapsed against him like a wilted rose. He slowed his horse to a walk and headed for a grove of sycamore trees alongside a streambed.

Chan dismounted and lifted Angie gently from the horse, depositing her on the soft grass.

Shitears had run so far, it took almost an hour for the herd to catch up, and by that time, Angie and Chan had become very good friends.

Chan convinced her that it was unhealthy to get back on a horse immediately after a runaway and that she was likely to have after-effects of shock from the terrifying experience. He insisted that she let him take her to a doctor to make sure she was all right. She might need a sedative. Angie started to protest, then reconsidered and consented modestly.

As they sat along the bank skipping pebbles across the slow-moving stream and chatting, Lindsey rode up. Her expression stiffened at the resemblance to the leafy green glade of her dream. But she was not the one Chan was bestowing his attentions on. It was Angie, younger and prettier than she. Wordlessly, Lindsey turned her horse back to the herd, unnoticed by the enraptured pair.

When the others caught up, Chan handed Shitears's reins to Jake. "This girl's a little overwrought from the frightening experience," Chan announced. "I'll take her into town to see my doctor. She'll no doubt need to rest a few hours."

Jake and the clustered Foofwahs could only stare at Angie, so high-spirited, even wild, and now so fragile. Lindsey busied herself away from them, checking on strays.

"You take care of her," Jake said, looking uncertain as to what this was all about.

As Chan, cuddling Angie in his arms, spurred his horse toward town, Angie caught CC's eye and winked. The wink wasn't lost on Jake, who turned back toward the herd disgusted.

Angie still felt shaky from the experience until they were half way into town, then she began to enjoy herself as Chan walked the horse slowly along the road. He paused again under a shady tree to adjust his horse's cinch.

Captivated by everything the man said or did, Angie realized she had never been so instantly excited by another person. Chan laughed easily, and acted as if everything she said was brilliant or witty. In her travels around the country, she met many fascinating people, especially men. But none had interested her like this one. She felt so safe with his arms around her, and she liked his warm, masculine smell. As she stood watching him pull the cinch, she wanted him to touch her again, to fold her in his arms.

"You know, Chan," Angie said, "I think I've recovered enough that maybe a little rest away from my horse for a bit is all I needed. Seeing a doctor won't be necessary."

"You're the boss," Chan said. "Would you like to go on into town anyway?"

"Maybe ... No. Let's just walk along by the stream again. It's cool under the trees and such a nice day." Her eyes gleamed with infatuation mixed with triumph at the success of her scheme. CC's scheme, really. Angie was merely an eager participant.

"What do you do to keep busy when you're not herding cattle?" Chan asked.

Angie told him about the Gypsy Spirit and her life on the road. He wanted to know all about fortune telling and how she had come to take on such a life.

"Tarot cards, fortunes? I don't believe it. Tell mine," Chan said. His steely gray eyes sparkled with merriment.

"Your what?" Angie asked.

"My fortune, gypsy lady. I want to know what a red-haired gypsy sees in my future." He grabbed both of her hands and held up her palms as though he would read her fortune.

"Well ... I could." Angie thought frantically about the gap between the bullshit she dispensed for a living and the halfway belief that she maybe really had psychic powers. Certainly, she had accurately predicted the disorganization and confusion of this cattle drive. Was that real or was it magic?

Chan sat on a fallen log in front of her. She kneeled before him and turned his strong, tanned hands so that his palms were upward. Chan had beautiful hands for a man. They were squarish and firm, with long-tapered fingers. Uncalloused, they still revealed the toughness of a man accustomed to heavy work, like handling horses.

"I see that you have a very long life line and that you will love many women. But you will have difficulty finding happiness." Her chance to gossip with CC was paying off. "Oh!" Angie dropped his hands and walked to the edge of the stream to better study a large rock in the middle.

"What?" Chan looked puzzled.

How could she tell him she had found a line that revealed falseness? Could Chan be false? Above everything, she wanted Chan to be the perfect Adonis he appeared.

She turned back, kneeled, and lifted his hands again. What do I know, anyway? she thought. Palm reading is not an exact science. But she couldn't conceal a tautness in her expression. She concentrated on the lines in his palms. "You will become greatly enamored of a beautiful, exotic woman, who will bear you many children."

Chan laughed and cupped her face in his big hands. His eyes delved deeply into hers and drew from her a sense of oneness. Then he broke the moment with a gentle smile. "Now you're putting me on. I've already met a beautiful, exotic woman, one with red hair, to boot. But she'd better not bear me many, no, *any* children, or I'll turn her out." He pulled her across his knees, turned her over, and gave a smart snap to her behind.

Then he turned her over again to face him and gave her a long, satisfying kiss.

Angie tingled with pleasure. Had she ever known such joy?

They held one another for a long while, content in their shared pleasure.

Finally, Angie said, "I hate to bring this up, but it's time for me to go. My friends will be worried."

"Surely they could get along without you."

"Possibly, but this job isn't easy for tenderfeet like us, and we've had our tender hands full herding cows, let alone staying in the saddle. We take turns riding watch, and I'm up for the early shift tonight."

"Aha! Maybe some handsome bandit will abduct you and carry you away to his tent for endless lovemaking."

"Always a hope ... but so far the closest I've come to a bandit out there at night is Jake."

"And you seduced poor Jake?" he laughed.

Angie grimaced. "I'd become celibate before I'd roll in the hay with that old boy."

"Yes, I suspect Jake is America's answer to birth control." Chan chuckled and led her to where his horse grazed near the road. "When can I see you again?"

"That's hard to say. We have a pretty full schedule," she smiled. "I'd guess it would be whenever you take a notion to rove around the range again."

"Let's make it more formal than that. How about dinner tomorrow evening in Los Vaqueros?" he asked.

"Sounds good to me," Angie replied, excitement sparkling in her dark eyes. Chan looked at her as if, more than anything, he wanted to remove her clothes, and she knew, more than anything, she'd like to help. Instead, he helped her into the saddle by placing his hands around her waist and lifting her easily from the ground. His touch lingered a shade longer than could be thought casual. She felt a warm flush of desire for this elegant, charming man and regretted that her circumstances were so inelegant.

"On second thought, Chan, as much as I'd like to go to dinner, I have nothing decent to wear," she apologized.

"If that's the only problem, I think I can solve that one. You're about the same size as my ex-wife. There's a closet full of clothing she's never worn. The price tags are still on them. Shopping was one of Yvonne's most notable talents. We could go to my home first for you to freshen up and change."

Angie hesitated only a moment. "In that case, I accept. I'll ask the boss for a night off so I can go out on the town."

"Good." Chan's gray eyes flashed a triumphant beam, and his tanned face broadened into a playful smile. He swung up behind her and took the reins. She could feel his arm under her breast, touching, exhilarating her senses as the horse bobbed along. With his right hand, Chan played with her hair. Before they reached the camp, he pulled back her long hair and lightly kissed the nape of her neck. She turned her cheek toward him for another kiss, and he didn't disappoint her. Angie thought she had never been so happy as she hopped down from the horse, no longer aware of stiffness or pain. She smiled up at him, memorizing his handsome features. "Until tomorrow."

"Tomorrow."

CHAPTER EIGHTEEN

PRICKLY BUSINESS

The third morning started out simply for Jake. While Chloë prepared breakfast, he saddled his horse, then sat down to enjoy coffee, bacon, cottage fries, and hot cakes with warm maple syrup. Even a little bacon gravy. Chloë was a fine cook, and Jake hoped never to miss one of her meals. Good thing she's married, he thought. I might make a mistake I'd be sure to regret. The promise of good food can ruin a man.

Jake was working on his second stack of hot cakes before any of the women appeared for breakfast. CC was the first to arrive, bubbling spirits in full surge. Such cheerfulness turned Jake's stomach sour. Never a morning person himself, conviviality at breakfast made him feel downright mean.

"And what exciting new adventures can we look forward to today?" CC asked.

"Don't you have no aches and pains?" Jake answered. He thought he could count on the old broads to be so laid out in misery he could throw it back at them that this was no place for women. He might have felt sorry for them if they hadn't seemed so smug about taking over his territory.

"Nope. No pain," CC replied. "But then I'm in good shape physically. I swim every day and play tennis three times a week."

"Umph," Jake belched. He put his head down and shoveled in a load of hot cakes. Maybe he could ignore her until he finished his meal.

"Oh, Jake," CC said. "I wish you'd check out Shitears. I think the shoe is loose on his back right foot."

"Hoof, lady. Horses wear shoes on their hooves, not their feet." There was no hope for silence.

"It wouldn't do to have a horse's shoe come loose on the trail, would it?" CC persisted.

Without answering, Jake took his mug of coffee and moved off to sit on a log facing his tethered horse.

Lindsey arrived in time to overhear CC's question and notice Jake's reaction. Several of the women were staggering around, helping themselves to coffee and taking in the conversation.

"As soon as you finish breakfast, Jake," Lindsey said, "check CC's horse's shoe. We need every horse we've got, and we sure don't want any horse to go lame." Lindsey's voice asserted more authority than she felt. Not a commanding person by nature, she felt especially uncomfortable giving orders to an old, experienced hand like Jake. But Jake had ignored CC's legitimate concern, and if she allowed personal animosities, some very real grief could result.

Jake resented receiving orders from anyone, especially from a woman. And to have to take orders from a woman, even Lindsey, in front of these fluffheads was more than he could bear. He was the trail boss here. Cody told him he was in charge. Now Cody's wife was ordering him around like he was a greenhorn. Jake took a pinch of Copenhagen to ease his battered ego. He'd be damned before he'd take any more orders from a woman. He decided to ignore Lindsey. The insult to his manhood rankled, and he sulked off to spend the rest of the morning by himself.

After the testing of wills reached an impasse, the rest of the morning went smoothly. The stiff leg muscles and sore backsides from the day before subsided as the women became used to the gait of their horses and learned how to lean into the motion rather than plopping up and down on their saddles like big bags of meal being pounded into dust. The liniment Jake had insisted on bringing helped somewhat during the night but time and experience helped more.

Now that the women were able to keep the cattle from straying into the brush and were even pretty good at bringing up the drags, Jake relaxed a little. By early afternoon, responding to the steady rolling gait of his horse and ignoring the hunger pangs starting up in his stomach in spite of the huge breakfast, Jake nodded off. He had learned many years ago how to nap in the saddle.

The women were drowsy and unusually quiet. The boredom of pacing themselves to the slow-moving cattle in the hot September sunshine lulled them into listlessness. Horse flies buzzing and diving around their heads were all that prevented them from falling asleep too. And the risk of severe injury from falling out of their saddles was never far from their thoughts.

Suddenly, Jake was shocked awake by a woman's screams. The shrillness went through his nervous system like an electric current. Jake looked around at the cattle but saw no panic so far. The riders were all present except CC. Drat the goddam woman. She's nothin' but trouble. She and that horse oughta run off a cliff.

Jake stood in his stirrups, straining for a better view as he searched the rolling plains for a sign of CC and Shitears. She was nowhere in sight, but her screams still washed over him like a flash flood.

The screams seemed to be coming from beyond the hillock on his right, a long way off. What in hell would she be doing on the other side of that hillock?

All the riders stopped, looking startled and defenseless.

Shitears loped over the hill, riderless, and heading hell-bent toward the cattle. Jake turned his horse quickly and headed off the runaway horse before he could spook the herd. The horse looked unhurt, just nervous, making it difficult for Jake to gather up the reins. After a few misses, Jake grabbed the reins and turned Shitears over to Gina.

Jake took off over the hill at a gallop. The astonishing sight on the other side of the hill stopped him, and he had to laugh. CC was spread-eagled on the ground, lying on her stomach with her Levi's at half-mast. Her face was smeared with dust, her exposed backside covered with cactus needles. When she saw Jake, she finally quit screaming.

"Are you all right?" Jake dismounted and bent over the sobbing woman.

"No, of course I'm not all right, goddammit! I'm lying here because I like lying in a cactus patch with my pants down and my face full of dirt!"

Jake tried to make her feel better. "Yer rump looks like a pin cushion. Guess you landed in that bed of prickly pear." When her howls commenced again, he decided to change tack. "Just lie still and I'll git some glue."

"Glue?" Her panic was unabated. "You're insane!"

"No, ma'am. Elmer's Glue is the best danged stuff in the world for takin' out cactus needles. You just spread it on like butter, and let it dry, then peel the little cusses right outa yer hide."

"Oh, my God. Does that mean I'll have to lie here until it dries? And where are you going to find Elmer's Glue out here in this Godforsaken country?"

"I wasn't born yesterday, missy, in case you haven't noticed. I always carry Elmer's Glue in my saddlebag for gittin' out cactus needles. I just hope I got enough to cover yer big ... uh ... to git 'em all."

"You didn't answer my question. Will I have to lie here?"

"No, but you might prefer to. Unless you like to wander around naked. I don't believe you'd want to put clothes on over all those needles and that wet glue."

CC groaned and buried her face in her hands, resigned to the indignities forced on her.

After rummaging through his saddlebags, Jake returned with a container of Elmer's Glue and, taking out his pocketknife, smeared the white paste liberally over CC's backside, like an artist working with a pallet knife.

"Usually, these barbs will break off and stay inside a person's skin until infection sets in. Then the pus pushes the barb out."

"Oh, thanks, Jake. Just work a little faster, please." CC was grateful for his help, but profoundly embarrassed by her nakedness and, almost worse, for losing control of her horse. "What in the hell's taking so long?"

"Now you just hold on, missy. You've probably got ten thousand of these mean little barbs."

"Ohhh," CC groaned and laid her face back down on her arms. Humiliated, she was determined not to let Jake know how much she hurt.

Lindsey rode over the hill and stopped, her mouth agape at the unbelievable sight.

"What happened?" she asked.

"I had to—you know—pee," CC said. "I got off my horse and had just squatted down when I heard this funny sound, like paper being crushed. I looked around, and there was this huge rattler. I swear it was as big as my arm, not two feet away. It wasn't coiled to strike, but it raised its head and looked at me, then slithered away into the brush. I screamed, and the horse reared up and took off. When I started to get up, I tripped over my Levi's and landed in the cactus."

Though sympathetic, Lindsey couldn't suppress a laugh. "Rejoin us when you can, but you might not want to sit in a saddle for a while." She returned to the Foofwahs to report the cause for the commotion.

When the barbs were finally removed, Jake reached in his pocket for a pint of Jack Daniels and grudgingly covered the wounds with his precious alcohol.

"Yeow!" CC screamed. "What was that for?"

"It'll keep the infection out, missy."

"Oh, fine, now I'll smell like a distillery." Then, fearful of sounding ungrateful, CC added softly, "But thanks anyway, Jake."

He mounted Tonto, and CC walked behind them.

"You'll be a real tender-ass for sure the next few days." Jake grinned privately and muttered, out of her hearing, "It couldn't happen to a more deserving bitch."

When they reached the others, Jake checked CC's horse, which looked none the worse for the escapade with the rattler and the wild race over the plains.

Remembering the order he'd received that morning, the order he'd elected to ignore, Jake lifted the horse's right rear hoof. Sure enough, the shoe was missing. Damn! Jake thought. That means he can't be ridden and will have to be shod before the day's over. Damn wimmen. More trouble than a whole passel of snakes!

Lindsey rode by and, seeing that Jake was checking the horse's shoe, stopped. Jake looked up and knew instantly what she was thinking, but he stubbornly refused to make excuses.

"Didn't I tell you to check the horse's shoes this morning?"

"It was all right this morning."

"Take care of it. We have an extra horse, but CC probably isn't going to want to ride for the rest of the day anyway.

Jake knew he'd been caught in a lie. Horseshoes didn't look all right in the morning, then fly off in the middle of the day, even if a horse did race a bit. He blamed CC for his predicament. The more he thought about it, the more he resented being placed in a position of having a whole mess of women for bosses.

When they reached the campsite, Angie drove the Gypsy Spirit back to pick up CC, who had tired after crippling along for a couple of miles and chose to stand and wait at a road crossing.

Jake used the campfire to heat a new shoe and shape it to fit the horse's hoof. Working on a rock didn't help. Jake didn't mind shoeing a horse, but an anvil made shaping much easier. Every time he hit the horseshoe with his hammer, he named it for a different Foofwah. It made him feel better but not good enough.

After supper, the women gathered around the campfire to tell stories and sing. They invited Jake to join them, but he made the excuse that he had some business to attend to.

Lindsey and Angie were both unusually subdued, wondering why Chan hadn't arrived to take Angie on their date. Usually the star performer whenever music and storytelling began, Angie sat as though in a trance, studying the fire. Lindsey sat opposite, quietly practicing tying different types of knots. With her eyebrows furrowed, she appeared completely absorbed in her task.

* * *

Earlier in the afternoon, Angie had followed CC's example from the day before and, passing a small reservoir, took time out to bathe and wash her hair. Invigorated by the coldness of the water, she quickly dried off and changed into clean Levi's. As she fluffed her bright hair and relished the warm sunshine, the fragrance of the shampoo made her feel fresh and alive. Thoughts of spending the evening with Chan aroused in her a desire for his touch, so gentle and firm. She shivered in anticipation at the memory of his kisses and the promise in his eyes.

Chan was to pick her up by five o'clock, but the hour arrived and no Chan. At first, she thought he had merely been delayed so didn't say anything to the others.

Two hours later, when he still hadn't appeared, her humiliation peaked. I've been stood up. No one has stood me up since I was a teenager. I can't deal with this.

Rather than reveal her distress, Angie quietly withdrew from the merriment, which was somewhat flat this evening anyway with everyone so tired. Everyone but her. She'd been in wonderful spirits. Now her aching muscles and soreness reasserted themselves. She wondered why she'd signed up for this friggin' chain gang in the first place.

By eight o'clock, she retreated to the Gypsy Spirit and her bedroll, where she lay wondering what it was about her that Chan felt he could afford to miss. If an emergency had come up, couldn't he have sent word by one of his men? This was unacceptable. If she ever saw the man again, she would freeze him out. Turn him to stone with her eyes and a few choice words. He couldn't give her the come-on with those sexy, knowing eyes and thrilling little feels and expect her to fall at his feet like a school girl.

* * *

Lindsey watched Angie leave the campfire, sensing her pain but feeling at the same time a nasty little worm of satisfaction that Angie had no doubt misinterpreted Chan's intentions. She forced herself to empathize with her friend, for, after all, hadn't she herself felt exhilarated by the man's attention, his knowing looks and touches? How much deeper must the hurt be for Angie, who didn't have the watchdog conscience posted by an absent husband.

But then, she hadn't thrown herself at Chan, the way Angie did. The poor man could hardly get out of Angie's way. She thought again of the looks she and Chan had exchanged in his bedroom and wondered how differently that scenario might have played out had she given in to her urges. Then she thought of the scenario were Angie to be given Chan's "house tour," how *she* would answer the invitation in his eyes. The thought was intolerable. An inner voice shouted, "He wants *me*!"

Lindsey laid aside the rope and clasped her arms around her knees. She put her head down on her knees and felt like crying for something. But what? Angie has a right to pursue the man. I don't. It's just that it's been so long since Cody has touched me in a special way. Rather than lovers, we're like old friends when we get it on.

Now she longed for the intimacy they'd shared in the early days of their marriage, feelings she'd not realized were missing until Chan awoke her sexuality. She told herself maybe she was at least partly to blame for the interest dying out of her love life with Cody. She was glad she had remained faithful. At the same time, she knew she'd always be curious about what she'd missed with Chan.

There's no point grieving over a thwarted love affair with a man, who in truth, probably comes on to every woman and doesn't give a fig about either of us. No point in both of us moping around here. If Angie wants to risk getting burned, that's her business. As far as I'm concerned, *forget him.*

* * *

When the evening watch started, Gina and Lindsey took the early shift. Jake had disappeared. After Angie crawled into the Gypsy Spirit to mope, a low murmuring had passed among the women about Chan's failure to show up. No one wanted to add to Angie's heartbreak, so they agreed to avoid the subject. He had seemed so enchanted with Angie the day before, and as unremitting matchmakers the Foofwahs were for the most part thrilled at Angie's opportunity to have some fun. Those among them who had reservations about Chan's sincerity kept it to themselves, thinking it possible they'd misunderstood the man.

* * *

At four-thirty, Chan called his men together to give them a verbal thrashing. He planned to drive out and pick up Angie after the "pep talk." He had big ideas for tonight, and she'd looked like she could use a little lovin' up. Chan liked his women spirited, and she showed the fire he needed to light his stove. Fortune-teller! That's a good one, he thought. If she could read fortunes, she'd sure as hell think twice about getting mixed up with me.

The men, looking uneasy, gathered in Chan's study where the wet bar was open. Chan served drinks as each arrived. The only times Chan invited them to the privacy of his home were when he wanted to chew on them a little. Chan liked his "boys" and, while they needed a good cussing out, he didn't intend to shitcan any of them.

The first to arrive was Billy Ray Worthman, the clean-cut young man who had caused Lindsey so much disappointment with the consequence of setting the Foofwahs in action. Chan viewed him like a son, indeed Billy Ray looked a lot like Chan when he was young, and Chan sometimes wondered if ... nahhh.

"Billy Ray, beer?"

"Yessir, Mr. Reed."

The next to arrive were Sam Saulie and Jimbo Crawford, two experienced hands who were top-drawer cowboys but meaner than catshit when they were mad or drunk. The last to arrive was Art Sheedy, the town bully. Each picked up a highball glass as he passed into the room. Chan knew what they liked. It was always scotch neat since they never spent their own money on anything but rotgut. He had the drinks poured and set on the counter to save time. He wanted the men comfortable before he laid into them. He let them settle down on the red leather sofa and club chairs before he began.

"Look, you men. Relax. But goddammit! Pay attention!" He kicked Art's boot off the glass coffee table, then sipped from his own vodka tonic. "You all get high wages for being the best there are. Now, I'm not complaining about the quality of your work. I couldn't hire any men who were more competent to run a ranch and work cattle than you four. But—and this is why you're here—I'm going to kick butt if you don't get off your asses and deliver Simon's goddammed cattle before another twenty-four hours go by.

"I don't have to tell you again how many thousands of dollars I've got at stake—and you can worry about your jobs—if those stupid women stumble their way to La Chulla and get Simon's herd to the auction. I can't believe you namby-pambies haven't been able to politely encourage the goddammed women to abandon their mission and go home to their quilting by now. What in the living hell is going on? Have you all become sissies?"

Chan took a break and offered another round of drinks, to everyone's relief. They weren't expecting Chan's wrath to be this bad. A little annoyance maybe, but the man was acting unhinged. His eyes glinted dangerously and white lines had formed around his tense mouth. What were they supposed to do? They weren't killers, and these old girls were tougher than Chan gave them credit for. They'd ignored taunts and humiliation, even kept cool when their horses were cut loose. They had other work to do than spook women, lots of work keeping Chan's ranch and herd together. Did he want them out there all day hassling a bunch of female dipshits? Besides, the women had that old reprobate Jake to protect them. Jake wasn't too smart, but he was cagey as all get out when it came to looking after cattle.

Chan continued. "We've tried the subtle approach. I've been trying to grease the Taylor woman with soft soap, but she's not buying—or selling, for that matter. You bunch of choirboys didn't even faze them, so it's time to get tough. I mean, MEAN!"

"You want us to kill someone, boss?" Art, the bully, asked. His colorless, piggy eyes squinted at the thought that he'd do it if he had to. He had three kids and an ex-wife to support, and the alimony and child support were choking him.

"No, you asshole, we don't have to go that far." Chan had started drinking before the men arrived. "I said 'mean,' not dead. We'd get strung up good if we resort to knocking off dingbats. Now here's what I think we've got to do ..."

The men sat with their heads together for the next two hours, drinking Chan's scotch and plotting a simple but foolproof method for disposing of the Foofwahs. With luck, no one would get hurt, but accidents could always happen. "Nothing intentional," Chan exhorted his men. "That is, nothing traceable to us ... to me."

"Okay, okay," the men muttered. The heavy responsibility laid on them and the generous supply of liquor gave them a dangerous bravado. They shambled from the room planning to head off to town and the Purgatory Saloon for supper and to drink some more. Billy Ray started to stay behind to go over the day's ranch business with Chan, but seeing his boss's mood decided it could wait until tomorrow.

Chan flipped on the television to watch the end of the network national news. Putting his feet on the coffee table he'd forbidden Art to use, he settled down with a fresh drink.

Before Peter Jennings could say "Goodnight," Chan's head drooped, and he sank into a deep slumber.

When he awoke and checked his watch, he groaned and staggered upstairs to bed. Catching sight of himself in the mirror over the sink, rumpled and needing a shave, Chan said, “Shit. Sorry, Angie kid. Prince Charming’s taking the night off.”

CHAPTER NINETEEN

JAKE'S NIGHT OUT

After dinner, when Jake went off by himself to sulk, he found he had a little Jack Daniels left in his saddlebag, so he soothed his injured pride with what he referred to as "the sippin' stuff." There wasn't enough left to make him feel much better, though, so he decided it was worthwhile taking a trip into Los Vaqueros for a fresh supply.

Without a word to the women, Jake saddled Tonto and led him quietly away from the camp until he was sure he wouldn't be heard. Then he mounted and headed off toward the tiny town. He'd noticed a roadhouse at the edge of town, the Purgatory Saloon, when they'd passed through Los Vaqueros a few days ago. There was sure to be liquor and music and maybe even a woman or two in a saloon. Not that he expected any woman to get excited over the likes of him at his age. But by golly, it was a free country, and he could look at 'em. And how he loved to see a pretty woman dance.

Jake's arrival at the roadhouse created little stir. He ordered a straight shot, then another, and leaned against the bar. A couple down wind of him moved away, and the man behind him found he had friends at a table. Jake soon had the bar to himself. On the dance floor, cowboys doing the two-step pranced and twirled their partners, throwing them out and reeling them back in with skirts swirling to the fast swing music followed by cowboy laments. Jake was particularly entranced with the intricate line dances, wishing he could join in without looking silly. On the sidelines, cowboys still wearing their spurs and hats drunkenly celebrated their winnings or bemoaned their losses at the roping contest. Several local girls looked like they came from the high school, but no one bothered to check for ID's.

Sadie Mawhinney owned the Purgatory Saloon, and tonight, as usual, she tended bar. Sadie was not beautiful, but she wasn't ugly either. A certain strength of character gave her face a carved-in-granite aspect. She was tough on the outside, but an occasional glimmer of sensitivity leaked through her steely eyes. Though she refused to wear makeup to cover her freckles, Sadie frequented the beauty shop weekly. No one was sure why. She wouldn't let the beautician dye her hair, laughing that she might have problems from looking too good, and her colorless fine hair, cut in the latest style, still lacked modishness. It just hung limp. Built like a stevedore, she had proven on many occasions that she could hold her own with drunken cowboys and truckers alike, priding herself on the ability to keep her premises under control.

Jake's drinks had barely begun to take effect when he noticed a mismatched couple on the dance floor. The pretty little filly, about sixteen he guessed, was getting a pretty good feeling up by one of the cowboys. Without prior acquaintance with the man, Jake nevertheless recognized his type instantly as the town bully. The girl tried to pull away several times, but the bully refused to release her. Verging on tears, she kept looking around to see if anyone would come to her rescue. The cowboys pretended to ignore her. Jake thought of his younger sisters and wondered if they ever had help from anyone when they got into a jam like this kid.

The more he thought about his sisters, whom he'd not seen for a lifetime, the angrier he became. He watched the scene for a few minutes, finished his last shot, and decided someone had to do something. If no one else was going to, he'd have to be the one. Pretty well fueled with liquid courage, he sauntered onto the dance floor. His target was a head taller, but Jake figured he had an advantage. No young whippersnapper would hit an old man. After all, cowboys had their own code of ethics. He weaved his way to the man and tugged on his arm to attract attention.

"I think what the young lady is tryin' to tell you is, she don't like none of your huggin' up. So let her go."

"Huh?" The bully's mean little bloodshot eyes sought to focus on the voice that seemed to be directed at him. His eyelids at half-mast and his face flushed from the exertions of the dance floor and the booze, the man turned in a circle and nearly lost his footing. "Whut'd you say?"

"I said, take yer hands off the young lady." Jake's hands were shaking, but his voice was strong and powerful.

"Mind your own goddam business," the man said, pushing Jake roughly with the intention of returning to his dance. Jake didn't notice, but a hush had fallen on the room. Every eye followed him and the mismatched couple.

Jake raised his voice. "I said ... what'sa matter with yer ears? I *said*, let the lady go." Jake grabbed the man's arm, but the man whipped his arm free, nearly knocking Jake to the floor. The bully hovered over the reluctant girl again, his feet barely moving, but his body swaying suggestively to the music.

Jake knew no rules for fighting. He'd learned to fight like he'd learned cowpunching, by wading in and doing what self-preservation told him was right. He placed his hands together for a hammer blow and swung with all his might at the bully's neck as he bent low over the girl. The punch jarred Jake almost as much as it jolted his opponent. But it got the man's attention.

"G'wan home, old man. You're botherin' me." He swatted at Jake as he might a pesky gnat, but seeing that Jake dodged too skillfully, the man placed his free hand on Jake's forehead and pushed him toward the door, knocking Jake's hat to the floor. Jake knew by now that he'd gotten himself into a real hassle. His only advantage, since he had neither strength nor youth, was experience. He hoped he was less drunk than the bully, but he wasn't sure. Jake kicked out with his leg and caught his spurs on the man's spurs, pulling the man's foot out from under him. The man went down but was up almost before he hit the floor.

"By Jeezus," Jake said under his breath. He was getting winded and sobering up enough now to begin to be nervous about the man's strength and agility.

The young girl backed away into the crowd gathering around the fighters.

The man lunged at him. "Now you're makin' me mad! Git the hell outta here before I beat the shit outa you. This ain't none 'a your business."

Jake was ready for him, dancing around in a boxer's pose with both fists doubled up to protect his face.

The lightning fast poke to Jake's jaw demonstrated all too well how wanting Jake's boxing skills were. He dropped with a thud. Instantly, he was up and back on his feet with the persistence of a mosquito at a picnic. Jake threw one punch, but it missed. The bully laughed, reared back like a maddened grizzly, and with an arm like a jackhammer struck Jake squarely in the middle of his jaw. Jake went down and lay on the floor for a moment, too stunned to rise. More slowly this time, he got to his feet. His lip bled profusely. The man waited, poised for the next blow.

Jake didn't see the tall young cowboy who disengaged himself from the crowd and headed toward the pair, flexing his shoulder muscles. Jake didn't know Billy Ray Worthman, but Billy Ray cut in between the fighting men and pushed Jake aside. Turning to the bully, he said, "Art, you're drunker'n a skunk. Get outta here and beat it before the boys and I get our dander up real good and do somethin' we're not responsible for." Billy Ray nodded toward a menacing line of cowboys in various stages of inebriation, all hankering to jump into the fray. Art Sheedy eyed the new foe he'd not counted on having to fight, then picked up his hat and spit on the floor as he swaggered toward the door.

"And before you go," Billy Ray added, "the next time you come in here, don't park your manners at the door. Treat your lady with respect, or you'll have all of us to contend with."

Only after the door closed behind Sheedy did Billy Ray turn to Jake and offer his hand.

"Guess it took an old-timer like you to remind us of things our grandpas taught us, like respect for our women and elders."

* * *

Sadie had watched the fight with considerable interest from behind the bar, keeping a gun ready if the fracas got out of hand and she needed to intervene. The grit and courage of the feisty little man impressed her. He was the only cowboy there big enough, despite his slight build, to take on that half-ass Art Sheedy. Art was becoming something of a local problem so that even the sheriff admitted the man was causing him trouble.

"The little old shit has a lot of courage to take on the big guy," she said to no one in particular. Sadie knew what she had to do. She wiped her hands on her jeans and came out from behind the bar to approach Jake and Billy Ray.

"Sadie's my name. I'm the owner of this bar. Mister, you got a lotta nerve taking on that ornery sonofabitch," she said to Jake. "Come with me, and I'll see what I can do about the bleeding. Your lip's cut bad." Sadie took Jake by the arm and led him past the bar and into the back room that served as her office and living quarters. Jake was too dazed to protest. He still wasn't sure what had happened to the bully.

"That'll teach you to mix it up with one of Chan Reed's boys," she said. "Now Reed himself, there's the one to keep an eye on."

"Yer not tellin' me nuthin' I don't already know," Jake said, wiping blood from his lip.

"You're lucky young Billy Ray was there to help you out. I don't know how he come to get in with that tribe."

Sadie offered Jake a chair and went into the bathroom to rummage around in a medicine chest. Soon she came out with a damp washcloth, a spray can of antiseptic, and bandages. Sadie found his bloody lip amid the scruffy beard and had him hold the washcloth to his mouth to mop up the blood, then she gave it a squirt with the disinfectant.

As she worked, Jake looked up into her eyes. Sadie had the same feeling she'd once experienced when she rescued a dog with a broken leg after it had been hit by a car. The little varmint looked so soulful and grateful, she wanted to give him a hug. But Sadie had a long-standing practice of not getting too affectionate with wounded animals or men. You never know when one of them's going to bite you.

"Guess these bandages aren't going to do much good on your mouth," she laughed. When she smiled, her eyes crinkled up in a good-natured expression Sadie took pains to conceal most of the time. She didn't want it thought that she might be an easy mark.

"I know a few folks might like you to give it a try anyhow," Jake chuckled. The whisky and the blows were beginning to wear off, and he thought he might like this Sadie if he got to know her. He wondered if she could cook as good as Chloë.

"Tell you what," she said, reasserting her business-like manner. "I gotta go back to the bar, and I'll be closing down in about an hour. In the meantime, whyn't you just take it easy. Looks to me like you could use a good bath. You just make yourself at home and soak in this bathtub. It'll help the sore muscles you're gonna feel in the morning. When I close up for the night, I'll come in and fix us some bacon and eggs. Meanwhile, if you'll just step outta them duds, I'll throw them in the washer, and when you get outta the tub, you'll have fresh, clean clothes to put on."

Jake hesitated. She made it sound so simple, but stepping out of his clothes when any woman was closer than forty acres wasn't something he intended to do. Then again, she'd been awful nice to patch him up, and he guessed it wouldn't hurt to have some clean clothes, though they wouldn't stay that way very long. Wimmenfolk! They've got the strangest notions about what's important, he thought, reluctantly pulling off his boots.

As she talked, Sadie ran the bath water then went down the hall for a set of towels. Jake quickly hopped into the bathroom and closed the door so she wouldn't see him naked. When Sadie returned, Jake's arm was hanging out the bathroom door holding his grimy, foul-smelling, clothing.

"Sure do 'preciate this, ma'am," Jake said in his politest manner.

Sadie held her breath as she hurried the offensive heap of rags to the washer. "Whew!" she said, thinking she'd hate to embarrass him, but the poor man was sure in want of a good woman to look after him. "I'll be back in about an hour," she called as she returned to close the door.

* * *

At the campsite, Lindsey decided to have a little talk with Jake, maybe apologize if she'd hurt his feelings. She found his bedroll laid out, but his horse was gone, and so was he. The empty bottle of Jack Daniels provided the only clue she needed. She and Cody had stopped at the Purgatory Saloon when driving through Los Vaqueros on their trips to La Cholla during the summer, and with Jake's fondness for hard liquor, she had a pretty good idea where he might be.

She caught Gina preparing for bed and told her she was going to look for Jake. Gina offered to go along, but Lindsey knew Gina was tired after taking the first watch with her.

"Don't worry about it. He's not far off."

* * *

A little past midnight, Lindsey reached the roadhouse. She wouldn't have minded stopping in for a beer if Cody was along, but she detested the idea of going into this kind of place alone at such a late hour.

Jake's horse Tonto was tied to the hitching rail along the side. The other cowboys had arrived by pickups and motorcycles. Trust Jake to carry out the image of the Old West, she thought, as she walked up the steps to the veranda. I hope he left his six-shooters at home.

Inside, Lindsey checked among the patrons, still fairly numerous considering the late hour. She ignored the raised eyebrows and heightened attention her presence aroused among the cowboys. She finally approached the bar and the big, homely woman wiping out beer glasses with a large white towel. Somewhat intimidated by Sadie's suspicious look, Lindsey cleared her throat and plunged in.

"I'm looking for my top hand. He's kind of a small man, around sixty or so. Got a pretty good thirst, so I thought he might be here. Jake's his name."

"Are you the undercover woman cop I been hearing about?"

"No, I'm a rancher."

"The man you're lookin' for, hon, he your father?"

"No, just an old friend. He's worked for my husband off and on for a long time. We're driving a herd of cattle through this area, taking them to auction, and he got his feelings hurt. Guess he left in a huff. I need to tell him I'm sorry if he's feeling unappreciated. The truth is, I can't do without him. He's a gamy old guy, but he sure knows his business."

Sadie beamed. "I know just who you're talking about, hon. You've come to the right place. He's in my apartment back 'a the bar. He got hisself cut up a bit in a fight, and I got him back there taking a bath."

Lindsey's mouth dropped open wide enough to accommodate the entire D-Day landing at Normandy.

"Taking a bath? I think we're talking about two different people."

"You said his name was Jake, didn't you, hon? This one sure is a Jake. Sure was in need of a bath, too."

"That sounds like my Jake," Lindsey conceded. "I don't know what you had to do to get him to take a bath. Jake would be afraid he'd lose what he calls his natural protection against evil spirits and flu bugs."

"You gotta understand these old-timers, hon. They ain't had the advantages of you younger folks. And I'd say off-hand Jake's closer to seventy than he is sixty. The only place the old-timers coulda taken a bath was in the middle of the kitchen floor. And if they had folks that cared, they got to take one once a week, usually Saturday night, so they'd smell sweet for church the next morning. But some weren't so lucky and didn't have nobody that cared, so they got outa the habit. Nobody to love 'em, see to their bath and clothes and things. All it takes is a little lovin' kindness, and you got these contrary folk eatin' outa your hand. Come on back here."

When Lindsey entered Sadie's living quarters, she hardly recognized Jake. He was shining like a sunbeam, wearing clothes that actually had some color to them. And he was grinning from ear to ear.

"How about this little lady?" he asked Lindsey. The big woman he nodded to, half again larger than he, had the grace to smile with modesty. "Ain't she sumpin' special?"

"Yes, Jake, she is. And you know what?" Lindsey laughed. "So are you, Jake! So are you!"

CHAPTER TWENTY

STAMPEDE

Wednesday morning dawned bright and fair. Overhead, jaunty white clipper ships sailed across the deep blue of the boundless sky. The horizon was flat in all directions but the west, where the recumbent Rockies quietly watched the little troop's progress.

By the fourth morning, the groans about sore muscles finally subsided. The Foofwahs had selected the better of the only two apparent choices: lie down and die, or get back on your horse and ride, ride, ride. At last, they faced their horses without despair.

New pain, however, sprang from a source not physical. Angie's downcast face told more than anyone wanted to know about her disappointment over Chan. Lindsey was unusually quiet, and Jake, always somber in the mornings, chattered away like an old magpie. What was his problem? the women wondered.

When Gina rubbed the sleep from her eyes, she glanced around at the glum faces until her eyes lit on Jake. "Jake, there's something different about you!"

Everyone's eyes turned in his direction. Indeed, something was different about Jake. His clothes were clean, his boots polished, and his whiskers trimmed.

Felon strolled through the gathering and paused long enough to sniff Jake's pant legs then followed Chloë while she poured hot coffee into everyone's mug. Chloë thought briefly of scalding the cat with the coffee but knew she couldn't do it. "Tell us, Jake," she asked, "what have you been up to?"

"So," Jake drawled, "what's it to ya?"

Lindsey, to avoid embarrassing Jake, hadn't mentioned to anyone her version of the evening before. Now she could contain herself no longer. "Jake has a lady friend in town."

Six pairs of curious eyes focused on Jake and, as one, the Foofwahs chanted, "Aaah-haah!"

"Don't want to talk about it," Jake said, the back of his neck turning red. He stomped off toward the horses, muttering his disgust with nosy women.

Lindsey filled in the details about Sadie, who she was and where. The women were impressed with Sadie's ability to maneuver Jake into a state of near-cleanliness. None of them had been able to taunt or intimidate him into taking a bath. In fact, he seemed to take pride in his filth.

"Do you think anything will come of it?" CC asked. Her matchmaker's acuity sensing romance, she poised for action. "Maybe we should have Angie tell Jake's fortune."

"Forget it," Angie said. "I blew it reading my own. If I gaze into my crystal ball, I'd likely see Chan and Jake as star-crossed lovers." She handed her empty coffee cup to Chloë and followed Jake toward the horses.

"I feel real bad about Angie," CC said. "I kind of felt all along that Chan was a skunk, but you'll have to admit, he hides it well."

Lindsey turned away to conceal any trace of guilt that might show in her eyes. She still felt uncomfortable about her meetings with Chan and her sensitivity toward him. Now, with Angie's interest in the man, she wanted no hint of rivalry between them. As far as anyone knew, her relationship with Chan was strictly business, and she cringed at the thought that the Foofwahs might recognize her foolish, romantic yen. She refilled her coffee and leaned thoughtfully against the Gypsy Spirit.

Gina's quick glance at Lindsey's stony face made her wonder if Lindsey felt a little envious of Chan's attention to Angie, at least before he stood her up. He was truly a remarkable looking man and polite too, the kind of man it would be hard to resist if he turned his attention your way. She was sure Lindsey's strong moral background had forced her into refusing the dinner date she'd been offered, though she'd joked with them earlier about Chan's offer to take her out.

Had she been in Lindsey's shoes and *her* inheritance at stake, Gina was certain she would have gone to dinner with Chan. As a businesswoman, she had spent many luncheons and dinners talking financial deals over cocktails beforehand. The implicit camaraderie had sealed numerous bargains to her advantage, and no one tried any hanky-panky with her! Well, maybe one or two entertained ideas, but it's all in how you handle the situation, she assured herself. Perhaps Lindsey had been too much of a prude for her own good this time. In spite of his good looks and charm, Lindsey could have trusted herself to use *him* rather than let him use her. She would have a talk with Lindsey.

Gina finished her coffee and, satisfied that she had worked through the vague something that had been bothering her, joined the others.

Jake sat impatiently astride his horse, chewing his whiskers and staring off toward the mountains in the west. Bundled with jackets and kerchiefs, the Foofwahs waited patiently, though their horses stomped and whinnied, breath rising as steam in the crisp morning air. The women weren't eager to be off, even if the horses did follow Jake's lead. The Foofwahs felt they would be happier sitting quietly, listening to the bird songs in the clear air than trudging off after a bunch of mindless cows.

* * *

Penny's agile mind found the six or so hours on the trail each day unbelievably dull and monotonous, though she loved the outdoors as much as anyone. She delighted in the bounteous splendor of the fields of golden wheat they passed and the green stalks of corn-like milo asserting its importance as a fall crop. She reveled in the beauty the myriad lakes and dams lent to the countryside, reflecting the breathtaking blue Colorado sky with such crystal clarity.

But six to eight hours of following the rear ends of cattle tended to deaden a person to the surrounding grandeur of nature. Certainly, a deep breath brought sneezes from dust and goldenrod if you were lucky enough to miss inhaling the ever-present stench of cowflop and horse piss.

After an hour of riding, the sun brought its usual warmth, and everyone began pulling off jackets and scarves. Penny rode forward to ask Lindsey about their distance today. Lindsey had only slept for three hours, and the morning's unrelieved dullness made her feel semi-comatose.

"You look as cross as a one-eyed bear, Lindsey. Do you want me to take the lead for a little while?"

Lindsey grunted, grateful to be snapped out of her lethargy, but she said, "No, thanks." She'd studied the map the night before and was a little worried. The original plan was to camp beside Caballero Creek, but now she wondered if the goal was realistic. It had been set at the beginning of the drive, before she realized how wearying the four-hour watches at night would be for the inexperienced women. Lindsey estimated that the distance to Caballero Creek meant riding twenty miles today instead of the usual fifteen. As tired as everyone was, she doubted they could make that distance.

She searched her saddlebag for a copy of the map. She needed to know where she was and what to expect along the way. She blamed herself for not riding over the route to check it out before they started. Worse, here she was leading them down the road to what? Maybe Chloë was right. Maybe this is the Purgatory Trail. Certainly they'd had a few misadventures. What hell might she be leading these dear friends into?

"Where is Jake, anyway?" Lindsey called to Penny. She turned in her saddle to look back over the cattle, but she couldn't see Jake or any of the women. They were letting the cattle stretch out too far and wide, considering the distance they had to cover. Oh, well, it's early still, she thought, determined to set her worries aside.

Lindsey turned to thoughts of Jake and how frisky he seemed this morning. Even Tonto seemed livelier. She chuckled. I wonder if Jake got more than a bath? Before she lost track of him, she'd heard him chatting lightheartedly with Penny and CC as he worked his way to the back. He even told CC a joke, and she heard them laughing together. Lindsey smiled at the thought of Jake telling a joke.

What a funny little old man he is with blue eyes that twinkle whenever he's amused or pleased with himself. He hasn't had many occasions for that lately! But today he's different. At breakfast, when he took off his hat for a moment, his hair, usually greasy and plastered to his head, was so shiny clean it fluttered in the breeze.

Thinking of Jake's good turn of spirits raised her own, then she heard Penny singing from her repertoire of camp songs. She looked over her right shoulder and saw Penny bobbing along, singing and talking to Old Bushmills, and Lindsey felt maybe things were okay after all.

On Jake's next round, Lindsey saw him pause to adjust one of Penny's stirrups without being asked. "If you're not careful," she heard Penny say, "all the Foofwahs will fall in love with you. You're outshining the sunflowers today, Jake."

Instead of his usual glower, Jake beamed with pleasure for a moment. Then he harrumphed and rode off, sitting a little taller in his saddle than before, Lindsey noticed.

* * *

Around noon, they crossed Arcilla Creek and came to a farm road. Neither presented a problem, though it was necessary to run the cattle along the road for a mile to get from one open range to another where they had permission to cross. Lindsey sent Gina ahead to act as a flagman at the front end in case any cars came along, and Jake took the duty at the rear.

To Gina's annoyance, she came upon Chan in his silver-blue pickup, which he'd swung cross-wise in the road and parked.

"I'm here to help you, ma'am, in any way I can," he said, leaning out the door and doffing his Stetson.

"Well, I guess the first thing you can do is move your pickup," Gina said. Why should she be polite to someone who had hurt her friend?

Chan appeared not to hear her, but sat in his pickup with the door open, his feet perched up on the dashboard while he listened to country western music.

"Cows like country western," he volunteered. "Makes them feel real calm and good about themselves."

Gina snorted. What a strange mixture of chivalry and chauvinism this man is.

Chan eased out of the pickup with the studied nonchalance and agile grace of a celebrity, obviously aware of his audience and ready to impress them with his magnificence. It occurred to Gina that his casual flair reflected the attitude of a man who made a career of having nothing really important to do.

When Lindsey approached, still riding on point, Chan saluted her with a hearty, "Hello, sweetheart, how's it going?"

Lindsey scowled, her expression clearly aimed to discourage any connection that would make her look like one of Chan's girlfriends. If he caught it, he gave no sign.

Few cars ever used the road, and this afternoon no one was in sight other than Chan. The barbwire fences on either side of the road served as barricades to keep the cattle between the fields of crops, and the passage went easily. Chan opened the wide cattle gate and held it until the herd and drovers passed through.

As each Foofwah passed Chan, he touched his hat, offered a dazzling smile, and bowed his courtly best.

When Angie rode through, he dropped the gate, and walked over to take her horse's reins. Angie reacted with icy politeness, her dark eyes masking the hurt she felt.

"I'm sorry about last night," Chan said. "One of my prize cows tried to deliver a breached calf. My men and I had our hands full trying to save her. By the time we got through, it was late. Very late. So I thought I'd just trust you to understand."

"Did you save her?" Angie asked.

"Who?"

"The cow." Angie winced at Chan's failure to follow the question. He could be lying, The excuse sounded pretty lame. On the other hand, if he were lying, why would he be here now? If he didn't want to see her, he could stay away.

"We lost the calf."

"Oh. I'm sorry."

"No, no. A pretty lady like you mustn't be sorry about anything on a beautiful day like this. Here, let me help you down."

Angie accepted his offer to help her dismount.

"Going my way?" Chan smiled with a mind-numbing pluck of her heartstrings as he lifted her from her horse.

"Is there any other way?" She sighed, looking up into his deep gray eyes, eyes that wrapped her into a tight little bundle of unrequited desire and consumed her.

"No."

They laughed together like two confederates, and Angie knew she couldn't remain mad at him. Chan offered her his arm in his mock-courtly style.

He led Twinkle to Jake and tossed him the reins as though Jake were a stable boy. Jake's amiable smile disappeared like the sun behind a cloud. His face flushed with humiliation and anger. Lindsey watched and sympathized. Jake did nice things for people if he liked them or because he wanted to but not when they treated him like a flunky.

The Foofwahs waved good-bye, and Angie and Chan walked through the gate, leaving it open. Each of the women watched, wrapped up in her own thoughts as the pickup roared to life and blasted off down the country road.

After the pickup disappeared, CC interrupted the silence. "Oh, shit! Seeing Angie go off with her hopes so high makes me feel mushy inside. I want so much for her to be happy! But at the same time, I have the same kind of emotions I felt when I helped my daughter dress for her high school graduation prom. She was so fresh, so innocent, so beautiful. I ached for her. I felt like I was dressing her as an offering for the gods, a sacrificial virgin to be slung over the precipice and crushed on the rocks below."

"Well, you can at least relieve your sentiments about Angie's virginity," Gina said. "She's a big girl and knows what she's doing ... I guess." She looked skeptical as she turned her horse to start rounding up cattle.

Jake secured the gate, scowling murderously under the brim of his cowboy hat while he worked.

* * *

As they rode, Penny could see Caballero Creek Reservoir toward the north, but she had seen few people this morning and many of the frame houses along the way stared across the prairie with vacant eyes. Built before the 1920s, the houses stood abandoned, the yards overgrown with weeds.

Twice they passed school buildings that once rang with the voices of children but now were empty, echoing only the wind. Blackened tumbleweeds from prior years laced themselves along the barbwire fences, a skeleton-like barricade for the newer crop already turning brown and taunting the wind, like an army of marauders poised for the attack. The grasses, high after the heavy rains of the summer, were turning a pinkish-blue from the recent dry spell.

Penny tried to relieve the monotony of the ride by identifying grasses but recognized only the wheat-like grama grass and Mormon tea. A taller, unfamiliar bush grew tiny, pointed hollow reeds that were like miniature organ pipes. Wind whistled through their stalks, accompanying the prairie's lonesome song. Attempting to invent a melody to capture the sound of the wind, she reached around the horse's flank to unhitch her guitar from its canvas cover.

Penny strummed and sang and thought how ironic it was that she'd hiked and biked across Europe and America but never had she moved at a pace so slow.

"I could have been in Canada by now if I'd been on foot, OB," she leaned forward and spoke into the horse's ear. He whinnied as if in acknowledgment that he too could have reached Canada, or even Mexico, if he weren't stuck with these plodding cows.

She stood in her saddle and looked around to see what the others were doing. Kai-ling was unusually subdued. For the first couple of days, she had squealed with delight whenever she spotted a baby rabbit hopping to safety or reveled at the beauty of a wildflower. Today, apathy seemed to have overwhelmed her. *Another twenty-four hours, just hang in.* Penny urged thought waves to Kai-ling who was too far back to hear her call against the wind.

* * *

Chloë had more or less mastered the tricky business of finding the roads where she could drive the Gypsy Spirit between campsites.

Relieved that she didn't have to ride with the herd, she rose earlier than anyone else to get the fire going and prepare breakfast. She often was the last to retire, leaving a thermos of hot tea for her friends when they came off duty. She even numbered Jake among her friends, unlike the other Foofwahs who were still halfway trying to figure out why they really needed him.

Thanks to Chloë, breakfast was the best time of day for everyone. The mornings didn't remain cold for long, just long enough to be invigorating. The cowboy coffee was strong and hot. Breakfast was the only time all of them ate together, so they took the time to enjoy a leisurely meal, joking and teasing each other and comparing notes on the day before. Then they would prepare for each day's drive.

Before breakfast, the riders fed and brushed down their horses and led them to the nearest lake or stream for a drink of water. After breakfast, the drovers, or droverettes as Jake persisted in calling them, saddled their horses and rounded up their cattle. Now, Chloë noted, four days into the drive, the Foofwahs seemed to be feeling fairly competent.

After everyone else left, her real work began: she packed up the food, cleaned the campsite of trash, washed CC's ceramic plates and mugs and the pots and pans. She doused the campfire, making sure no sparks could escape into the dry grass, and then carefully studied the map to find the roads to the next campsite—with Felon looking over her shoulder. She could almost tolerate the sight of the cat by now but refused to touch the filthy animal. At least, his breath had improved now that he was eating people food rather than mice, but she suspected he sneaked a few at night.

By the time Chloë finished her chores, the herd had already traveled several miles across the high plains but was still in sight.

The routine established the first day worked well: by the time the herd arrived at the prearranged campground, Chloë had the camp set up, a fire built, and dinner waiting. The variety in the menu never failed to surprise and delight the hungry drovers. To Jake's disgust, the Foofwahs voted to eliminate gravy from the menu, but the ever-popular biscuits remained.

* * *

Penny felt uneasy. The weather hadn't been a problem, but this afternoon thunderheads were gathering in the north and the breeze had a coolness to it. She'd heard frightening stories about the changeable weather on the high plains. One moment a beautiful, warm September day and with little warning a downpour could turn into a raging blizzard. Weather charts showed this part of the country to be among the coldest in the United States. She was glad it was still late summer and near the end or their trip, so below-zero temperatures were unlikely. "We'd be in deep cow-do if that happened, old boy," Penny said to OB, stroking his mane.

She wondered what Joe was working on today, then, feeling a little guilty about running off and leaving him to his carpentry, she turned her thoughts to the pioneers and their tribulations crossing these very plains, along the Santa Fe Trail. "What gritty women they must have been to have stuck it out with their men," she told OB. "Now we don't even have Indians looking to scalp us. We're surrounded by paved roads and interstate highways, our chuck wagon has a gasoline engine, and we think we've got it tough. Did you know this is called the 'High Lonesome,' OB?"

The horse nickered and tossed his head.

"You did? Well, aren't you the smart one?"

Glancing behind her again, it looked like everyone but Lindsey—still in the lead—had learned from Jake how to sleep in the saddle. What a crew, she thought.

Suddenly, Old Bushmills's ears pricked up, his attention riveted toward the north. Penny noted that the reservoir had disappeared behind a large hummock about a half-mile away, but nothing seemed unusual. Ahead but at some distance, she could see Tut racing toward Lindsey. He had been sitting managerially in the seat beside Chloë when the Gypsy Spirit passed near the herd earlier.

Penny searched the horizon, but nothing appeared out of the ordinary. OB continued to keep his eyes pinned toward the north.

"What is it, OB? What's so interesting out there?" She could see one of his nostrils flare.

The horse snorted but didn't take his eyes from whatever fascinated him.

She called to Lindsey, but Lindsey's attention was distracted by a wandering calf that needed to be brought back to the herd.

As Penny started to rein OB around, he whinnied and danced a little sideways step. Clearly the horse was uneasy. Penny sniffed the air. Smoke? She scanned the horizon. Surely it was her imagination. Soon she noticed a thin gray wisp rising from behind the hummock. Tut was drawing nearer and she could hear his urgent bark. The smoke must be from a rancher burning trash or clearing a field of stubble. Nothing to get excited about.

Risking a yell, she called again to Lindsey.

"Can you see that smoke?" Penny pointed toward the hummock.

"Yes," Lindsey returned her call. "Smells like grass smoke. Probably someone clearing off a field."

Tut's actions drew their attention. The dog pounced, backed up, barked, and pounced again. He wasn't just being playful. Whatever he was excited about was serious business. He ran toward the hummock and circled back toward her, all the time barking furiously.

"Tut, what's the matter with you?" Lindsey decided to ride over to the knoll and look around. "Penny, take over my position while I try to find out what's got Tut crazy," she called over her shoulder. "I hope it isn't a snake or a skunk."

Lindsey whistled to Tut but he didn't respond other than to continue barking and circling back and forth.

As she rode toward the knoll, the smell of burning grass became stronger. Then she could see smoke, lots of smoke. She spurred Ringo to greater speed. As she crested a second, larger knoll, she stared in horror at the scene spread out before her.

Below lay a shallow valley about ten miles long where Caballero Creek Reservoir nestled and sparkled in the afternoon sun. But between Lindsey and the lake a grass fire raged over an area at least two miles wide. Flames leapt high in the air and the acrid, white smoke stung her nose and eyes. The fire roared toward her at an alarming speed, whipped by the constant wind that blew across the prairie.

She had warned the Foofwahs that the recent dryness had made the high grass vulnerable to fires, and it was obvious this one was out of control.

"Oh, my God! Tut! Come boy!" Without waiting to see if the dog obeyed, Lindsey turned her nervous horse and galloped back to the herd.

"Grass fire! Grass fire!" she yelled. Jake was at the rear with CC and Kai-ling. They were too far off to hear her shrieks of alarm. Penny and Gina were near enough to hear but hadn't reacted yet. They appeared stunned as they tried desperately to recall Lindsey's instructions in case of fire.

Lindsey raced toward the rear shouting, "Grass fire!" and pointing toward the knoll. "Stampede the cattle! Caballero Creek's not more than five miles ahead. Get them out of here!"

Jake snapped to attention when he finally heard Lindsey's frantic cries. "What the ..." He took off toward the knoll to verify for himself that Lindsey's panic was well-founded. He soon realized she was right and fell into helping the women draw the cattle into a tighter group before frightening them into a panic.

"Whooee hah!" The women yelled like drunken cowboys, waving their hats and spurring their horses to run at the startled cattle. As though a single body, the herd, already nervous from the smoke smell, took off at a breakneck run. Gina and Penny moved out of their way, then raced alongside to keep the cattle from veering in the wrong direction. Penny's guitar worked loose from its tie and flew through the air, to be crushed by the onrushing herd.

Riding at the front of the herd again, Lindsey gasped in horror as she saw Chloë and the Gypsy Spirit approaching over the rough ground. She doesn't realize what's happening. She'll be in the way of the herd!

Lindsey spurred Ringo to even greater speed as she raced toward Chloë to warn her out of the way.

"Chloë! Head to your left," she screamed, waving her arms. She could see Chloë's startled expression through the windshield. Felon's wide eyes peered from the cottage window over the bookshelf.

Chloë swung the truck wide to the left of the onrushing cattle, then turned and began to herd stray calves with the bumping, jolting Gypsy Spirit, at times blasting the air horn to get their attention.

Tut joined CC and Kai-ling and nipped at the heels of any cow needing motivation. If a cow or calf fell behind or tried to feint to the right or left and leave the herd, the dog gave it his special attention.

The flames swept over the crest of the knoll like a giant harvester devouring the grass and leaving behind a smoking, blackened wasteland. The distance between the herd and the fire narrowed. Everything appeared to Lindsey to be happening in slow motion except the encroaching fire.

Lindsey's review of the map earlier had revealed Caballero Creek was west of them about five miles but meandered southeast. It doglegged and turned to flow due east for about three miles before again turning southeast. It was to this eastern flowing leg of the creek that she aimed the herd.

"Faster, Ringo, faster." She spurred the horse again and again.

Suddenly, Lindsey had a horrid thought. She needed to confer with Jake. She could see him over her right shoulder and yelled, "What if Caballero Creek has no water? What if the trees catch fire?" She quickly realized the futility of his hearing over the noise of the pounding hooves and bawling cattle.

After covering what Lindsey estimated to be three miles, she could see a line of trees ahead that surely bordered the banks of Caballero Creek. Any creek will do, she thought, if it only has water!

Jake seemed to share her worries, for when he saw her waving frantically, he caught up with her and called, "If there ain't enough water in the creek to protect the cattle or stop the fire, keep 'em moving down the creek bed. Don't let 'em out of the creek unless the trees catch fire. We'll drive 'em on down to the Arkansas River. We can't be far from the Arkansas."

Angie isn't the only one reading minds these days, Lindsey thought, then forced back hysteria. How did Angie miss this in her crystal ball? She slapped Ringo across the rump with her reins. She had to keep ahead of the herd. How hard can you run a horse before you run him to death?

CHAPTER TWENTY-ONE

BOGGED DOWN

Jake raced beyond the pounding cattle to position himself on the bank and turn the animals down the creekbed. Lindsey joined him, understanding exactly what he planned. Gradually, they turned the stampeding herd and guided them into the trees and toward the creek. At the point Jake selected for the herd to enter Caballero Creek, both sides of the creek had a skirting of trees, but little brush. The creek flowed southeast and its bed was as wide as a two-lane road, protected by the deep embankment.

But the first cattle to reach the creek milled about instead of heading down the steep slope into the water. The embankment proved to be a bottleneck. Gina and Penny worked among the milling cattle, whipping them across their rumps with ropes to force them into the creekbed. In a frenzy of terror, one by one, the cattle slid down the bank.

The creek contained little water and wouldn't provide much protection if the trees caught fire. The smoke could trap and suffocate the cattle if they weren't roasted alive first.

"Keep the cattle moving," Jake yelled as the other Foofwahs approached. "We have to keep the herd moving toward the Arkansas."

The cattle were winded and tiring as they crashed among the trees lining the creek. Slowing down kept them from tumbling pell-mell over the embankment into the creekbed, breaking legs and crushing the smaller calves. Once they reached the streambed, being thirsty, the animals wanted to stop for a drink. The early arrivals could not be allowed to blockade the progress of the others or the result would be disastrous. Forcing them to move down the narrow ravine would be slow and cumbersome, but the eight-foot walls of the embankments on both sides kept the cattle from escaping once they entered the creekbed.

From her position on the edge of the embankment, Gina flailed angrily at the stupid beasts that had succeeded for the time being in outrunning the flames themselves but blocked the progress of the unfortunate animals that were still in danger.

"Hoy! Hoooeee! Giddup there!" she yelled. Even lashings with leather reins had little result. The cattle moved sluggishly, grudgingly, into the creekbed. Later arrivals continued to pile up behind them, and those on the edge of the embankment were crowded and pushed into the stream below. Pandemonium resulted.

CC and Kai-ling arrived and with Lindsey's help coaxed their horses down the embankment so they could urge the lingering cattle out of the way. Lindsey and Penny stayed above to check the progress of the encroaching grass fire and to make sure all the cattle entered the ravine.

The fire, less than a mile away, continued to roar and gain on them. Lindsey could see it would take more than prayers to keep the dry leaves of the trees and the brush beneath the trees from catching fire.

The next time Lindsey looked back, she saw, silhouetted against the flames and smoke, the Gypsy Spirit driven hell bent toward the creek. As Lindsey continued to flail the cattle, she kept her eye on the Gypsy Spirit until she was sure Chloë would outrun the flames. From the many cattle scrambling down the embankment, the slope eroded enough to make the leap less steep and frightening for the later cattle.

When Chloë reached the grove of trees alongside the creek, she plowed the truck into a fallen log and could go no further. As she fled from the Gypsy Spirit, she tripped over an exposed tree root but picked herself up and hurried down the slope to the streambed.

The drovers were having trouble forcing the herd down stream, for once in the creekbed and away from the smoke and flames the panic of the animals subsided. Exhausted and thirsty, they advanced slowly.

Lindsey turned her attention to the sparser grass growing beneath the trees. With luck the thinner growth would diminish the fire considerably as it approached the tree trunks, but she was all too aware that it would take only one little patch of dry grass or brush to kindle the trees.

"You can ride the spare horse," Penny told Chloë. The spare horse had a halter, but it didn't have a saddle.

"Fine with me," Chloë said. She struggled up on the animal's back, assisted by a push from Penny.

"Sorry you have to ride bareback," Penny said. "Jake has Angie's horse up ahead. You can switch when we catch up."

"This'll do," Chloë said. A wallop against her back and the rearing of her horse almost tossed her from the nervous animal. Reaching back, she felt the rough fur of Felon. "Oh, gawd, no!" Tingles ran up her spine at the thought of touching the thing, but she didn't have the heart to push the frightened cat to the ground to be trampled by the cattle. "Well, hang on," she relented. "I guess you're one of God's creatures too and deserve to be saved." With Tut circling, Chloë clung frantically to the horse, and Felon dug his claws into the thick back pockets of Chloë's jeans as they followed Penny.

Lindsey eased her way through the herd toward the head of the line of cattle. It was slow working her way among the tight knots of cattle trying to move down the streambed. But Gina and Jake were busy keeping the cattle moving and someone needed to be riding in front.

They came to a clear section free of trees for as far as Lindsey could see. She viewed the clearing with relief. It removed the danger of fiery trees falling on them. But the grass fire was burning within twenty yards of the embankment.

She saw Gina scramble up the embankment with a towel soaked in creek water. Gina began furiously beating at an encroaching arm of flames that threatened to reach a crevice filled with dry leaves and dead brush. If the fire entered the ravine, there was little for it to feed on, but the cattle nearby would again panic and cause untold havoc.

When the towel became too charred and shredded to use, Gina grabbed her Stetson, Revenuer model, and flailed madly at the fingers of flame still eluding her authority. Finally, the danger past, she slid down the embankment and looked as though she might collapse.

"I can't believe I did that," Gina cried, her face and arms blackened by the smoke. "I'm scared to death of fire."

Lindsey helped her to her horse, and Gina stood with her face pressed against the saddle for a few seconds while she shuddered with relief.

Continuing toward the front of the line, Lindsey saw that the fire was losing momentum and beginning to sputter and die out. That's odd, she thought. The grass is equally thick here and deep. Why would it be dying out?

She decided to investigate. Turning a reluctant Ringo up the now shallow embankment, she rode into the path of the fire. As she watched, flames all around her diminished and disappeared. Lindsey was shocked to note the earth outside the creekbed was neither firm nor dry but moist and soggy. The fire was dying because the grass and soil were no longer dry.

From her vantage point on higher ground, she could see off to the south and east miles and miles of cattails and tall reeds. Oh, dear God! Swampland!

Lindsey's minds-eye recalled the map. Arcilla Creek and Caballero Creek were very close together when they entered the Arkansas. The herd was now behind or west of the Arkansas River dam and the lake. The dam backed the lake into the mouth of the creeks, forming a swamp several miles long. She knew they had to stop the cattle before they ended up in the swamp.

Lindsey rejoined the refugees in the creek and raced ahead to the front of the line. But she was too late. The creek banks gradually lowered until they completely disappeared allowing the stream to spread out and form the miles-long marsh.

Already, the twenty or thirty head of cattle in the lead were up to their bellies in the black, boggy water. Lindsey was the first on the scene, and the first to discover this newest crisis.

We saved the herd from the fire and will lose it in the bog—or in quicksand, she realized. I've got to stop the rest of the cattle. We could lose the whole herd.

She wheeled her horse to retrace the route back down the creekbed. It wasn't easy bucking the traffic of the oncoming herd, though the exhausted cattle had slowed to an amble.

The first rider she met was Gina. "We have to stop the herd and hold them here," Lindsey cried. "We've run into a marsh and twenty or thirty head are already mired down."

Gina understood. "I'll tell the others we can't force the cattle any further."

Gina worked her way to the end of the line, shouting, "Stop! Stop! There's a marsh and possibly quicksand ahead!" Jake was now bringing up the rear of the herd and the last to get the news.

If the creek water had a calming effect on the cattle, the marsh had a paralyzing effect. The bull Fernando had led the first couple of dozen head twenty yards into the bog before the mud forced them to halt. The combined efforts of the drovers stopped the remainder of the confused cattle, so no others waded into the bog. Lindsey knew they had nothing more to fear from the fire. It had begun to die out for lack of fuel at about the same time the leaders of the herd reached the marshlands.

One by one, the Foofwahs left their positions and rode forward to see for themselves. Their hearts sank. The cattle that weren't up to their bellies in the deadly muck were struggling to lift their feet out of the black ooze. A cow would strain mightily to pull one leg free from the sucking mud, then put it back down into the same spot to lift another leg. Each time she changed feet, she sank lower into the mire.

The women were silent as they realized the magnitude of the job lying ahead.

CC was the first to speak. "How in hell do you get cattle out of a marsh full of cattails and water moccasins?" Frozen horror on each face told the story. No one answered, but no one turned away.

"We don't have to worry about water moccasins this far north," Jake offered, to make them feel easier. He felt kind of sorry for the women, getting into more than they bargained for, but he'd be grateful to have their help, *any* help getting the bogged down animals out of this mire. He knew the burden of the work would fall to him. "Rattlers is the worst we have to worry about around here."

"Indeed," Lindsey said. "What do we do now, Jake?" Her tone reflected her exhaustion, frustration, and a hint of annoyance that he'd felt it necessary to comment on rattlers.

The sun was getting low and Jake estimated they had less than two hours of daylight left. To Lindsey's question, Jake removed his hat and scratched his head, then answered, "Waalll, I dunno. I think the first thing we need to do is find a dry spot on the other side of the creek so the rest of the herd can be controlled. And we gotta send someone back to make sure Chloë and the truck are safe."

"I mean about these cattle, Jake. What do we do about the ones in the bog? Chloë and the truck are safe. Anyway, I'm not worried about the Gypsy Spirit. It can be replaced, but cattle can't." This time, Lindsey was openly cross. She turned to Kai-ling and asked her to backtrack along the creek and find a place where the cattle could be contained on the other side, a spot with enough forage for the cattle to graze.

"I'm a thinkin'," Jake responded with equal irritability, "this ain't the sorta position a cowpoke is called upon to get hisself out of ever' day. Though it ain't unheard of either. But I never been in this kind of jackass mess in my life."

The women winced. Did he think *they* were responsible for the mess they were in now?

Jake replaced his hat and sat on his horse, staring off at the cattle in the bog. "It requires a bit of thinkin'. If we had some ropers now, it'd be simple enough. We'd just rope 'em and pull 'em out one at a time. Some of 'em are already strainin'. But them cattle's too tired to try very hard and ain't got the strength to work at it for long, so we go at it fast. A cow that's bogged down gets excited and struggles until she's plumb tuckered out and dies. We don't have the manpower to handle that much bogged down beef."

"You're a top-notch roper, Jake," Lindsey said, "and I can rope some."

Gina spoke up. "CC and Chloë can keep the rest of the herd together in the creekbed until Kai-ling finds a place to pasture the herd and camp for the night. Penny and I can haul the cows out after you and Lindsey rope 'em. It will be slow, but I think we can do it."

"I'm afraid once we begin to rope them," Lindsey said, "the others will get excited and start to mill around. Then we'll be in bigger trouble. What scares me is the possibility of quicksand." Lindsey was too tired to think clearly.

"Ain't going to do much millin' around in that bog, and can't be no quicksand in there. If there was, them cattle'd be sunk outta sight before now," Jake argued. "What we gotta do is git them critters outta there. *Raaght* now! Let's git started!"

Lindsey showed Gina and Penny how to dally their ropes around the saddle horn to gain enough leverage to pull the cattle out.

Jake spurred his horse gingerly into the bog and roped the nearest cow. Then he dallied his rope around the saddle horn and let the horse pull the cow forward until she realized she either had to move or be strangled. With a valiant effort, the cow struggled to free each leg, taking painfully slow steps until Jake pulled her to the edge of the bog. Gina exchanged Jake's rope for the rope that had dangled uselessly on her saddle for the entire drive. She dallied the rope around her saddle horn and urged her horse to gently force the cow to take the last four or five steps out of the bog and up onto the dry bank. She was grateful now for the ugly, coarse gloves CC provided when the trip began.

Lindsey eased her horse into the muck, threw the lariat and connected on the first try. After much struggling on the part of the cow, Lindsey led her to the side of the bog and turned her over to Penny.

* * *

CC and Chloë were having their own problems. All too soon, the cattle in the creekbed became restless. They were tired and hungry. Their thirst slaked by the creek water, they now wanted to graze. All the grass on the east side of the creek was blackened by the fire. Some spots in the burned grass still smoldered. The cattle began to mill about and slip through gullies and bushes to find their way out of the imprisoning creekbed.

Sensing they wouldn't be able to hold the cattle much longer, CC was becoming frantic by the time Kai-ling returned from her reconnoitering mission. She'd found a spot where the riverbed made a slight cradle, leaving about a five-acre area of dry, swamp-free grassland on the other side of the creek. And she'd found a wide enough cut for the cattle to get out of the ravine.

With the advantage of high creek banks on both sides, CC, Kai-ling, and Chloë—still bareback astride her horse with the cat managing to hang on behind—blocked the cattle from pushing further upstream. Tut at Chloë's side barked orders. Together, they turned the cattle around and drove them back north for a mile to the dry grassland. Though cramped for space, the cattle gradually eased into the dry area and settled down to graze.

* * *

An hour later, with darkness fast approaching, CC joined the rescue team along the edge of the bog. She reported that the rest of the herd was now pastured and being guarded by Chloë and Kai-ling.

CC edged her horse into the bog and quickly picked up the technique of dropping her rope over a cow too mired down to shake off the loop. With an extra pair of hands to help, the work went faster. Several times, Jake dismounted, and, standing in muck over his boot tops, urged and yanked a calf to firm ground. Thirty-seven head had entered the bog.

The evacuation process was long and arduous. The cattle unused to being roped, fought against the lariat.

Shortly before sundown, Chloë went back to check on the Gypsy Spirit to see if it was still intact and if she could scavenge enough food for dinner. She was relieved to find it had not burned, nor had the fire reached the trees bordering the stream.

The thicker grasses leading up to the trees were now blackened, and here and there dried cowflop still simmered and smoked, reminding her that pioneer women used dried buffalo patties as fuel for preparing meals. She wondered how long they burned and, if the wind changed, would there be any danger from straggling grasses beneath the trees catching fire.

She hurried to gather up a few utensils and found a canned ham and bread. At Kai-ling's campsite, Chloë made sandwiches and a pot of coffee and had a meal ready when the group finally finished their backbreaking job.

* * *

When Jake roped the last cow and walked it to the edge of the bog, he looked like a swamp zombie. He was almost completely covered with black muck. The women looked only slightly less vile, and all were deathly tired. Together, they drove the rescued cattle back up the creek to rejoin the herd. Two of the cows stumbled and fell from exhaustion. Only one bull, Fernando, had drowned struggling in the swamp before they could reach him. All things considered, it was a successful rescue effort, but they were too tired to congratulate themselves.

At the campsite, Chloë dispensed food to each grateful drover. When Jake reached out a hand for his sandwich, his eyes dropped to her chest. "Now ain't that a sight," he said.

Aggravated, Chloë's eyebrows pinched together. Can no disaster could stop men from ogling women's breasts? she thought. Glancing down, she saw "Chloë, Swamp Lady," colorfully emblazoned on her T-shirt from the writers' conference. She began to laugh and point and soon the whole crew began to whoop and carry on until tears made ruts through their blackened cheeks.

Suddenly, an ear-splitting "whoosh" filled the air, and the sky lit up in a resplendent display of flares and sky rockets. Exploding tin cans and shards of CC's ceramic plates rained on the surrounding countryside. The still-smoldering fire had reached the truck's gas tank and Angie's hidden cache of fireworks. That night the Gypsy Spirit fulfilled its destiny and entered into Colorado history.

CHAPTER TWENTY-TWO

ANGIE'S DATE

As they drove along little-used roads, Chan pointed out landmarks: the Arcilla Creek Reservoir, the once proud but now tumbling-down Olive Branch schoolhouse, boundaries of neighbors' property. He talked easily, his manner reflecting his love of the area and the land.

Angie began to wonder how much further they would drive when Chan pulled off the main road onto a lightly graveled dirt road leading to Bountiful Reservoir and Harmony Lake. He stopped the pickup at a point with a full view of pretty Harmony Lake. These reservoirs were much smaller and the waves less pronounced than the ones Angie had passed on the cattle drive. Nevertheless, Harmony was the most impressive of all. Surrounded by stubble from harvested crops rather than grassland, the area appeared richer, more prosperous than the grassy plains she'd become accustomed to on the cattle drive. Chan explained that the harvested corn, milo, and maize would be used as ensilage, winter feed for the animals.

"You'll find everything in this high plains country is geared toward raising cattle."

"This is all very lovely." Angie breathed in the fresh, pure air. "But why are we stopping here?"

"For this ..." Chan bent over to kiss her on the lips. A tentative kiss, inviting but lacking passion. Chan drew back slightly, while his eyes searched hers for a response. Angie found her emotions struggling mightily with the reality imposed by her mind. It had been several years since she'd been attracted by any man into an intimate affair. With such ambivalence, she hesitated.

"Nice?" Chan's gentle voice prompted.

Her slow reaction fumbled with a seriousness she didn't quite comprehend in herself. Hadn't she thrown herself at the man? Why was she holding back? Suddenly, Angie turned in the seat, placed her arms around his neck, and pulled him toward her hungry lips. Her kiss brimmed with fervor. Now she felt the stirring she'd suppressed as she sought his encouraging lips. His strong hands caressed her shoulders and held her close.

"Nice." She smiled into his eyes, capturing a look filled with promise and knowing her eyes radiated acceptance. But even as she yielded to his touch, she felt a sense of uneasiness. The sensation passed quickly, and she melted comfortably into his arms.

Without a word, Chan restarted the engine, turned the pickup around, and drove back to the main highway.

"My place is nearby," he said.

They soon turned off the road and passed under the archway leading to Chan's home. "There it is. Tres Alamos." Chan nodded proudly to the imposing Victorian mansion at the end of the long driveway. Resuming the role of gracious host, he told her, "I think you'll like the house. It was originally built in 1892, but Yvonne, my ex, spent a great deal of time and money refurbishing it. She did a wonderful job of decorating inside and having the lacework outside restored. I'll give her credit for that."

"It's beautiful!" Angie breathed, at a loss for an adequate reflection of her awe. She had long admired Victorian houses, but owning one had always been a remotely shimmering dream. The man beside her, displaying great pride and sentimentality, grew in stature in her eyes. What must it be like to possess such a grand estate? What a man! "The latticework is lovely."

"Yvonne called it latticework, but it looks like lace to me around the verandahs and eaves. Someone had removed all the lacework and destroyed the original character of the house."

Offering her the usual visitor's tour, Chan took her arm and guided her through the house. He smiled with pride and amusement at Angie's inability to express herself. She seemed usually so quick with words.

"You're almost as wide-eyed as your friend Lindsey was when she was here," he said.

"Lindsey? Lindsey here?" Something didn't compute. Lindsey hadn't mentioned being in Chan's house. She eyed him questioningly.

Chan was quick to read her expression. "She only stopped by a few minutes the other day on her way to town." He gave Angie a reassuring hug. "That's all."

"I'm glad to hear that!" Angie looked relieved. This would be a new ballgame if he were playing around with Lindsey. With a whole different set of rules. In fact, she'd have to tell Chan he'd struck out with her, and she didn't want to have to do that.

After showing Angie through the bedrooms, Chan led her by the hand downstairs and through a breezeway to the glass-enclosed swimming pool and hot tub. The roof had been opened to capture the sunshine and warmth of the September afternoon.

"Can we swim?" she asked. She longed for the coolness of a refreshing shower or a dip in the pool. What must Chan think of her? She felt like a dusty little brown toad but she'd far rather feel like a princess in these palatial surroundings.

"We can swim, but not until I show you my pride and joy."

A snicker slipped from Angie's lips.

Chan pretended to be hurt. "You're laughing at me."

"A friend of mine once asked if I wanted to see his 'pride and joy.' I leaped to the conclusion that he meant his ... you know."

Chan grinned. "And it was ...?"

"Two photos, one in black and white and one in color, of household cleansers, Pride and Joy."

"I can guarantee you my pride and joy are not household cleansers. But let me modify my offer first. Would you like to see my most prized collection? I'll save the 'pride and joy' for later, and I don't think you'll be disappointed."

Angie's heart raced. Things are happening so fast, she thought. I'm an experienced, mature woman. Why is it I feel like a foolish schoolgirl?

Chan took her through his walnut and red-leather office and on into the adjoining saddle museum. He was proud of his tooled leather-and-silver-bedecked saddles and gave her a lengthy explanation of the history of each. He was even prouder of his horses, stabled next to the museum. He introduced Angie to each of the eight horses, but he lingered longest over his white gelding, Challenger.

"This is the horse I've dreamed about all my life. He's so well trained, I had to attend six sessions of classes in Brussels before the Belgian owners would sell him to me for forty thousand dollars. I ride him in parades."

"You must be quite a lady-killer," she smiled, stroking Challenger's white neck. "I assume he's a thoroughbred, but what kind is he, quarter horse, Morgan, Tennessee Walker, Peruvian Passo?" Angie wanted him to know she was somewhat knowledgeable about horses.

Chan laughed. "Peruvian Passos are all roans, a deep reddish color. Actually, this one was bred for hunting and jumping, though I've never used him for that, and I purposely selected one that had not yet been trained in those specialties. It means they are warm-bloods or pedigreed non-thoroughbreds. My experience with thoroughbreds has been that they are hot-blooded, unpredictable, and fragile, and most of them were behind the door when digestive systems were given out. I've had a couple of thoroughbreds. One of them jumped when frightened, and the other got his front feet caught beneath the lower corral railing. Both of them twisted their intestines, and there was nothing we could do to save them." Chan patted the neck of Challenger lovingly.

Angie looked on admiringly as Chan divulged his lavish, extravagant lifestyle and passion for good horses. She thought about her nomadic lifestyle in the Gypsy Spirit and wondered how much the freedom of the road was worth.

Despite niggling self-pity and envy, Angie raved about everything. She raved so much, she ran out of superlatives and feared sounded monotonous, or worse, insincere when she was truly impressed.

After the tour, Angie asked if she could be excused to go freshen up. Chan told her to use the pink-and-white bedroom and bath she recognized as Yvonne's.

"Look around. Help yourself. I think you'll find most everything. When Yvonne left, she didn't take much with her but some good, *very* good jewelry," Chan said. He turned away, speaking more to himself than to Angie, "But then she didn't have to. The divorce settlement gave her enough to redecorate the Taj Mahal."

They stood in the doorway to the elaborately chandeliered dining room. "Put on a bathing suit and a beach robe. I thought we'd swim for a while, then cook steaks on the patio. But before you go, I'll mix you a drink. What's your choice?"

Angie started to say "beer," then thought better of it. The ambiance seemed to demand something more genteel than the favored libation of her vagabond lifestyle. "White wine?"

"Hmmm," Chan nodded. He disappeared into the adjoining wet bar and lounge, with its gleaming crystal and red leather nearly as elegant as the dining room.

When he returned, he handed Angie a stemmed glass of sparkling clear liquor. "I thought a martini more appropriate to the situation," he smiled, looking deep into her idolizing brown eyes. He pulled her close. She carefully juggled the glass and lifted her face to receive his kiss. The kiss, at first a gentle teasing of her parted lips, became an exploratory probing with his tongue, long and hard.

Her body already awakened, Angie felt her toes curl.

"That was to hold me until you return, my adorable little gypsy. It's the last time you'll be out of my sight this evening," he promised, seeming reluctant to release her.

"I won't be long ..."

* * *

Upstairs, Angie found Yvonne's room quickly. It fairly shouted of the feminine presence of its former occupant. Angie stood on the pink hooked rug and slowly took in the snowy white lace, lace, lace everywhere and the high, canopied bed, its lace curtains tied back at each post with enormous pink bows. The bed was covered with a pink-and-white down comforter and skirted with white lace dust ruffles. The headboard was piled high with white lace and pink taffeta pillows. Angie had never seen a room like this.

"Right out of *House Beautiful*," she breathed. She resisted the temptation to leap into the middle of the high bed and make angel's wings on the billowy down comforter. "Stop it! You're a grown-up!" She chuckled to herself delightedly as she continued her inspection. A delicate little Empire writing desk in front of the lace curtains at the corner windows, a pink-and-white tufted chaise longue, and white Louis XIV furniture etched with gold attested to the exquisite taste of Yvonne.

Halfway expecting to see Chan's ex-wife step from behind the long wall of mirrored closets, Angie soon located a drawer filled with bathing suits. Chan was right. Most still had store tags. She tried on several before picking a royal blue bikini trimmed with white. Pleased that it fit, she was nevertheless somewhat unnerved over being so close in size to Yvonne. Angie posed in front of a closet mirrored door, surprised at the shapely figure she had developed after the exercise and weight loss of the past few days. She had to admit she looked great in the bikini. Smiling, she sipped from her cocktail while continuing to admire herself in the magnificent room, surrounded by lavish furnishings. Even this room had its own crystal chandelier.

"Not bad—but spooky," she smiled to the figure in the mirror, then hurried to find a robe before the specter of Yvonne could catch up with her.

She hated to delay getting back to Chan but decided it would be wise first to rinse off the layers of dust and sweat. She stepped inside the clear glass shower stall and indulged in a fragrant cleansing with pink soap that left her scented deliciously of lilies-of-the-valley. She even shampooed, thinking her hair would be wet soon anyway but how much nicer if it smelled good. In the mirror, her tanned cheeks glowed not just from being scrubbed but from the excitement of romance.

Isn't it interesting, she thought, that Chan and his wife kept separate bedrooms. She liked the idea of the strain in their intimacy long before they separated.

Before returning downstairs, she selected an ankle-length patio dress in earth tones to wear during dinner. The bodice was strapless but Angie found a simple white linen jacket to add later when the evening would grow chilly. She spread the outfit on the bed for a quick change after swimming.

Unable to find sandals small enough ("Ha, Yvonne had big feet!"), Angie descended the sweeping, carpeted staircase barefoot. Chan was sprawled casually on an enormous divan, already dressed in a beach robe, and, she assumed, bathing trunks underneath. Seeing him thus, a sensuous, warm feeling spread through her body, and she anticipated his embrace.

Chan rose, martini in hand, and took a few steps toward her, then abruptly halted. The startled expression on his face was that of a man who'd seen a ghost. Confused, Angie stopped too, her hand still on the banister.

"What's the matter?" she asked. Her alarmed first thought was that he was having a seizure, he appeared so stricken, so cold. Then, an unwelcome fear gripped her as she returned his frozen stare. This man she so greatly admired was really a stranger. What if he's a serial killer? Or a Bluebeard? What do I know of where Yvonne is? Maybe he tortures his women and throws them into a dungeon for his pleasure when it needs sating. "What ...?" She stood rigid, unable to continue.

Chan shook his head, then laughed, embarrassed.

"Nothing. It's just that, for a moment you looked ... Never mind. You look wonderful. In fact, ravishing. I had no idea ..." He untied the sash of her robe and his glance traveled slowly, appreciatively, over her well-developed figure.

"That I was so nearly the same size as your ex-wife?" She unconsciously adjusted the bikini bra that was just a little too small. She looked down and quickly retied the sash. "I was a little surprised myself." Angie tried to keep her voice light to conceal her nervousness. "I hope the outfit I've chosen for dinner won't bring back unhappy memories."

"Nonsense." He pulled her close and led her toward the patio door.

"I have to admit," he gave her a squeeze, "your appearance gave me a start. It's not as if Yvonne died or anything like that. In fact, she's very much alive, dating, and having a wonderful time."

"Does that bother you?"

"Hell, no! Well ... sometimes. But we're not here to talk about my ex-wife. Here, let me freshen your drink." He stepped to the portable bar and picked up the frosty martini pitcher.

"I left my glass upstairs. I'll go get it."

"Oh, no. You're not leaving me again." He took her arm and led her to the bar where he poured another glass and lifted it to her lips. She took a tiny swallow and removed the glass from Chan's hand before setting it down.

"I gather you're not much of a drinker," he said, running his hand inside her robe and around to the back of her bra. The warmth and sureness of his hand against her skin filled her with a desire for intimacy but instead she moved away.

"On the circuit, the carnies and the concessionaires get together in the evenings for a beer occasionally. I was raised in the Bible belt by strict fundamentalist parents. Everything fun was a sin. That included having a cocktail, playing cards, dancing, you name it." Angie took a sip from her martini. Its warmth spread through her, and she began at last to relax.

She continued. “My mother had nine children. Apparently sex was allowed since begetting was mentioned in the Bible, but I don’t think they were supposed to think it was fun.”

“Bet they lied,” he grinned, “the men, anyway.”

“Bet you’re right,” she agreed.

Chan stepped behind the bar and miraculously appeared with a tray of hors d’oeuvres. “Millie, my cook, made these before she left for the day. Let’s take them to the pool.”

Angie was starved. She’d had no lunch, and the tiny sandwiches with a variety of fillings and crackers topped with a medley of cheeses looked terribly tempting. She selected a cracker with cream cheese and caviar.

“Mmmm, delicious!” She resisted taking another.

They each took a tray of snacks, and Chan carried the martini pitcher into the pool house. The dying sun’s rays gave the pool a pink, misty glow that made the room look like the end of a rainbow.

Angie’s work schedule seldom allowed time for relaxation such as swimming. She’d learned to swim as a child but hadn’t been near a pool for several years. It wasn’t her favorite sport.

She was relieved when Chan sat down, placed the tray of appetizers in front of them on a glass-topped table, and helped himself. Angie did the same, nibbling daintily to take the edge off her appetite so she wouldn’t embarrass herself by gobbling down her food later. After six years of preparing her own meals and eating alone, she hoped to avoid such a social faux pas, but she sure was hungry.

They talked casually for a few minutes, then Chan stood and slipped out of his robe. “Race you to the water,” he said, pulling Angie to her feet.

“No contest,” she laughed and followed him to the pool.

Chan, poising on the diving board, dove cleanly into the water. He swam easily, his strong strokes cutting through the water with scarcely a ripple. Angie watched, admiring his well-muscled, trim physique. Unusual for a man his age, she thought.

Far from being a competent swimmer, Angie envied Chan's skill. She eased into the shallower water and paddled toward him. She could see Chan approaching under water and prayed he wouldn't pull any stunts to be funny, like pulling her under by a leg or tossing her into the deep end. As a child, she'd been tossed into the deep water by an older brother and in her panic nearly drowned. She'd never been particularly fond of water since that experience.

When Chan surfaced and pulled her to his side, she clung to him, feeling her breasts pressed against his firm, hard body. Her bare legs intertwined with his. They floated and bounced around the pool, clinging together and laughing at the splashes to their faces, their weightless buoyancy, the smooth water against their skin.

"Don't turn me loose," Angie said when they were in deep water.

"You're safe with me. Just relax. I'll take care of you."

Ah, wonderful! Angie thought. Someone to take care of me. She dipped her head back into the water to get her long hair out of her face. She was in paradise. She began to float away from him but he quickly caught and lifted her high out of the water, then pulled her close, letting her body slide slowly down his own, an inch at a time, until her breasts lingered above his face.

"Peaches," he murmured like a man enjoying a private joke.

"Peaches?"

"When I was in high school, the boys had all the girls' breasts categorized by size. Tiny ones were strawberries, perfect-sized ones were peaches, the bigger but still okay ones were cantaloupes. Watermelons were beyond the limit. Girls who were perfectly flat were called boards," Chan laughed.

"We used to have the same kind of rating system for the boys when I was in high school," Angie lied. "Only we called them beanies, weenies, bananas, zucchini, and gourds."

Chan was shocked. "Did you really? I may be a little old-fashioned, I guess, but I didn't realize nice young girls made such observations."

"Come on, Chan," Angie teased. "What makes you think we didn't use our imaginations just the way you boys did."

"Touché." They laughed together. Chan climbed from the pool and returned with their martini glasses refilled.

"A third one for me?" Angie smiled uncertainly.

"You only sipped at the first two and left them behind. You have some catching up to do." Chan put his arm around her neck and sipped his martini over her shoulder. They clung along the edge of the pool, sipping and bantering until the glasses were empty.

Once again submerged in the water, Angie realized Chan had deftly removed her bikini bra and was lifting her out of the water again. This time as her body glided down his, he was virtually smothered by her breasts pressing against his face. She ached for him to fondle and kiss her breasts, and she wasn't disappointed. Her body tingled and arched with desire. She knew Chan was aroused too, for she could feel his hardness against her legs.

Laughing and forgetting her fear of the water, she teased him by pushing away, diving deep and swimming between his legs. His hands caressed her body as she glided by. The two cavorted like playful porpoises. Once, she wrapped her legs around his waist and offered her breasts for more nibbling.

Another time, Chan erupted from the depths of the water directly in front of her, folded her in his arms, and kissed her passionately. She could feel the heat of his lips as his tongue stole stealthily past her lips and searched her mouth like a hungry panther on the prowl. When he released her, shc slipped behind him and pulled him close, wrapping her arms around his body. He turned in her arms and slid her bikini panties over her legs.

As the water eddied about them, they shared long, satisfying, demanding kisses, deepening their passion until, without releasing her, he placed his hands on her hips, pulled her close, and they began a long, slow, undulating water dance of love.

Gently at first, then as his passion took control, with a fierceness that bordered on animal savagery.

At some point, Angie wasn't sure when, Chan carried her from the water to a chaise longue where they lay like spent kittens, purring in each other's arms, drained and content.

CHAPTER TWENTY-THREE

FREE ADVICE

After Angie dried her hair and changed into the patio dress, she was still barefooted. She grinned at Chan. "Do you have a minimum dress code here, sir?"

"The toenails must be the right shade of pink, milady." Chan looked her over from top to toe. "You'll pass."

Angie flew into his arms for a long and satisfying kiss.

Chan put on some danceable country western music and mixed another pitcher of martinis. They sipped while they worked, preparing dinner. Chan grilled thick steaks on the back patio, while Angie put potatoes in the microwave. Together, they made a salad. They ate their steaks at the kitchen table, since the evening air had already turned chilly.

Angie declined another round of martinis and wine with her dinner, but after the meal they sat at the table enjoying Irish coffee and listening to the music. They talked contentedly, learning more about one another and comparing likes and dislikes.

Angie told of the Foofwahs' running feud with Jake and complained about the complications the ride had made in her life when she should be in San Antonio right now. They laughed together at some of the funny experiences and outrageous people she'd met on the circuit. Chan told about his days as a football star in college.

Twice Chan pulled her to her feet to slow dance around the spacious kitchen. Angie couldn't recall a time when life had ever been as good as it was this evening. She felt like an actress playing a role in a movie scene. Angie the teller of fortunes no longer existed. And a good thing! She certainly hadn't called this one. It was all too wonderful, too grand. She would wake up soon and find this day was nothing but a fantasy.

"What are your plans for tomorrow?" Chan asked off-handedly as he refilled her glass with the rich, sweet coffee.

"Well," Angie had to shift mental gears and return to the real world. "Our plans were to drive the cattle to Caballero Creek Reservoir, or as near as possible tonight. Then tomorrow we'll only have seven or eight miles to go before we cross the Arkansas River and on into La Cholla. We'll travel west until we reach the state highway then go south two miles to the river." She paused, hating to waste time talking facts when there was so little time for them to be together.

"Go on," Chan urged.

"We were told the cattle bridge over the river connects there, so we should be at the auction by noon, in time for Lindsey to get the cattle into the sale. After she sells them, she can pay you whatever Uncle Simon owed for the year's lease, and we can all go back to our normal, everyday lives." A wave of sadness swept through her.

Chan looked at the ceiling with a thoughtful frown on his face. He stroked his chin.

"What's the matter?"

"Nothing's the matter. I'm a little surprised no one told Lindsey about the shorter route. Just a minute, I'll get a map." Chan hurried to his office and returned with a Colorado map. He spread it on the kitchen table before them.

"Let's see, now. You say the cattle are here on Caballero Creek, just a little south and east of Caballero Creek Reservoir. You'd cross a farm road about here," he pointed. "You could cut off four, maybe five miles if you turned south here. Forget continuing west until you reach the highway. That will leave you four or five miles too far west of the cattle bridge. With the short cut, you have to cross the highway here." Chan marked the map. "That will give you access to the cattle bridge over the Arkansas here." He marked the map again fully four miles east of the highway where they planned to cross on the bridge.

"Four miles less could mean the difference of several hours getting to the cattle auction," he said. "I don't know where

Lindsey or Jake got their information, but they aren't as familiar with this country as I am. It takes an old-timer like me to know the short cuts. We used to herd cattle over this route all the time before we used trucks. It's too bad that the truckers' strike came along at such a crucial time."

"You're right. Four miles could make a big difference in getting to the auction in time." Angie's gratitude shone in her dark eyes. "Thanks for the suggestion. I'm sure Lindsey and Jake will appreciate your help." Angie folded the map and tucked it in her pocket.

* * *

After a while, they mounted the stairs and made love again, this time in the waterbed in Chan's master bedroom. Angie was more relaxed, and this time Chan pleased her more than she believed could be possible. Afterwards, they napped for an hour or so.

When Angie awoke, she was startled to see the lateness of the hour. "Look at the time! I need to get back to the cattle drive. I've enjoyed this evening tremendously, but I'm needed for the night watch."

She dressed quickly, wrinkling her nose as she started to put on her dusty jeans and flannel shirt. Anticipating her distress, Chan had slipped down the hall and returned with a fresh change of clothing. "Here, take these. I can't stand to see you going off in those old things."

Gratefully, she stepped into a new pair of jeans Yvonne had left behind. The shirt was snug, but it would do. She found the map Chan had given her and tucked it in her jeans' pocket. "Thanks. And incidentally, making love in a waterbed beats making love in the water."

"I'll remember that," Chan laughed. "My lily of the water-bed."

* * *

"I feel like Cinderella," Angie said, "and my evening ended all too soon." God, I really could fit into Chan's lifestyle without any trouble at all, she thought, snuggling close to him in the pickup.

"You didn't leave a glass boot behind, I hope."

"No, only my heart."

He leaned over and kissed her. "I'll keep it safe."

"Mmmm." She leaned her head on his shoulder and wished her happiness would last forever.

The thin crescent moon floated high among the stars in the dark sky, and the wind had died, giving the night a magic, dream-like intimacy. The only sound for some time was the purring of the pickup's engine. Angie silently watched the landscape rush past the headlights.

"A penny for your thoughts," Chan said. He placed his firm hand on her thigh, creating in Angie a renewed tingle of desire.

"I was just thinking that today was nearly perfect. Thank you for giving me this lovely day."

"It's been special for me, too. It seems we have a lot in common. This doesn't have to be the end, you know."

Her thoughts raced, but she tried to sound casual. "What do we have in common?"

"Well, we both like sex. We both like country western music. And we both like each other."

Angie pondered her next question before asking, "Prioritized in that order?"

"You know better." He took her hand and gently kissed each finger.

She laughed and hesitated again before asking the next one. "Would you write to me?" She felt like a schoolgirl at the end of summer camp. "After I take my friends back to Phoenix, I'll be heading east. I'll be in New Orleans for ten days. You could send letters in care of general delivery."

"I was thinking along the lines of us *seeing* more of each other. Not writing. I'm not much of a letter writer."

Angie giggled. "Does that mean you're going to pop in at the fairs and carnivals around the country to be with me?" The idea of making love to Chan in the Gypsy Spirit intrigued her. "The show circuit gets mighty lonesome."

"No, I was thinking of something a little more permanent. I like to travel as much as anyone, but I can't see myself following the show circuit or even 'popping in' as you call it. The next thing I'd know, you'd have me in a turban, telling fortunes."

"You could exhibit your 'pride and joy' among the world's wonders."

Chan cupped her chin and pulled her face close to his for a quick kiss. "I was thinking perhaps you might like to, ah, settle down in Plainview so we could see more of one another."

Angie's heart missed a couple of beats. She was sure he was about to propose that she move in with him but had thought better of it. He was probably afraid of rushing things. So was she, for that matter.

"That would be wonderful," Angie breathed. "There's only one problem. I have to work, and I'm good at what I do. But my résumé doesn't exactly inspire prospective employers. I chose this gypsy lifestyle because it's the only way I knew to be my own boss. I can't exactly see myself behind the check-out counter at Kmart."

"I've got friends. I could help you find a good job here. One that pays as much, I'm sure, as what you must be bringing in."

"You're tempting me!" Angie's heart sang with sheer joy.

"That's what I'm trying to do." Chan slowed the pickup but kept his eyes on the road as he leaned over to kiss her again. "Speaking of tempting ..."

As Chan sought her mouth again, she pulled away, laughing. "Watch out! You'll kill us both."

"Then I may have to stop along the road and settle your hash, you minx."

"Well, as romantic as that offer sounds, I simply must remind you that duty calls ..."

"I know. I *know*. You prefer cows to me." Chan laughed heartily. "You won't forget to tell Lindsey and Jake about the short cut now will you?"

"Absolutely not. And thank you again for the tip."

"Anything to help out a friend. Simon was special to me, and any relative of Simon's is like a relative to me."

They rode again in silence. Chan's eyes searched the grasslands on either side of the road.

"That's strange. I thought surely the herd and your friends would be camped alongside Caballero Creek right about here, but there's no sign of a campfire. Nothing at all."

Angie sat up straight, alarmed.

"I'm pretty sure the plan was to make it to Caballero Creek if possible. Are you sure you're in the right area? Can you shine your spotlight over there?"

"No, it's not working."

The acrid smell of grass smoke lingered in the still night air. A sense of foreboding gripped Angie that her friends were in trouble.

Chan backtracked along the road bordering the rangeland where the cattle were expected to cross.

"I knew they were to cross Sid's place, entering the gate right here, and there are the cattle tracks. It's plain the herd entered here, but from the road it's hard to determine where they camped. We should be able to see a campfire."

Chan drove south slowly, scanning both sides of the road for several miles. Then he drove east for several more miles. "They can't have gotten off their planned route this far south," he worried. They drove around for forty-five minutes before they finally found the campsite on the western side of Caballero Creek and about five miles south of where Chan had expected to find them.

Angie was concerned when she found her friends sleeping under the stars in their bedrolls. Where was the Gypsy Spirit? Tut stretched and welcomed them as they stepped from the pickup.

Chloë and CC were the only ones awake. They sat beside the fire sipping coffee from tin mugs. Angie could see the huge herd of cattle lying on the ground, resting. Against the background of the starlit sky, the silhouette of two riders could be seen tending to their night watches.

"Where's the Gypsy Spirit?" Angie asked.

"You won't believe what happened this afternoon after you left," Chloë answered. "We still don't believe it ourselves. Some stupid camper must have left Caballero Creek Reservoir without putting out his campfire, and it started a grass fire."

CC took over. "We got caught in the wall of fire but managed to stampede the cattle ahead for about five miles into Caballero Creek. Some of the cattle got bogged down and all of us have been busting our butts pulling cattle out of the bog. We've lost three head of cattle and may lose more that are in bad shape."

"Lindsey and Jake are taking it pretty hard," Chloë said. "At any rate, we're all okay, and most of the cattle will be all right. Thank God we only have a few miles to go tomorrow."

Angie turned pale thinking of the danger to her friends while she was off having fun. Seeking selfish pleasure when they needed her most, more than she'd ever been needed before. "And the Gypsy Spirit?"

"We thought it was safe ..." Chloë began.

"Then 'whoosh' and it was gone," CC finished. "But it went out in a blaze of glory."

"*What*?" Angie cried.

"Remember the fireworks you said you bought in New Mexico?" CC asked. "The rockets lit up the sky in a spectacular display."

"I can't believe this," Angie said. She sat on a boulder and stared into the fire. "My truck, my livelihood—gone!"

Chan walked to her and placed his hand on her shoulder. "Now you have even more reason to stay here. And you won't need to go back to Phoenix."

She patted his hand and looked at CC. “Who’s on night watch?”

“Gina and Penny. Gina was supposed to be relieved by you, but when you didn’t show up, she volunteered to stay on the watch.”

“After everything you’ve been through today. I’m so sorry! I feel like such a rat for not being here to help. And then being selfish, worrying about the Gypsy Spirit when my friends have been risking their lives. I’ll never forgive myself!”

“You needn’t feel that way.” CC said. “You couldn’t have known this would happen.” She gave her friend a reassuring hug. “Even if you are a fortune teller.”

“Where are the horses? I’ll get Twinkle and relieve Gina right now.” She turned to Chan, her look mixed with anxiety and frustration.

“I’m sorry about the trouble you folks have had today,” Chan said. “I’ll call Sid in the morning and tell him to be more careful who he lets in to camp around Caballero Creek. Some people are downright irresponsible. I guess they don’t know how much damage they can cause when the grass is dry and they don’t put out their fires. I wish there was something I could do.”

CC had something for him. “Don’t forget to call Ace in the morning. Let him know everything is just fine. And don’t you dare mention the fire.”

Chan looked at her as if she were a martyred saint. “You’re *so* brave. Each and every one of you. I feel so inadequate.”

“Don’t worry,” Chloë said with a sad and gentle smile. “It’s not your problem. But thanks for your concern just the same. Will you be at the auction tomorrow?”

“Of course.” He turned to Angie. “Don’t forget to tell Lindsey and Jake about the short cut. Well, I’ll be going.” He waved goodbye to Chloë and CC. Angie walked with him to the pickup where she kissed him a sweet but distracted goodnight.

CHAPTER TWENTY-FOUR

THE LAST DAY

Breakfast the next morning was a skimpy affair. With most of the food and utensils lost in the fiery explosion of the Gypsy Spirit, only the meager supplies Chloë rescued the night before sustained the dispirited drovers.

Chloë had salvaged enough to prepare bacon biscuits and a pot of coffee. The riders were so relieved that this was to be their last morning, no one complained about the short rations or the inconvenience. Felon left Chloë's side long enough to scrounge his own victuals, since she refused to drop him tidbits.

"He's fat enough," she said. "Probably had a feast of fried rats last night." Out of everyone's sight, she sneaked a biscuit to Tut.

The tension of the final push into La Cholla showed in the tiny, taut lines around Lindsey's eyes and mouth. She mourned the loss of the cattle too, not for their monetary value, but as a shepherd who has failed her charge.

After the riders showed up for breakfast, she raised her voice so all could hear. "Gather around everyone. We need to be sure you know what to expect today."

Jake reported two more head of cattle died from exhaustion during the night. The rest of the herd looked tired, but he thought they'd be able to continue the last eight or ten miles today.

Angie spread the map Chan had given her on the ground so all could see. "Chan says there's a shortcut we should use. It will save four miles, maybe more, and will be a better approach to the cattle crossing over the Arkansas. He said this is the route all the cattlemen used before they had cattle trucks to do their hauling."

Jake and the Foofwahs studied the map while Angie pointed out Chan's markings of the night before. On the map, the route did look much shorter, but Lindsey was uneasy.

"I don't know, something doesn't add up here," she said. "Before you guys arrived, I went into the La Cholla auction yard and talked to the manager. He suggested the route on a big wall map he had. I understood the only approach to the cattle crossing bridge over the Arkansas was by driving the cattle due west to the state highway. I distinctly remember he said we'd have to drive them through North La Cholla, about two miles on the paved road. He stressed that, because he said we'd have to get a permit, but he would take care of it. I understood this was the only approach to the bridge over the Arkansas and the railroad tracks. That's four miles west of the point where Chan's marked the crossing here." She pointed to Chan's markings on Angie's map.

Lindsey had been alone when the man at the auction yard gave her the instructions. She had no one to call upon for verification.

"Jake, you're familiar with the area. Have you heard of this shortcut?"

"I only been up this way a few times and I never had no reason to discuss the cattle crossing."

Lindsey regretted again that she hadn't taken time to ride the trail before the Foofwahs arrived. She'd mapped out the trail as suggested by the auction yard manager and checked it by driving up and down the main roads in a pickup. She'd called five or six ranchers to get permission to cross their rangeland, and none had suggested a shortcut. But maybe she'd misunderstood the directions. She tried to recall the auction manager's exact words nearly a week ago, a week that now seemed like a long month.

She checked the map again. She mentally worked out the timetable with the mileage chart and knew the cattle had to be in the auction yard no later than noon to be included in the sale. If she insisted they drive the cattle to the highway and then had to backtrack four miles, she would lose four hours, two each way. She couldn't afford to take any chances.

"What do you think, Jake?" Lindsey asked. A worried frown darkened her expression. The tension of the drive and the responsibility for decisions were wearing her down.

"Did Chan say anything about what kind of land we could expect before we get to the Arkansas here?" Jake directed his questions at Angie. "Any danger of running into swampland like we done before?"

"No, he said after we cross this farm road," she pointed to Chan's mark, "we should go about two miles west then head straight south, and it will give us a straight shot onto the cattle crossing bridge. He stressed if we went to the highway we'd be going four miles further west than we need to go, then it would take us several hours longer than if we take this cut-off."

Jake sat hunched on his heels, his whiskers dancing in the early morning breeze. He rubbed his chin and eyed Angie speculatively. "Did he say why he was so all-fired anxious to git us to the auction sooner?"

"Chan said he and Simon had been good friends for years, and any relative of Simon's was like a relative of his. He wanted to do everything he could to help Lindsey."

"Hmmmm," Jake rubbed his chin and slowly shook his head.

Gina spoke up. "While riding night watch, I kept wondering why no one, the owners of the land for instance, reported the fire. Why didn't someone come to investigate? If the land belonged to me, I'd be concerned enough to drive out and check a grass fire. Unless, of course, I thought it was being controlled."

"Why would anyone fishing at the lake have a campfire going in the middle of the day?" Kai-ling asked.

"I wondered the same thing," Penny broke in. "But I assumed someone cooked the fish they'd caught. Funny, though, none of the other lakes or dams has had campers or fishers around."

"And it isn't white geese season for hunters," Lindsey offered.

"I'm positive Chan was following us the day I met him after my swim," CC said. "He was surprised to see me but pretended to be on his way to talk to Lindsey when I told him who I was. He just struck me as acting a little sneaky. AND THEN HE BROKE MY CELL PHONE! IT WAS INTENTIONAL!"

"Possibly," Lindsey said. "But that could have been an accident."

"It sure put us out of touch with anyone we could call for help!" CC's brown eyes snapped with anger. "Any one of us could have been killed or badly injured."

"*Maybe* he was planning to set the fire that day, and you fouled up his plans. There's been a lot of strange things happenin' on this drive that don't make no sense to me," Jake added, shaking his head. "Appears to me we've had about as much luck as a jackrabbit at a coyote convention."

"Don't be such a pessimist, Jake," Lindsey interrupted. "I think the man is just trying to be a good Samaritan. He's trying to help out a relative of an old friend. I can't believe he'd stoop to endangering our lives by setting a fire."

"Waaall, it appears to me that he's got a whole lot more to gain if you miss that auction today. If he's such a good friend, why didn't he stay and help Angie ride herd last night? He knew what had happened, that all of us were so tuckered out we were more dead than alive. Yet he walked away. That ain't the way westerners do things. Neighbors help neighbors."

Angie had stepped away for another cup of coffee. Returning to the circle studying the map, her face flushed with anger when she heard Lindsey's and Jake's remarks. "Are you suggesting Chan had something to do with this fire? How could Chan have set the fire? He was with me all afternoon."

"He's got several cowboys who follow his orders," Gina said. "If Chan said, 'Set a fire,' they'd set a fire. Remember the men who were checking us out when we left Uncle Simon's place?"

Jake turned to Angie. "I'm sayin' that yer friend Reed has worked awful hard convincin' us he wants to help, for someone who hasn't lifted a finger when it comes right down to it. Reed has three hired men who had time to come razz us the day we took off, but he never once offered Lindsey the use of them hired men. No, they were going to be too busy off at a ropin'. Where I come from, when a neighbor has a drive, the whole neighborhood turns out to help, and they don't expect a cent in return. Here, nobody showed up 'cept Reed in his white hat and fancy clothes, offerin' a lot of chin music and nothin' else."

"I think you're all so worn out you're letting your imaginations run crazy," Angie said. She didn't try to conceal her anger. "We've had a run of bad luck, but you don't have proof that Chan has anything to do with the problems we've had. You aren't being fair!"

"Waaall, missy, I don't mean to step on no toes, but if you recall the first morning of the drive you had to sober me up before I could hit the floor with my hat. Wanna know what I think? I think Reed's men came to the bunkhouse the night before on purpose to git me too drunk to be of any help the next day. They were trying to slow us down or, better yet, convince Lindsey she couldn't git them cattle into La Cholla."

"You didn't tell me about that," Lindsey accused.

"I was kinda 'shamed. Didn't want to worry you none, thinkin' you had a useless old man who'd let someone flummox him like a flippin' greenhorn."

"And that first night out," Kai-ling interjected, "I found Romancer with her tether rope cut. And there were other horses loose."

"What?" Lindsey looked astonished. "You found horses cut loose? Why didn't anyone mention this to me?"

Kai-ling related the story of discovering Romancer and smelling the cigarette smoke. "I knew none of us smoked, so I thought an outsider was in the darkness among the trees. But then I told myself it was my imagination. Now, I don't think so."

Penny and CC added their observations about finding their horses loose and thinking Jake had been careless.

"Sorry, Jake," Penny said. "We should have known better."

Jake looked pained but accepted the apology with his usual graciousness. "You wimmen!" he said before shooting a stream of tobacco against a tree trunk.

"What you're saying then is that someone has been sabotaging our drive from the start?" The idea shocked Lindsey. She looked inquiringly from one face to another. Then she remembered the cocklebur she had found in Cody's saddle blanket. "Chan certainly has a lot to gain if we don't make it. Do you really think he or one of his men could have set the grass fire?"

"I'm sure of it," Gina said. "Of course, ranchers clear off land by burning it, but the rancher who owned that land knew we'd be passing through yesterday and that smoke could frighten our livestock. He could have warned us. An accident? Maybe, but not likely. Someone still would have shown up to help us."

"And like I said," CC offered, "Chan was stalking us the day I went to swim."

Angie glared at CC. "Why do you hate Chan so? What has he done to you? What has Chan done to any of you?" Her anger crescendoed and spread as she took in the whole group. "You're adding two and two and coming up with twenty-two. Frankly, I think you're all jealous because Chan has been paying attention to me. One thing I know, you'll be sorry if you go the long route and miss the auction this afternoon, and we're wasting a piss-pot lot of time now!" She marched off toward the saddled, patient horses, mounted Twinkle, and rode away to round up the cattle.

Heated discussion followed Angie's departure. Lindsey argued that despite their suspicions about Chan, they couldn't afford to take a chance on the longer route and then have to double back. The four hours they'd lose would jeopardize reaching the auction in time.

"But what if we run into a swamp there like we done here?" Jake posed his final argument.

"I'll be riding point, making sure we don't run into any more swampland. We can surely keep north of the bog and go west to the highway without losing time. There must be farm-to-market roads that aren't on the map."

Finally, Jake allowed Lindsey to convince him the shortcut was worth trying. "They're yer cattle, Lindsey. I've said my piece."

Jake turned to the other Foofwahs. "Okay, the way I figure it, we'll cross the road right about there and drive the cattle a couple of miles for an hour, then head due south and come out on the Arkansas about here. Reed says that's where the cattle crossing is. We should be able to make that about ten o'clock and have them cattle in the auction yard thirty, forty minutes later."

Jake looked around at the women. "Any questions?" Everyone looked worried, but no one had questions. Jake took a final gulp of coffee, threw the dregs into the grass, and rising from his heels, said, "Ladies, this is our last day. Let's head 'em out!"

* * *

They crossed the farm road within an hour after leaving camp and soon turned south. Gina was still uneasy, an alarm ringing in her head. Something wasn't right here.

A student of geology years before when she was in college, Gina scrutinized the changing landscape. The terrain had become desert-like with grass becoming sparse and finally non-existent. Pear cactuses grew thicker. The soil beneath Mouse's feet was no longer black loam but had become white and chalky. It reminded her of Fossil Canyon in Arizona. Fossil Canyon had once been the bottom of an ocean and the white chalk-like cliffs were formed by sedimentation from plankton and other tiny sea creatures that died and sank to the bottom of the sea where they calcified. It was evident that here too the land had once been under water.

The rolling, grassy plains were gone. Now the riders and their herd moved through a moonscape of bare, white hills. It looked as if a childlike giant had taken a scoop and piled up white caliche mounds fifteen to twenty feet high, side by side, some on top of one another. Gauging from the sweating exertion of Mouse, Gina guessed they were on a gradual rise. It was hard to be certain because the herd seesawed up and down the hundreds of small hills. There was constant danger of losing a cow or calf behind the hills.

Odd, she thought. Angie said if we turned south here, the route led directly to the cattle crossing over the Arkansas. But if the land is getting higher, doesn't that mean the cattle crossing will have to span a gorge? No one mentioned a gorge. If little Caballero Creek could have embankments eight feet high, how high might the embankment of a powerful river like the Arkansas be?

Gina was positive Chan was leading them into a trap ahead. She doubted the bog could extend this far west, since it was formed primarily by water backing up from the lake made by the Arkansas River dam. Besides, a bog would have shown up by now. After a while, the scooped hills began to level out, and Gina's suspicions about the upward gradual slope were confirmed.

* * *

Jake was unhappy about giving in to Lindsey's judgment. Still edgy from the grass fire the day before, and naturally distrustful to begin with, he felt sure Reed was trying to pull a fast one. The death of five head of cattle added to his disgust with himself, taking the loss of the cattle as a reflection on his competence. And he'd been shamed in front of the women with his admission about Reed's men plying him with drink the night before the drive started and Angie having to get him sobered up. He was distressed too because Angie was angry with him. She was making a mistake messing around with that skunk Reed, but Jake didn't like being on her bad side.

There were a lot of questions that needed answering. The most important one that kept popping into his mind was why Reed was so anxious to appear helpful without ever actually doing anything. If he was so all-fired anxious to help, why hadn't he offered the expertise of his hired hands to Lindsey for the past five days? Maybe they were at a roping for a couple of days but what were they doing the rest of the time that couldn't wait?

And, if Reed had been trailing the herd the day CC slipped away to swim in the lake, why? Was CC right? Had she interrupted his plans to start a grass fire then? That bothered him.

Jake hadn't forgotten Kai-ling's story about Romancer and the other horses being cut loose the first night. At first, he dismissed it as a schoolboy prank, probably some campers nearby. But she claimed she smelled cigarette smoke. He knew Reed's man Jimbo smoked.

Jake recalled a comment Sadie had made during the midnight supper they'd shared in her Los Vaqueros bar. "That Chan. He puts up a good front all right, but that's all it is, a front. He's a man to steer clear of."

Chan had everything to gain if the cattle didn't make it to the auction in time. But what it boils down to, Jake thought, is I don't trust the sonofabitch. There will be no second chance for Lindsey. The auction is held once a week, and if she misses this one, next week will be too late. Lindsey will have to forfeit the cattle, and Reed will be a couple of hundred thousand richer. Not bad returns for a small amount of effort.

Jake mulled these questions over and over in his mind. He wished he could get to a phone and call Sadie. He'd ask her to explain her remarks about Reed. What did Sadie know about him? Was she trying to warn him of something? He hadn't paid too much attention at the time, and now he wished he had. With every half hour that passed, Jake became more convinced he needed to do something, but what?

Jake glanced at his watch. They'd been on the trail for almost three hours. It was a little after nine o'clock, and they should be getting near the crossing. He thought maybe he should ride ahead and look around. What wouldn't he give for an all-terrain vehicle right now? Then he wondered if someone might be following them today and decided it was more important to ride back and check for himself. He told Lindsey, who was in the lead, that he was going to check on the drags. When he passed the Foofwahs, he slowed to ask each of them if everything was all right. Angie ignored his overtures of friendliness.

Jake shrugged, at a loss to know how to sweeten her feelings, then continued toward the rear. He backtracked toward their morning camp for almost a mile, then paused, thinking he might as well turn back. Before he could act, he heard a horse's hooves approaching from the other side of a twenty-foot high mound. Pulling Tonto off into a crevice created by the white cone-shaped hills, he dismounted and waited.

Jake didn't have to wait long. The horse and rider appeared around the hill that concealed him. It was Billy Ray Worthman.

"Hello, Billy Ray," Jake said. He stepped in the cowboy's path.

"My God, Jake. You nearly scared the piss out of me." Billy Ray reined in his horse and dismounted.

Jake's thoughts wobbled in a riot of confusion. Billy Ray sure as hell don't have no business following us. Did Billy Ray set the fire yesterday? Shit, I hope not. I thought there might be some hope for this youngster.

Billy Ray looked uncomfortable. He didn't step too close, as though he weren't certain of his welcome. He glanced around nervously.

"Yer as jumpy as a bit up old bull in fly time, man. What's eatin' you?" Jake asked.

"Jake, I been wantin' to talk to you. Been doin' a lot of thinkin' lately, and I don't like the way things've been goin'."

"Why in the hell are you people followin' us?" Jake asked. "If you got time to do that, why aren't you bein' useful?" Jake's ire was working into a lather at the thought of the danger the goddammed women had been through and now suspicious that the trouble didn't stem from accidents but from intentional malfeasance.

Again looking around nervously, Billy Ray rubbed his hands on his Levi's like a schoolboy faced with a dilemma. If he lied, he was in trouble. If he told the truth, he was in deep shit. He used the schoolboy's defense. Evasion.

"What I'm *askin'* you, Jake, is *why* are you drivin' these cattle straight onto a bluff?"

"What do you mean, 'onto a bluff'?"

"Why, hell, man, everyone around here knows that the bank of the Arkansas River on this side of La Cholla is a white chalk bluff, and there's no way in hell you can get cattle down that thirty foot bluff to the river. Worse yet, it'll take you half a day to follow the rim and circle back around to North La Cholla. If you don't get them cattle turned west soon, you'll lose four hours. If you turn west now, you can still hit the state highway and approach the only crossing over the Arkansas, through the break in the cliff cut by the state highway."

Jake's stomach turned over twice before he could respond. "You wouldn't be lyin' to me, would you, Billy Ray?"

"It wouldn't benefit me none to lie to you. But there'll sure be hell to pay if word gets back to my boss that I tipped you off. If you tell anyone I said this, I'll have to say you're lyin', because my job'll sure be on the line." With that, Billy Ray swung up to his saddle, turned his horse, and rode away.

Jake stared after him a full minute before he knew what he had to do. He turned and rode back to the herd.

Jake found Gina first. "Gina, we're bein' led into a trap. If we continue goin' south, we'll end up on a thirty-foot bluff above the river, and it'll take us extra hours to git the cattle turned around. We gotta git them cattle turned back west raaght now! We gotta approach the cattle crossin' bridge like Lindsey was told in the first place!"

"How do you know that?" Gina asked.

"I can't tell you how I know, just have faith in me, will you? We gotta work fast and begin turnin' the herd west, pronto."

Gina didn't push for more information. It didn't matter how Jake knew. Gina's doubts had been well founded. And she already knew Jake could be stubborn when his mind was made up.

"Can you spread the word to the other wimmen?"

Gina nodded. Jake raced ahead to talk to Lindsey while Gina circled the cattle to tell the rest of the Foofwahs. Without argument, they started the slow process of turning the herd westward.

* * *

Lindsey thought hard about the events unfolded by her helpers at breakfast this morning. Added to her own suspicion that Chan had placed a cocklebur under Cody's horse's saddle blanket the afternoon Cody'd been thrown, evidence was adding up fast that the man was treacherous.

When Jake rode up beside her, Lindsey jumped nervously. Worry lines creased her brow. The stress of working against time was destroying her self-confidence. When Jake repeated the message he'd delivered to Gina, Lindsey stared at him angrily for a moment.

"How do you know we're being led into a trap?"

"Lindsey, I been workin' for Cody nigh onto ten years now, and not once did Cody ever doubt my loyalty. I know you've had cause to wonder 'bout me, but this is one time you'll have to take my word on faith."

"You can't just ride up and say you've learned we're being led into a trap, and we're going to end up on a bluff. I need to know how you came by this information, Jake. You're obliged to tell me!"

"You got to trust me, Lindsey. You got to take my word for it. I made a promise to Cody to do the best job I could. I also made a vow to someone else to keep my mouth shut. And I don't go back on a promise. I can't tell you who or how I got the information. Just say it came from God, if that makes you feel any better."

Lindsey shrugged and turned in the saddle to give the signal to shift west again. She was surprised to see the herd already turning. "If we're acting on bad information, Jake, I'll never forgive you. You know it means the cattle won't get to the auction in time."

"You got to trust me, Lindsey."

Before riding off to take the lead, Jake told her, "Someone's got to break it to Angie that she's playin' catspaw, doin' Chan's dirty work."

Lindsey thought about it and decided the only person who could tell Angie and make her believe it was CC. She motioned to CC to ride forward then explained the situation to her.

CC wanted no part of it. "Angie really believes in that asshole, and, for her sake, I hope she won't be hurt. I couldn't, no wouldn't, be the one to break her heart for anything. But, Lindsey, look at it this way, Angie is one smart cookie. She'll figure things out."

Lindsey agonized for her friend. If Jake was right that they'd been led into a trap, there could be no doubt that Chan Reed manipulated Angie to unwittingly betray her friends.

CHAPTER TWENTY-FIVE

BITTER VICTORY

For the first three hours that last morning, Angie sulked, angry with everyone. CC professed to be her friend but was bad-mouthing the man Angie had fallen so desperately in love with, the man she hoped to spend the rest of her life with. She couldn't understand why CC took such a hard attitude about a man she barely knew. And he had been nothing but mannerly toward CC. CC even claimed now that the accident with her stupid phone was intentional! When CC met Chan riding to catch up with them that one day, she leaped to the ridiculous conclusion that he was *stalking* them. For God's sake! What's wrong with these people?

Then there was Jake. She had stood up for Jake when everyone else made fun of him. On the first day of the ride, who was it that found Jake so drunk he was barely able to function? She was the one who sobered him up so he could still take part, much as the others wanted to dump him from the start. She had kept his secret. She thought of Jake as a special friend. Now, he too had betrayed her.

Angie's thoughts of Gina were equally bitter. Gina was sure Chan was behind everything bad that had happened to them. Another ridiculous assumption! Lindsey was the only one who seemed to want to give Chan the benefit of the doubt, but Lindsey was half out of her mind with worry about failure and half-believing the accusations of the others. None of them were being fair. Chan was trying to be a good neighbor and little thanks he got for it.

Even Kai-ling, who never said a judgmental word against anyone, thought Chan or one of his men had cut the tether on her horse the first night out.

Feeling outcast, weary, and heart sore, Angie rode alone on the left flank of the herd. She decided to ignore her friends and turn her thoughts to the fabulous day she'd spent with gentle, fun, wonderfully sexy Chan.

Gina interrupted her reverie when she rode by to break the news of the change of route. She offered no explanation, and Angie vowed to herself she'd be damned before she'd ask why their plan to take Chan's shortcut had been reversed. Someone had made the decision. She wished she knew who and why but would not risk the indignity of inquiring.

She felt left out, no longer a member of the group. Too, she was disappointed that CC made no overtures toward soothing her anger or apologizing for her accusations against Chan. She hurt deep inside with a pain she hadn't known since the death of her son.

By ten-thirty, they reached the state highway and turned south again on a narrow road that was paved but little used. For almost an hour, the cattle plodded along. A couple of cars pulled to the side of the road and stopped until the herd went around them. On the outskirts of North La Cholla, the road cut through chalky cliffs and dipped sharply down into a three or four block Mexican barrio. Behind a tall cyclone fence, closely packed prefab homes huddled beneath a grove of sycamore trees. Worried mothers and excited little kids with barking dogs watched the progression from behind the safety of the fences. Tut ran alongside the procession, periodically announcing its importance and keeping the cattle in line. Felon lay flopped sideways over the horse's mane in front of Chloë so she could keep him from digging his claws into her horse whenever something made the cat wary.

Passing through North La Cholla's main residential area, Angie held her breath while Lindsey led the herd to the bank of the Arkansas River. Would the cattle bridge be here as everyone else believed? Or had they missed it?

When the road cut through the cliffs, Angie had a flash of doubt about Chan's directions and markings on the map, but the doubt quickly succumbed to faith born of love. He'd said they would be going four miles too far if they went to the state highway. Chan had lived in the area most of his life, and few people knew the country better than he. She knew his intentions were honorable. He surely had Lindsey's best interests at heart when he suggested the shortcut. If she weren't so angry, Angie would grieve for Lindsey. They were this close to the auction but would have to double back miles to locate the bridge. They'd never make it in time.

A grove of trees closed in above the roadway and cut off Angie's view ahead. Anxiously, she watched Lindsey, waiting for a signal that the bridge was not there. The success or failure of the last four days of agony would rest on whether Lindsey located the bridge. If it wasn't there, it meant Chan was right. They should have listened to him. The drive had failed for lack of trust. On the other hand, if it was there, that meant Chan had deceived her. Impossible.

After what seemed hours but only fifteen minutes passed, Lindsey yelled and waved her hat. She was too far away for Angie to hear, but Penny relayed the news. "It's here! It's here! The bridge is here!"

Everyone cheered except Angie. Tears sprang to her eyes, and her heart sank into her boots. She tried to smile as though the tears were from happiness for Lindsey's victory, but deep in her heart she knew she cried for a loss that was profound. The location of the bridge clinched it: Chan had used her to give wrong information, and she had been a fool to believe him.

Wave after wave of conflicting emotions trembled through her small body, the news a knife wound in her heart. One more dream in her bleak life shattered. She was an idiot to think this one would work, that Chan really cared for her. Chan had deliberately given her false information to pass on to her friends. Worse, she had been angry when they rejected his plan.

A few minutes later, she was near enough to see the bridge. It was a wide, cement viaduct arching high above the river and leading directly into the auction yard.

Jake rode ahead, positioning himself to guide the cattle onto the bridge from one side while Lindsey steered them from the other.

The first cattle stepped onto the bridge and became alarmed by the roaring of the swiftly moving water below and the hollow thunk of their hooves. They tried to turn back but were forced to turn again onto the bridge when the cattle behind crowded forward. Once above the fast-flowing Arkansas, the animals complacently eyed the concrete before them as they paced stolidly onward to the end of their journey. Mother cows bawled for their calves, and their pace stepped up at the sight and smell of the corrals. Food and water were near.

As Angie helped herd the drags over the bridge, she stopped at the highest point to glance back, beyond the barrio, beyond the tops of the trees. Her eyes traveled along the cliff edge that formed a backdrop for North La Cholla, then eastward several miles toward the juncture where Chan had indicated the cattle bridge was located. As far as the eye could see, white cliffs lined the northern bank of the river.

The endless chalky cliffs and the location of the cattle bridge off the state highway were the final evidence she needed to prove betrayal by the man she loved. She was sick at heart.

Chan not only used me, she thought ruefully, he tricked me into betraying my friends. He wasn't interested in me. His lovemaking was nothing more than a one-nighter, an inducement. Be honest and call it by its rightful name: I was a shill in his confidence game. All for the sake of delaying Lindsey by a critical few hours. What a blind, stupid fool I've been. I trusted him.

* * *

Chan sat in the bleachers at the auction yard, watching as pen after pen of cattle were run through, bid on, and replaced by another lot. On his knee, he had a pad on which he occasionally penciled notes about the animals milling around in the arena below. He chatted amiably with his friends and compared opinions on the quality of the lots of cattle being offered for sale. He was not buying today, for he expected to be the owner of four hundred sixty head by this time tomorrow. Of course, he couldn't mention this fact to friends or neighbors. Not yet, anyway.

He nodded across to his attorney Sleighton Lerner seated in the next section over. "How's it going, Sly?"

Lerner only nodded in return, continuing his conversation with one of the cattle buyers. Lerner always attended the auctions, picking up a fair amount of business settling disputes. As Uncle Simon's probate attorney, Lerner would be present to assure that payment for the sale of Simon's herd, if there was a sale, was funneled through the estate. No illegal side transactions among his clients. He had the law on his side and ten percent interest in the proceeds to motivate him.

Beside Chan sat two gray-haired cattlemen he'd known since high school.

"Hey, would you look at that!" One of the men pointed past the auctioneer and beyond the innumerable cattle pens toward the bridge. "I've not seen the old cattle crossing used for years, but here comes a herd over the bridge. Now that's as pretty a picture as I've seen for a long time."

Chan's jaw dropped. He stood up and stared in disbelief. He snapped his fingers at Jimbo, lounging nearby, and snarled, "Get the binoculars from the pickup."

Chan's lips moved, but the words caught in his throat. "It can't be, it can't be ... It just *can't* be!"

When Jimbo returned with the binoculars, Chan focused on the riders and turned white with anger. He cursed under his breath. It was Lindsey's herd all right. She'd made it in spite of everything he and his men could do to stall them.

"You know that herd?" one of the cowmen asked.

"I sure as hell do. That herd wasn't supposed to show up here till tomorrow. I've been double-crossed and, by God, someone's going to pay for this!" The two cattlemen exchanged knowing glances and suddenly decided they had important business elsewhere. Chan's temper was dangerous when he thought he'd been wronged.

Furiously, Chan stomped off the bleachers, his rage obvious to all whose paths he crossed.

You idiot, he berated himself. Do you want to blow everything at this stage in the game? What does that bitch know about selling cattle? She probably doesn't even know she had to arrange for a hauling or moving permit. Or she might have forgotten to bring the necessary proof of inoculation or ownership papers. At any rate, she'll have to tangle with probate, and that takes time. She'll lose on a technicality, but, by God, she *will* lose!

He strode through the narrow passages, between hundreds of loaded pens until he arrived at the entrance of the bridge where Lindsey and Jake were trailing the last of the herd into the receiving pens. Fortunately for him, the distance he had to walk gave him time to think and gain control over his anger.

Chan felt better. An inner, small voice warned him to keep cool. Don't lose everything now. By the time Chan approached Lindsey and Jake, he was all smiles.

"Ahhhh, I see you made it! I was hoping you'd get here in time. Prices are good today, or at least they were this morning. Congratulations!" Chan extended his hand for Lindsey to shake. Lindsey smiled and took it. Jake wheeled his horse around and rode past.

"Chan, thanks for all your help." Lindsey's voice sounded triumphant, without rancor. "We'll be having a victory dinner tonight. We'd love to have you join us. And I'll have a check for you. We'd like a private room in the best restaurant in town. Maybe you can suggest a good dining place?"

"The Trail's End is the best in La Cholla. I'll be delighted to join you. What time do you suggest?"

"We'll need a few hours to rest and freshen up. How about seven-thirty?" Lindsey's heart was singing. She was relieved and happy that the long drive was over. She had won the race against time and the almost insurmountable odds. She could afford to be generous.

After they parted, Chan looked around for Angie. He spied her dismounting Twinkle, then turning the horse over to a young man, an auction employee. Chan didn't want to meet Angie now, certain she would know the map he gave her was a trap. He didn't feel up to coping with any more confrontations just yet.

Chan was not sure whether Angie had forgotten to tell them about the map or had been overruled. Obviously, they didn't take the route he advised. If Angie learned about the entrapment ... but how could she if they didn't go that route? How could he explain the displacement of the cattle-crossing bridge? He had a lot of things to puzzle out. Chan went out of his way to avoid meeting any of the Foofwahs, a fact that didn't go unnoticed by CC and Gina who watched as he hurried to his car.

* * *

The herd was taken over by auction yard employees who had been instructed to rush the animals through as soon as possible. They counted the cattle and assigned them various pens. One man with a clipboard took care of the necessary paperwork. Cowboys on horseback cut calves from their mothers and sorted the cows into weight and age lots; the bulls went into separate pens. Within an hour, they were watered, fed, and hosed down to wash away the mud of the bog and the dust of the road. They emerged with their red and white coats shining.

Lindsey supplied office personnel with the necessary hauling permit, the inoculation records, and proof of ownership as well as a copy of Uncle Simon's will. Attendants led their horses away to be unsaddled, watered, and fed. Uncle Simon's horses, except Ringo and Tonto, Lindsey decided, would be kept for a week then sold at the next auction. After they'd had a chance to rest from the hard drive and were fed some grain, the horses would look fresher and bring a better price.

Lindsey decided too to sell Old Bushmills and Mouse. She would keep Romancer and Shitears along with Tonto and Ringo. The horses would be boarded a few days until Jake could take them to Wickenburg.

Outside the sale arena, the Foofwahs wearily turned their horses over to the auction employees. As they dismounted, most of them hoped it would be the last time, ever, to climb off a horse. Kai-ling's eyes glistened with tears as she turned Romancer over to the auction employee, much to the dismay of the seventeen-year-old helper. "Don't worry, ma'am," he said. "Your horse will be well cared for. He's to be kept for a few days, not sold. We'll take good care of him till you're ready to pick him up."

CC was surprised to find she'd become, if not fond of Shitears, at least more understanding of his special problems.

"I'm sorry I threatened to send you to the glue factory, Shitears. I guess I gave you as rough a time as you gave me. It couldn't have been easy putting up with such an inexperienced rider. I'm glad you'll be going home to Wickenburg."

Gina hugged Mouse good-bye. She'd learned to love and trust the beautiful mare. The last couple of days, she'd been thinking of buying the horse from Cody. She was planning to continue riding once she returned to Phoenix, but she understood Lindsey's reasons for selling the older horses.

Penny too was having problems handling the idea of Old Bushmills being sold at auction, but she considered herself a practical person who could face the situation realistically.

"When I sold my horse just before I went to college," she told her friends, "it nearly broke my heart. I can't let that happen again. Someone will buy him, surely. He'd make a good kid's horse. I'm just glad the ride is over and relieved to be going home." She turned away to hide the tears in her eyes, for she knew Old Bushmills was too old, no one would buy him. She knew very well what happened to a horse once he became too old.

Chloë slid off her unnamed horse, grateful to have survived the journey, and kissed the ground. "I will never ride another horse. Come on, Felon. Let's get out of here." She pulled the traumatized cat from the horse's neck and set him on the ground.

Tut was on his best behavior among the cattle pens, a true professional in this realm. Felon stayed close by his side.

* * *

Angie wasn't thinking of her horse as she dismounted, collected her sleeping gear and duffel bag, and turned Twinkle's reins over to the young man who stood waiting. She had more important things to think about right now. All Angie wanted was to get away by herself, some place she could be alone. She needed to think, to cry her heart out.

She'd been looking forward to the end of the trail so she could spend time with Chan, planning their future. Now, there would be no future with the man, and she hoped never to see him again. The hurt would be too great.

Since she had no place to go or transportation to get there, she was stuck. Though she wanted to avoid Chan, she found herself looking around for him, even knowing she needed to work things out in her head before she could face him. At the door of the sale arena, she paused to search among the cattle buyers to make sure Chan wasn't there. He'd said he would be at the auction. Apparently, that too was a lie.

She entered the sale barn and climbed up the bleachers to an empty seat, as far back as she could get. She looked around again. From this different, higher vantage point, she was both relieved and disappointed when she could not see him.

She sat alone, chin in hand, oblivious to the activity and excitement around her while she thought through her dilemma. She entertained images of revenge. She wrote mental scripts telling him off with brilliant dispatch. But no punishment seemed drastic enough to express her disappointment and rage. She felt like putting her head between her knees and howling with anguish and humiliation. She hated to admit it, but CC was right. Chan was an asshole. Once she reconciled that thought with what it would be like to spend the rest of her life with a man like that, she relaxed. After a while, she stretched out on the hard wooden bleachers and slept.

* * *

One by one, Jake and the Foofwahs slipped into bleacher seats to watch the sale. Tut settled down at Chloë's feet and took a well-earned nap. Felon snuggled up to her side causing her to move to an empty seat down the row, but the cat followed, purring loudly when she reached down to scratch his head.

Within the hour, Lindsey's cattle began to appear in the auction arena in lots of ten, twelve, or twenty, all well matched by gender, age, and size. With their coats washed clean, their thirst quenched, and their hunger assuaged by a satisfying meal of grain, the cattle looked almost as good as they had the morning the drive started. The Foofwahs found it hard to believe this was the same herd they'd been driving for the past four-and-a-half days, the herd that had looked so distressed only last night. They also felt compassion for the confused animals, though they were to be sold as a breeding herd, not headed for the slaughterhouse.

Lindsey located the cattle broker Cody had contacted before his accident. She was worried that the broker's important client, a Mr. Eakins, might not have arrived, but sure enough Eakins was there and in a buying mood, the broker said. He pointed out a jolly-looking man surrounded by other buyers swapping stories and slapping their sides.

The auctioneer went into his tongue-twisting spiel. When a cattleman lifted a single finger to bid on a lot, the nearest ring man standing inside the arena went into paroxysms of leaps and shouts. "I got four and a half!" Another lifted finger. "I got four and three-quarters!" boomed the second ring man, who leaped into the air and twisted his body like a baseball umpire calling "Out!" Another lifted finger caused yet another ring man to slam his hat onto the straw-covered floor and yell, "A fiver here. I got five."

Lindsey made notes as each lot sold and was led out. Thanks to Mr. Eakins's interest in Uncle Simon's cattle, the bidding was well above Lindsey's expectations. In between lots, the auctioneer told corny jokes to the cheers and jeers of the cattle buyers.

Though the past week had totally exhausted Lindsey, she seemed to be suddenly electrified with energy, like a slot-machine player after the machine hits the jackpot. The Foofwahs didn't understand what was happening but could tell from Lindsey's smile that things were going well.

When the sale ended at three-thirty, every lot of cattle had been sold. Lindsey turned to her friends, and, smiling broadly, hugged Jake while jumping up and down with unrestrained glee.

"We did it!" she danced a little jig with Jake, squealing, "We made it, Jake. We made it!" Tut, startled from a peaceful dream, leaped up and began barking. Lindsey hugged the Foofwahs, danced around them, and cried, "We won the race against time. And, best of all, our bond of friendship forged a strength that J. Chandler Reed couldn't beat with all his petty, underhanded, thieving tricks."

After the excitement died down, Lindsey announced, "We'll check into La Cholla's finest hotel, freshen up, then have dinner at the best restaurant in town, The Trail's End. This will be our victory dinner, everyone."

* * *

Angie awakened to Tut's barks and the squeals and laughter of her friends. Before coming fully awake, she realized that the sale was over, and the jubilant voices of the Foofwahs indicated the sale had gone well. Warily, she stood up and approached her friends.

Lindsey met her half way up the steps. “Angie, isn’t it wonderful? I’ve a rough estimate that the cattle are bringing almost twice what we’d estimated! Far more than we’d hoped for.”

“I’m so glad.” Angie grinned, and she meant it. “I’m sorry I was such an idiot. I realize now that Chan was using me, and I fell for it. Lindsey, can you ever forgive me? I would never be able to forgive myself if I’d learned, too late, that my stupidity was the cause of your missing the sale.”

“Don’t worry about it,” Lindsey said, taking Angie into her arms. “Everything has turned out just fine. Fortunately, Jake got a message, he says from God, telling us to ignore Chan’s route. It came in time for us to change direction. You believed Chan because he can sound very convincing. I believed him too, at first.” Lindsey turned to the group.

“I have a surprise for all of you. I’ve invited Chan to be our guest at dinner tonight.” Lindsey grinned at the shock registering on the faces of her friends.

“What?” Angie asked. “Why? I, for one, never want to see the man again as long as I live.”

“Well ... we’re all going to prepare a little roast for our friend Chan. I’m sure he doesn’t suspect a thing. He thinks it’s in his honor.”

“What if he doesn’t show up?” CC asked.

“He’ll show up. I’ve told him I’ll have his check ready,” Lindsey grinned. “Come on, let’s gather our things and get a cab to the nearest hotel. I want to arrange some special treats for this evening’s affair.”

CHAPTER TWENTY-SIX

SWEET REVENGE

Two taxis deposited the bedraggled crew in front of the President's Hotel, so named as tribute to its most famous guest, Teddy Roosevelt, who stopped over in La Cholla in 1908. It was originally called the President Roosevelt, until the late 1930s when its arch-conservative owner came to resent newcomers assuming it was named for Franklin Delano. The owner depersonalized the name, hoping to encourage future presidents of the right party affiliation to take advantage of the hotel's sumptuous suites. Few present-day western towns sported such grand and well-preserved facilities.

Lindsey requested the presidential suite. "No Foofwahs have been elected president yet, nor have you, Jake, but I feel like a winner big-time today, and I say we live it up!"

The startled desk clerk took one look, hesitated, and excused himself to speak with someone in a back room before checking to see if he had rooms available.

"Son, there's a difference between dirty women and dusty women," the manager explained. "Keep in mind this is a cow town, and don't let your college degree get in your way. Unless we've got a president coming through today, book 'em in fast, before they change their minds!"

The desk clerk returned to announce that rooms were available, but no pets were allowed. A young bellhop stepped forward and suggested that, for a nominal fee, he would take "the pets" home with him. He would be off work in an hour.

Lindsey conferred with Chloë before accepting his offer.

"But I'll be back for the dog in a day or two," Chloë said. "My husband will love having a nice dog like this. I'm not responsible for the cat."

"I'll take Felon home with me," Lindsey said. "We'll appreciate your looking after them until then. They get along fine."

After approving the suite, which covered the whole top floor of the hotel, the women marveled over the prospect of a hot shower. Lindsey asked Gina to make certain arrangements for her while she called Cody and dashed to the bank.

The Foofwahs bathed and changed into what remnants of fresh clothing they could scrounge from their saddlebags, fussing over mud-encrusted Levi's and shirts they would have to wear until they could shop for replacements.

Meanwhile, Gina went into action. She asked Jake his pants and shirt size, before calling a local haberdasher who brought to the hotel a selection of sports coats, shirts, ties, pants, and boots. Gina helped Jake choose a dashing wardrobe for the evening. Afterward, Jake located a hardware store and purchased a red Swiss army knife and a Zippo lighter.

Gina also called a women's clothing store and asked the owner to hold the shop open late so her friends could select outfits for dinner that evening. After that, she called two beauty salons and arranged appointments for the Foofwahs to have their hair and nails done.

"Nails, my God!" Gina said after she hung up and looked at her ragged and split fingernails for the first time in nearly a week. What was left of the polish was scraped and grimy. But she smiled with pride when she thought what those hands had been through and rushed off to the beauty salon to see what repairs could be made.

* * *

Chan spent the afternoon at the Cattleman's Club, taking a long lunch and poring over stockmen's journals and guides, though he seemed unable to concentrate. Occasionally, an old friend would say hello, but their visits were brief. Chan wondered if everyone in town was laughing at him. If word got out that he'd been bested by a bunch of Brünnhilde's on horseback, he would never be able to show his face in Plainview or La Cholla again.

He tried to think positively about Lindsey's dinner invitation. While irritated and desperately disappointed to see the cattle arrive in time, he was sure Lindsey would stub her toe somewhere down the line. She'd forget important papers or fail to come up with the money until after the close of probate. He counted on Lerner to help him out there. As long as he didn't have the check in his hands before midnight, he was safe. No, there was no use giving up hope yet. And he was obsessively driven to mend fences with Angie. Chan believed the most difficult scenario he could expect would be handling Angie's anger, and he was fully prepared to deal with that. The *best* scenario would be that the entire episode would be forgotten once ownership of the herd became his and these good old girls, these "Foofwahs," high-tailed it back to Arizona.

After much sober reflection during the afternoon, Chan decided that Angie had not double-crossed him. Any number of things could have happened, and certainly Lindsey wouldn't have invited him to the party if she'd suspected the trap he'd set for them. Angie probably forgot to tell them about the shortcut. Maybe Lindsey's plans were so firm, her directions so clear, Angie decided not to mention it. Maybe she'd simply been overruled.

Chan regretted leaving the auction without first finding out whether Angie was angry with him. He felt bad about the way he'd used her and wanted to make it up to her. He wondered fleetingly how he would explain the "shortcut," if the subject arose but put it out of his mind. He assured himself he was never at a loss for words when it came to women. Words flowed easily. He would come up with an appropriate explanation. He always had in the past.

* * *

By the time the Foofwahs finished their beautification processes and selected elegant outfits and fancy shoes, it was too late for rest. There was time only to dress for dinner.

The hotel's car rental agency delivered a sleek dark-blue Lincoln stretch-limousine for their use. The Foofwahs didn't know the agency had sublet it from the local undertaker, who had the only limo in town, but that fact wouldn't have altered their euphoria.

When the party trooped out of the hotel that evening, all shiny and sparkly, they smelled like the aftermath of a raid on the perfume counter at Wal-Mart. Even Jake looked and smelled especially grand.

The Trail's End was as impressive as advertised, and the owner gave an admirable imitation of a New York maitre d'. He bowed and informed them he'd reserved a small, private banquet room looking out on an enclosure that sported a waterfall and his personal rare bird collection. He ushered them to their room and looked pleased by their exclamations of delight over the beauty of the exotic tropical birds displayed in their Edenic sanctuary.

Chan hadn't arrived yet, but Lindsey suggested they order a round of cocktails, wine, or whatever to toast their success. To nearly everyone's surprise, Sleighton Lerner entered the room and Lindsey stepped forward to greet him.

"Thank you for coming this evening, Mr. Lerner," she said, her manner polite but formal as she shook his hand. "I wanted you to share in our victory celebration."

The attorney smiled stiffly and ordered scotch on the rocks before retiring to a solitary corner of the room.

Thinking the man looked uncomfortable, Kai-ling attempted to put him at ease. "Isn't Colorado beautiful in the fall, Mr. Lerner?" she asked.

"Yes," he replied. Finding little to interest him in small talk, he turned his back and retreated into silence.

Kai-ling shrugged to Penny, "I tried," and the two joined CC and Gina. They were already in high spirits, figuring out what part of their adventure they would tell their husbands and what they might edit. Kai-ling laughed and chided them for their artfulness.

"You don't know Ace," CC defended herself. "If he suspected we'd been in real danger, he would never trust me to go off on a jaunt without him again."

"And Ted won't believe me, anyway," Gina said. "He'll say my overactive imagination manufactured half of it. Don't call us artful, Kai-ling. Call us discreet."

Chloë overheard them and entered in. "For that matter, who would believe our incredible story? I, for one, will never tell Ray that I rode on a horse bareback. He'd pester me to start riding again, and, frankly, I've already enjoyed all the riding I can stand."

"Maybe you're right," Kai-ling conceded. "Hanchen must never know about the fire or that we rode horses on lonely night watches. So ... what did we do that I *can* tell him?"

They all laughed and continued to refine their adventures to a husband-acceptable level.

Angie, standing quietly apart from the others, looked into her heart. She wasn't sure how she'd react to meeting with Chan tonight or for that matter how Chan would react to her. Isn't it ironic? she thought. This is the same man whose passion I shared only twenty-four hours ago. No, "ironic" isn't the word. "Moronic" fits better.

When Chan stepped into the room, Angie caught her breath. God, he looks good, she thought. Dressed in a conservative dark suit, he carried his white Stetson as jauntily as if he had no cares.

Lindsey caught Angie's expression and followed her eyes to where Chan stood in the doorway. Dammit! she thought. Why does he have to look so great?

Chan glanced around the room until he picked out Angie. The look between them tore at Lindsey's heart. They're truly in love, she told herself. For a moment, she envied the shared intimacy that passed so openly as Angie and Chan gazed achingly into each other's eyes. But Lindsey knew she'd better intercept their electric current before someone blew a fuse. She quickly welcomed Chan with a warm smile and with both hands outstretched.

"You look enchanting," Chan said, his eyes traveling over her gold lamè evening dress trimmed with black velvet.

Sensing the hushed expectancy of her friends, Lindsey accompanied Chan to the clustered Foofwahs who sipped their cocktails while trying to look friendly and nonchalant. Chan bowed gallantly over each hand offered him and complimented the ladies on their spectacular transformation.

When he reached Angie, Chan paused with the half smile that hinted at shared secrets and looked deep into her eyes as if waiting for his cue.

Angie smiled sweetly. "I missed you at the auction today," she said, her voice as smooth as honey.

"I was there until nearly one o'clock," Chan lied, his voice equally smooth. "I talked to Lindsey for a minute but had to tend to some urgent business that came up unexpectedly. I trust today's drive was less eventful than yesterday's?"

"No hitches today, thanks to God and Jake!"

Looking over Angie's shoulder, Chan's eyebrows lifted in surprise when he saw his friend and legal counsel, Sly Lerner. Lerner sauntered over, and they chatted briefly.

Angie could not take her eyes from Chan's face. She appeared to be memorizing every feature. Lindsey observed her fascination with the man and was troubled by a nagging doubt that Angie in the long run would not be able to follow through with her resolve to end her relationship with Chan.

Chan ordered a vodka tonic and another round of drinks for everyone.

Lindsey allowed her guests to finish their drinks before asking them to find their places at the table.

"Chan, you sit at the foot of the table next to Angie, please." Lindsey sat at the head with Lerner to her right.

After everyone was seated, Lindsey tinkled her glass with a spoon.

"Listen up, everyone. Tonight is extra special for me. This past week, as I rode along, I planned how I'd reward my wonderful friends who have sacrificed so much for me. They have proven that friends we make down the road of life are among our sweetest and most precious treasures."

She paused to moisten her lips. "We have all known friends who are there when the going is good, but rare are the friends who stay with us when the going gets rough."

Lindsey lifted her glass of champagne. "I propose a toast to each of you, the true friends who were there for me when I really needed you. To the Foofwahs! Without previous experience but with remarkable spirit and courage, you put your own lives on hold while you rushed to help a friend in need. You proved that friendship and a whole lot of determination can overcome impossible odds."

Turning to Jake, she smiled, "And to Jake! What can I say of an old and trusted friend who has seen me through one more difficult time? You've earned the respect of us all. I thank you, my friends!" She sipped from her glass.

Jake surprised them by rising to his feet, glass in hand, to propose a toast of his own.

"I got to hand it to you wimmen. I thought once you got away from the drug stores full of hair dye and oh-dee-cologne, you'd give up. I thought you was a bunch of hot-house flowers, but yer a tough bunch of old, uh ... Foofwahs! Lindsey and me sure couldn't a done it without ya."

"You got that right!" CC exclaimed. To everyone's astonishment, she jumped up, threw her arms around Jake, and gave him a loud smooch on his shiny, clean beard. Lindsey thought she detected a glisten in Jake's eyes as he removed his dirty, blue bandanna from the inside pocket of his sports coat and honked into it.

"Anyway, as I was sayin', here's to the droverettes!" He drained his glass and said, "Now, let's git on with the food. I got a purty little lady name of Sadie — Hell! Listen to me! You wimmen have got *me* makin' poetry. Let's just say I've got some unfinished business waitin' for me in Los Vaqueros."

As the laughter subsided, the waiters began to serve an exquisite green salad trimmed with miniature carrots and tiny ears of corn. Lindsey chatted with Penny on her left and tried conversing with Lerner on her right, but he was preoccupied with picking shiitake mushrooms out of his salad and stacking them neatly at the side.

Glancing toward Chan and Angie, Lindsey smiled. Ah! Everything's under control. She'd expected he might be leery about walking into a trap, but he looked as relaxed as if he were in his own living room—and in just as much control.

"After dinner," Lindsey announced, "we've planned a program for our special guest, Mr. J. Chandler Reed, who honors us with his presence. I'm sure Chan shares our joy at performing what everyone agreed was an impossible task for a group of 'over the hill broads.' We all want to share a few of our special thoughts. In the meantime, enjoy your dinner."

Dinner was a grand culinary event masterminded by the Paris-trained chef. Jake and the ex-droverettes had missed lunch and thought the portions of nouvelle cuisine too stingy, but the waiters kept everyone's glass filled with champagne. The dessert cart held temptations no one resisted.

Jake whispered to Chloë, "This frog food ain't half as good as yer biscuits and gravy," to which Chloë smiled and raised her glass, acknowledging his compliment.

No longer an outcast, no longer angry, Angie too seemed relaxed with her friends. Chan, cheered by the fact that Lindsey had never once mentioned paying off Uncle Simon's debt—and the clock was ticking toward midnight—took over his end of the table. With engaging and riotous stories, he kept everyone laughing.

Ho, boy! Lindsey thought. Is he in for a surprise.

* * *

Chan couldn't keep his eyes off Angie. She looked positively devastating in a low-cut, Chinese-red dress that accentuated her deep tan and her red hair, drawn back in a becoming French twist.

"You look terrific," he told her.

Angie smiled acknowledgment but said nothing.

Again, Chan's eyes strayed back to absorb her beauty. If she's upset, he thought, she gives no hint. She couldn't be sweeter or more charming.

Over coffee and brandy after the dessert plates had been removed, Chan picked up on the sudden lull in conversation and saw that all eyes were on Angie. Chan's defense mechanisms clicked into place. Something fishy's going on here!

"Well!" Angie said brightly, bending toward Chan, her low neckline revealing a tantalizing amount of cleavage. "I have wonderful news. I've made a decision. Since I no longer have the Gypsy Spirit and my fortune-telling concession has gone up in smoke, I'm going to take you up on your suggestion. I'm moving to Plainview."

Chan's eyes did not leave Angie's, his expression concealing his instinctual caution.

"What do you think of that?" Angie asked with a pixie twinkle in her dark eyes.

"Like you say, it's wonderful news!" Chan was not acting when he smiled his pleasure. "I'm sure it's a decision you will never regret."

From across the table, CC spoke up. "Did I understand you to say, Angie, that you're moving to Plainview?"

Angie nodded.

"Why, Chan, how nice that you two lovebirds can be together. It sounds like something very special is developing here. Congratulations to both of you."

Chan smiled his acceptance of her best wishes.

"Perfect!" Lindsey clapped with a little too much enthusiasm. The combination of no lunch, release from stress, and generous amounts of champagne was taking its toll. "I'm *so* happy for you! When you plan the wedding, I hope you'll include all of us. Jake, too. In his new finery, he'd make a wonderful best man. We've gone through so much together these past few days. We love Angie. We know her better than we know some of our own sisters. And, we already know you, Chan, almost as well as we know our own husbands." Lindsey blushed.

Chan was becoming uncomfortable, confused. What in hell had Angie told her friends? Moving to Plainview implied no future wedding plans. He'd made no commitment other than wanting to see more of her. Things were moving way too fast here.

"When do you intend to make it legal, Chan?" CC asked.

Chan could feel the sudden rise of color to his face. What in hell is going on here? He searched first Angie's serene face, then quickly scanned the faces around the table, frantic for some idea of where this was going.

For all I know, he thought, these idiot women have a justice of the peace hiding outside. This has to be a charade of some sort. Am I being set up, or are they sincere? And what in hell is Lerner doing here? Has he spouted off about some of our private conversations? No, he wouldn't do that. That's lawyer-client privileged information. I'd sue the son of a bitch, and he knows it. No, it's Lindsey's money he's after. But he looks as uncomfortable as I feel.

Angie's move to Plainview was one thing, but marrying her was out of the question. Beside him, a smiling Angie waited expectantly for his response.

He continued to remain silent, hoping an answer would come to him. His thoughts ran wild. All I wanted was to let her know I liked her and wished to see more of her. What's happening?

He cleared his throat, an action the entire room interpreted as a positive indication of his good intentions.

"Oh, darling!" Angie cooed. "You've made me so happy! I just want to run out to the street and shout to the whole world, 'J.

Chandler Reed has chosen me!' Can't you see the society page announcement?"

Chan's mind was filled with images of "Wealthy Rancher Weds Fortune Teller," "Former Carny Bags Playboy Rancher," "Society Leader Lusts After Bimbo on Horseback." He could see *The National Enquirer* on supermarket stands now. He closed his eyes, but the images grew worse.

"Angie dear, don't you think ..." Chan patted her hands between his own. "Don't you think we should take this a little slower?" But his words were drowned out by the table full of well-wishers.

"A toast to the happy couple!" Gina said in a lilting voice above the roar of approval as she lifted her glass. "Hear! Hear!" someone volunteered. The entire ensemble staggered uncertainly to its feet to honor the toast.

Jeezz, Chan thought, but managed to smile like a happy man. He wanted to run, but there was no place to run to. He had to bluff the evening out. Angie and I can work this out later, between the two of us and without the cheering section. He stood and raised his glass.

"And now, I want to offer a toast to Lindsey," Chan said, "a great gal with lots of guts. Congratulations on accomplishing what I truly believed was an impossible task."

"Hear! Hear!" The Foofwahs and Jake became increasingly boisterous with more toasts. The champagne had kicked everyone into high gear. After everyone at the table was thoroughly toasted in more ways than one, they all sat down, all talking at once.

Lindsey rose again and tinkled her spoon against the water glass. "Which reminds me, Chan. The time is now eleven fifty-five. P.M. Here is my check in full payment for the grazing fee. My friends here and our mutual attorney are witnesses to the fact that you received it before the deadline."

Stupefied, Chan blurted out, "What? How did you get the money? I thought you weren't able to come up with the cash. And the money from the sale will be tied up in probate for months to come." Chan's final ace-in-the-hole had collapsed. He looked around the room for support, but his astonishment was viewed with benign looks of "We told you so!"

Even Lerner looks smug, Chan thought. The bastard's thinking of his probate fee and no telling how much more he can jack out of the estate.

"The La Cholla banker was most cooperative this afternoon after I showed him the bill of sale from the auction." Lindsey glowed at the success of her coup. "He advanced the payment."

Chan slumped to his chair, defeated.

More good news awaited. Jake stood and addressed Chan. "Uh, Chan, I almost fergot. Will you please return this knife to Jimbo?" Jake held out a red Swiss army knife to be passed down the table to Chan.

"Sure, Jake, but how did you come into possession of Jimbo's knife?" Chan had a nasty feeling that he didn't want to know the answer. He had seen Jimbo's knife many times since Jimbo's son sent it from Germany. In fact, Chan had seen Jimbo etch his name on it with a nail.

"Found it where we picketed our horses at Comanche Reservoir on the first night out. The night the horses was cut loose."

Jimbo hadn't mentioned losing his Swiss army knife. Chan swallowed hard. But his quick wits seldom let him down, and they didn't fail him now.

"Are you sure this is Jimbo's knife? I'm positive he was using it at the ranch yesterday. A lot of people have knives like this."

"Naw, it's his awright! He showed me his knife where he'd scratched his name 'Jimbo' on it, the night yer men came to Simon's bunkhouse like skunks in sheep's clothing to liquor me up. His name's right there!"

Sure enough, "Jimbo" had been etched in the red plastic. Chan decided to ignore the reference to his boys plying Jake with liquor and concentrate on the knife.

"I'll check with Jimbo, but I don't really think this is his knife." Chan pocketed the knife. I've got to get out of here and the sooner the better. Why do I feel like every word I say gets me one step higher to the gangplank?

"Now, Chan," Lindsey said. "Kai-ling has composed a poem, and I've asked her to recite it in your honor."

Kai-ling stood, a mischievous smile playing on her lips, and proceeded to deliver another blow to Chan's comfort:

> A Prince of the Plains rode into our lives,
> Bowed gallantly, purloining our hearts.
> "At your service, my dears," his words to the wise,
> While counting our cattle and drawing his charts.
> Now we ask, "Whose service was served in *your* eyes?"
> Please, Chan, no more help till we're out of these parts.

Chan smiled weakly, while the Foofwahs applauded as wildly as though Kai-ling had been awarded the Nobel Prize for her contribution to Western culture.

"I have something that belongs to Jimbo too, Chan," Penny spoke up. She stood and held a silver-metal Zippo lighter. She passed it down the table. "I found this at the south end of Horse Creek Reservoir where the grass fire started. I'm sure Jimbo lost it the day he set the grass fire."

All eyes turned toward Chan, watching his face intently. The room was warm, and he began to sweat profusely. Jimbo did own a Zippo lighter with "JIMBO" scratched on the case. The idiot! Scratching his name on everything in sight. Sure enough, there it was!

Whoa! Chan thought. Something's wrong here. Jimbo didn't set the fire. I sent Art Sheedy to do that job. How could Jimbo's lighter have ended up there?

"But ..." he started to protest, then checked his tongue. If he denied Jimbo's responsibility for the fire because of Art's involvement, he'd give himself away. Keep your mouth shut, he cautioned himself.

Gina added to the festivities by announcing that the truckers' strike was a lie. She'd called the local paper to verify the fact.

Chloë added, "And I'll bet you're the one who turned away that lovely, intelligent dog."

"What?" Chan drew himself to his feet, a picture of injured innocence and righteous indignation. "I came here in the spirit of neighborliness, but I guess once again my intent has been misinterpreted. I sincerely hope all of you are having fun at my expense, but I certainly don't like your implications that I or my men had anything to do with cutting horses loose or setting that grass fire. And I assure you," he said, pointing to Chloë, "I know nothing about any dog. My lawyer will call this defamation of character and find it anything but funny."

His lawyer looked awkwardly at his fingernails.

CC spoke up. "You'll be getting a bill for my porcelain plates and their little baskets."

Lindsey raised her eyebrows. "Porcelain?"

CC grinned guiltily. "Well ... ceramic, but good ceramic."

Chan's aggravation reached its peak. He moved back from the table and reached for his hat.

"Before you go," Gina called sweetly. "I'm keeping your map, the one where you wrote your name and scribbled some phony mileage notes. The one where you marked a cut-off you insisted we should take. I took the liberty of picking up a geologist's map of the area showing that the route you suggested clearly ends at a thirty-foot bluff on the north bank of the Arkansas River. If we hadn't already wised up to you, we'd have missed the auction altogether."

Chan stopped in mid-stride, like a fleeing deer pierced by an arrow. He turned to see Lindsey rummaging through her purse.

"I think the county attorney might find this interesting." Lindsey held out a large cocklebur in the palm of her hand. "Do you know where I found this, Chan? It was under Ringo's saddle blanket the day Cody was injured. Ringo was trained by Cody and had never once bucked him, but he bucked him off a few minutes after you left. You placed this bur under Ringo's saddle when Cody turned his back the morning you made your ridiculous offer on the cattle, Chan. And, by the way, we'll be billing you for the five lost cattle—at today's sale price."

Chan stared at her balefully for a long moment. "You are mad, woman!" he hissed. He walked to where Lindsey sat and bent over her, his knuckles pressing against the table, his face less the six inches from Lindsey's. "MAD!"

"You bet I'm mad." She stood and faced him. "I'm mad because Cody will suffer for the rest of his life from a leg that's been viciously broken. I'm mad because I was deprived of Cody's help moving the cattle. I'm mad because you influenced Sleighton Lerner to put off reading the will until it was almost too late to protect my interest. I'm mad because you set up the roping to keep the locals from helping me, and you and your men lied about the truckers' strike. And let's talk about the fire. You'll be lucky if we don't press criminal charges. Angie's insurers *may*, when they seek recovery for the Gypsy Spirit."

Chan knew the time had come to retreat, and quickly, but he knew if he left without talking to Angie, there'd be no second chance to redeem himself with her. He glared at Lindsey, then turned to Angie and lowered his voice. "I need to talk to you!"

"And I need to talk to you too, Chan."

"Privately."

Angie smiled sweetly. "I think not, Chan. Anything you have to say to me can be said in front of my friends."

Again, Chan started to leave, then thought better of it. "What have you been telling these people about us, Angie? What kind of trap have you led me into here?"

"The same kind of trap you led me into, Chan. You used me. You pretended to care about me but you were lying. All you wanted was to use me as bait to keep Lindsey from getting her cattle to the auction on time. I can't tell you how humiliated, how disappointed, how *cheap* you've made me feel. I trusted you, Chan. I thought I loved you."

Angie brushed a tear away with the heel of her hand. "I believed you to be an honorable man who cared about me. But all you thought about was the money Uncle Simon's herd could bring. You schemed and plotted to take possession of a herd that rightfully belonged to Lindsey. Lindsey is a good person who loved her uncle and sacrificed months of her life taking care of him. She deserved to inherit the herd, and her uncle wanted her to inherit it."

"You've got me all wrong, Angie ..."

"I don't think so, Chan. For the first time in days, I've got you right. I'm sorry for you, Chan. You've put up a good front, pretended to be a good person, but somewhere deep inside, you're warped, evil. Money is more important to you than honor or people."

Weeping openly now, Angie spotted the brilliant colors of the South American toucan in the aviary beyond the window. No matter how attractively displayed, it was still a captive. She shuddered to think how easily she might have exchanged her freedom for security and beautiful surroundings, all shallow gains were she to pledge herself to a man she couldn't trust.

"But I do care about you, Angie. I care more than even I was aware. I know I treated you badly, and I regretted it the moment I let you go with that map, when I realized that sooner or later you'd know what a bastard I've been. I knew then I'd truly screwed up. You don't know the pressure I've been under. Sly could tell you." He looked to his friend for help.

Sly was deeply, profoundly involved with the study of his fingernails.

"The bank is pressuring me. I owe hundreds of thousands of dollars. If I don't pay it soon, I stand to lose a good share of my ranch. Tres Alamos is all I own that means anything to me, anything of real value. If I lose the ranch, I'll have lost my very soul, my only reason for existing. Can't you understand that?"

Angie looked at him sadly. "No, I guess I can't. I don't own a thing, not even a dilapidated truck designed in a cuckoo-clock factory. I've never owned a forty thousand dollar horse, nor have I ever had the money to live like you. But I have one thing you'll never have. I have self-respect and the respect of all my friends. You tried to take even that away from me."

"Angie, don't leave me this way. I'm sorry for what I did to you. You're the nicest thing that's happened to me since Yvonne left. Say you'll stay. I'm truly not the asshole you think I am. Please give me another chance. I'll even marry you if I have to!"

"If you *have* to, Chan?" Angie slowly raised her eyes to his, then turned from his mesmerizing look. Tears of rage burned her eyes. This was it. The end of her dreams. There would be no second chance.

She turned back to Chan and planted her feet. She had just figured something out.

"You blew up my Gypsy Spirit!"

"But, Angie ..." he started to protest.

"Well, *up yours*, J. Chandler Reed." Angie turned away and walked angrily toward the door, pausing long enough to call over her shoulder, "Up yours, you son of a bitch!"

CHAPTER TWENTY-SEVEN

SOMETHING OLD, SOMETHING NEW

The party postmortem didn't last long. The long day filled with cheers, tears, and free-flowing spirits ended by one a.m. In her room, Lindsey started to undress when she heard a knock at the door.

Who could it be at this hour? Surely her friends had settled down by now. Cautiously pulling the chain across the door before peeking out, she found Cody! Her husband, on crutches, leaned against the opposite wall.

He looked pale and grinned crookedly as he thrust toward her a silvery, gift-wrapped package the size of a shoebox. "Special delivery."

"Cody," she cried, throwing the door open wide. "I'm so glad to see you!" She ushered him in with a warm hug and a kiss. "How did you get here at this time of night? *Why* did you come?"

Our buddy Lerner phoned after you called and said he thought I ought to get here for the celebration party. Sorry I missed it. Couldn't get an earlier plane out of Phoenix to Denver."

"You drove from Denver? You must be a wreck."

"Naw, Lerner sent a car for me. I'm as fresh as a daisy." He looked a wreck.

"I can't believe Lerner did all this without saying a word to me." Lindsey frowned, uncertain where Lerner fit into the picture. She'd only invited him to the party to back up her assertions about the legality of the transfer of the cattle—and to make Chan Reed squirm, since she knew his lawyer wouldn't support him.

"Lerner thought there might be fireworks. He was trying to do a good deed, I think. Here." He placed the mystery box in her hands.

"Whatever can this be?" She studied his smiling eyes for a clue, then rattled the box, turning it over and over.

"Open it."

First, she opened a tiny card bearing the inscription:

You thought I'd forget? Hell, no! All my love, always, C.

Lindsey's hands trembled as she unwrapped the box and folded back the pink tissue paper to find gleaming, intricately crafted silver spurs like the ones Cody promised her so many years ago.

She looked up at Cody with tears glistening in her eyes. "Cody ... my dearest Cody." She threw herself into his arms and gave him a long and loving kiss. "After all these years, you remembered."

"I'm sorry they don't have garnets or rubies, like I promised—"

"Hush! They're beautiful."

"And you can tell Angie, we'll help her get a new set of wheels. I don't know how we can ever repay the others."

"I doubt anyone will expect it, but we'll find ways. Friends help friends."

Cody settled awkwardly into the wingback chair by the window to watch his deliriously happy wife dance around the room, jingling her spurs.

"Oh, Cody, I love you!" Lindsey laughed and cried and ran to the closet to dust off her boots. "Let's go home!"

She looked over at her husband who had fallen asleep in the chair. She smiled and set aside her spurs. "In the morning."

About the Authors

CLEO LORETTE, married to a cowboy, lived on an Arizona cattle ranch for many years—and claims she has never met a horse she could trust. She has published thirty-five magazine articles on subjects ranging from health and fitness to horsemanship and family relations. Cleo has taught creative writing at two Phoenix-area community colleges.

GRETA MANVILLE left a career in corporate management at a major transportation company in California to move with her husband to Arizona. She began writing fiction after enrolling in one of Cleo's classes and has earned several awards for both fiction and poetry in national contests.

Printed in the United States
1242300001B/49-132

9 780759 624597